Implementing Digital
Forensic Readiness

Implementing Digital Forensic Readiness
From Reactive to Proactive Process

Jason Sachowski

Dmitri Ivtchenko, Technical Editor

AMSTERDAM • BOSTON • HEIDELBERG • LONDON
NEW YORK • OXFORD • PARIS • SAN DIEGO
SAN FRANCISCO • SINGAPORE • SYDNEY • TOKYO

Syngress is an imprint of Elsevier

Syngress is an imprint of Elsevier
50 Hampshire Street, 5th Floor, Cambridge, MA 02139, USA

Notices
Knowledge and best practice in this field are constantly changing. As new research and
experience broaden our understanding, changes in research methods, professional practices,
or medical treatment may become necessary.

Practitioners and researchers must always rely on their own experience and knowledge
in evaluating and using any information, methods, compounds, or experiments described
herein. In using such information or methods they should be mindful of their own safety and
the safety of others, including parties for whom they have a professional responsibility.

To the fullest extent of the law, neither the Publisher nor the authors, contributors, or
editors, assume any liability for any injury and/or damage to persons or property as a
matter of products liability, negligence or otherwise, or from any use or operation of any
methods, products, instructions, or ideas contained in the material herein.

ISBN: 978-0-12-804454-4

British Library Cataloguing in Publication Data
A catalogue record for this book is available from the British Library

Library of Congress Cataloging-in-Publication Data
A catalog record for this book is available from the Library of Congress

For information on all Syngress publications visit
our website at https://www.elsevier.com/

Working together
to grow libraries in
developing countries

www.elsevier.com • www.bookaid.org

Publisher: Todd Green
Acquisition Editor: Chris Katsaropoulos
Editorial Project Manager: Anna Valutkevich
Production Project Manager: Punithavathy Govindaradjane
Designer: Mark Rogers

Contents

SECTION A DIGITAL FORENSICS

SECTION B DIGITAL FORENSIC READINESS

SECTION C APPENDICES

SECTION D TEMPLATES

Preface

The art of war teaches us to rely not on the likelihood of the enemy's not coming, but on our own readiness to receive him; not on the chance of his not attacking, but rather on the fact that we have made our position unassailable.

Sun Tzu
The Art of War

Introduction

Regardless of how strong an organization defenses, there will come a time when the weakest link is exposed leading to some type of incident. When that time comes, organizations turn to the highly specialized skills of digital forensic investigators to parse through and extract evidence from the complex volumes of data.

Unfortunately, there are times when an incident occurs and organizations are unable to support the digital investigation process with the electronic data needed to conduct analysis and arrive at credible and factual conclusions. Not only does this slow down the digital investigation process, it also places additional overhead on people and system to reactively identify where relevant electronic data is and work to have it properly collected and preserved to support the investigation. In comparison, the ability to collect and preserve electronic data before something happens enhances the digital investigation process by pro-actively streamlining activates and reducing overhead.

This book has been written from the business perspective of the digital forensics discipline.

This book is not designed to provide detailed technical knowledge of digital forensic science or how to perform digital forensic investigations. This book is written from a nontechnical business perspective and is intended as an implementation guide for preparing your organization to enhance its digital forensic readiness by moving away from being reactive and becoming proactive with investigations.

While the basic principles, methodologies, and techniques of digital forensic science are covered, this book focuses on outlining—in detail—where, what, and how an organization can enhance its people, processes, and technologies to implement effective and proactive digital forensic readiness.

About the Author

Jason has over a decade of experience in digital forensic investigations, secure software development, and information security architecture. He currently manages a team of forensic investigators and data breach analysts for the Bank of Nova Scotia, commonly known as Scotiabank, Canada's third largest and the most international bank.

Throughout his career, Jason has performed hundreds of digital forensic investigations involving enterprise servers, network logs, smartphones, and database systems. Complimentary to his technical experiences, he has also developed and maintained processes and procedures, managed large information security budgets, and governed the negotiation of third-party contracts.

In addition to his professional career, Jason serves as a contributing author and content moderator for DarkReading, a subject matter expert for (ISC)² professional exam development, and volunteers as an advocate for CyberBullying prevention and CyberSecurity awareness. He holds several information security and digital forensic certifications, including Certified Information Systems Security Professional—Information Systems Security Architecture Professional (CISSP-ISSAP), Certified Cyber Forensics Professional (CCFP), Certified Secure Software Lifecycle Professional (CSSLP), Systems Security Certified Practitioner (SSCP), and EnCase Certified Examiner (EnCE).

Acknowledgments

I would like to most of all thank my wife and my children for showing me that no matter what I do in my lifetime, they will always be my greatest success.

Thank you to my parents for providing me with countless opportunities to become who I am today and for encouraging me to keep pushing my boundaries.

Thank you to my colleagues for allowing me the honor to work with you and for the infinite wisdom and knowledge you have given me.

Lastly, thank you to Blair for opening doors.

Digital Forensics

Understanding Digital Forensics

This chapter provides an introductory into the history of digital crime and digital forensics as they evolved side-by-side over the last half century.

INTRODUCTION

Digital forensics has always been labeled as an "interesting" profession to work in. This comes as no surprise as public interest spikes; fueled by the works of novelists and film makers who made the world of digital crime and digital forensic both appealing and stylishly straightforward. But the reality is, there is a lot more discipline to the digital forensic profession that what is portrayed in the media.

While it is relatively known that there are legal aspects involved with digital forensics, most people are surprised to learn that the profession involves a great deal of scientific principles, methodologies, and techniques. Not only does digital forensics require a significant amount of specialized training and skills to properly apply these scientific fundamentals, digital forensics is also somewhat of an art form where analytical experience comes into play.

HISTORY OF DIGITAL CRIME AND FORENSICS

Information technology has been involved in criminal activities for more than half of a century. Dating as far back as the 1960s, computer crimes were first committed as either physical damage or sabotage to computer systems. But when technology first arrived, most people did not think that it would one day become such an integral part of our everyday lives. If history has taught us anything, it is that as information technology advances there will always be both new and evolved digital crimes.

With a growing commercialization of technology and the expansion of the Internet, computer crimes continue to take the next step in an ever evolving threat landscape. Moving forward from the 1970s and into the new millennium, computer crimes expanded out from just damage and sabotage into digital crimes such as fraud, denial of service, SPAM, advanced persistent threats (APTs), and extortion.

PROLOGUE (1960–80)

From the 1960s to 1980s, computers were primarily owned and operated by corporations, universities, research centers, and government agencies as industrial systems largely supporting data processing functions and were, for the most part, not connected to the outside world.

Responsibility for securing these computers was left to the system administrators with routine audits done to ensure the efficiency and accuracy of the data processing functions. These activities were essentially the first systematic approach to a computer security discipline. It was during this time period that the computer first became a point of interest to the information security, legal, and law enforcement communities.

Several government agencies started creating small ad hoc groups of individuals who were provided with basic training on computer systems. These investigators would then work with administrators to gather information from the computer systems to be used as evidence in criminal matters.

Computer crime dates as far back as 1968. In Olympia, Washington, an IBM 1401 Data Processing System was shot twice by a pistol toting intruder.

Following closely behind in February 1969, the largest student riot in Canada ignited when police were called in to stop a student occupation of several floors of the Hall Building at Concordia University. When the police came in, a fire broke out resulting in computer data and university property damages totaling $2 million.

Prior to the 1980s, computer crimes were dealt with using existing laws. In response to the increasing computer crimes, law enforcement agencies began creating additional laws to address them. The first computer crime law, the *Florida Computer Crimes Act*, was created in 1978 to address fraud, intrusion, and all unauthorized access to computer systems. The evolution of crime into computer systems during this time period instinctively coined the terms *computer forensics*, *forensic computer analysis*, or *forensic computing*.

INFANCY (1980–95)

With the arrival of the IBM personal computer (PC), there was a sudden explosion of computer hobbyists. These PCs had very few applications and were not user friendly which enticed hobbyists to write program code to access the internals of the hardware and operating system (OS). Among the hobbyists were individuals from law enforcement, government agencies, and other organizations who collectively shared their understanding of computers and how technology could play a larger role as a source of evidence. Much of time and money spent by these individuals to learn about these new technologies was done on their accord because their respective agencies did not necessarily support their efforts.

Investigations performed by these pioneers were fairly basic in today's perspective. The Internet was not yet widely available for consumers which limited the scope of most cases to data recovery on stand-alone systems. Cybercriminals mostly consisted of a mix between traditional criminals who used technology to support their activities (ie, phreaking[1]) and people who used their technical skills to illegally access other computers.

In this time period there were very few forensic tools available which left investigators to either build their own or use available data protection and recovery applications to perform their analysis. Additionally, the only means of preserving evidence at this time was to take logical backups of data onto magnetic tape, hope that the original attributes were preserved and restored it to another disk where analysis was performed using command-line utilities.

Throughout the 1990s, forensic tools began to emerge from both the hobbyists (ie, Dan J. Mares' Maresware, Gord Hama's RCMP Utilities) and larger software vendors (ie, Norton's Utilities, Mace Utilities). These applications and software suites were each developed to solve specific forensic activities (ie, imaging, file recovery) and proved to be powerful tools for the computer forensics practice.

As technology became more widely available and reports of different type of computer crimes were growing in publicity, law enforcement agencies around the world started responded by enacting similar laws. Canada was the first to respond in 1983 by amending their *Criminal Code*. Following suite, several other nations began implementing legislation in response to computer crimes including the *1984 U.S. Federal Computer Fraud and Abuse Act*, the 1989 amendment of the *Australian Crimes Act* to include *Offenses Relating to Computers*, and the *1990 British Computer Abuse Act*.

In parallel to the establishment of computer laws, the forensic community was growing in popularity and interest. Agencies recognized that the majority of forensic investigations were performed by individuals who had minimal training, operated on their own terms, used their own equipment, and did not follow any formal quality control. From this, efforts began to create a common body of knowledge (CBK)[2] of principles, methodologies, and techniques that could be applied to standardize and bring formal structure to computer forensics.

CHILDHOOD (1995–2005)

The years between 1995 to 2005 proved to be a major step forward in the maturity of forensics. Technology quickly became pervasive among consumers where it was embedded in elements of our daily lives which drove significant innovation such as cellular phones. Plus, the Internet had gained enough momentum where it was becoming more readily available for use in homes and businesses; introducing personal accessibility to e-mail and web browsing.

Accompanied by these technology advancements was the opportunity for criminals to commit new cybercrimes. An example of this opportunity being made available through technology occurred following the events on September 11, 2001; when investigators realized that digital evidence of the attack was recoverable on computers all across the world. This revelation reinforced the fact that criminals were using technology in the same ubiquitous ways as the everyday consumers were.

From the technology sponsored growth in digital crimes, the term computer forensics became increasingly challenging to use because both crimes and evidence could now be found throughout networks, printers, or other devices. In 2001, the first annual Digital Forensic Research Workshop (DFRWS) recognized that computer forensics was now considered a specialization and proposed the use of the term *digital forensics* to describe the field as a whole.

Expansion into this new digital forensic field resulted in the creation of specializations for investigating new technologies. In addition to the traditional computer forensics becoming a concentration, there was the introduction of *network forensics* and *cellular forensics*. However, with the formation of these specializations came increased technical sophistication and legal scrutiny over the requirement to follow standardized principles, methodologies, and techniques.

The formalization of digital forensics led to the first publication of digital forensic principles being issued between 1999 and 2000 from the combined work of the International Organization on Computer Evidence, G-8 High Tech Crime Subcommittee, and the Scientific Working Group on Digital Evidence. Likewise, forensic tools underwent an evolution away from the simple homegrown application, used by the hobbyist, and into sophisticated commercial suites of tools. At the same time, the digital forensic community continued to mature where professional certification programs had been created to not only recognize individuals with the appropriate knowledge and experience but also acknowledge the laboratory environments that met the requirements of forensic science principles, methodologies, and techniques.

ADOLESCENCE (2005–15)

Attributed to the academic preparation required, in addition to formal training, the maturity of digital forensics has grown exponentially to a point where it is now recognized by the Information Security profession as a core skill area. Colleges and universities have recognized the popularity and appeal of digital forensics leading to the creation of numerous academic and professional education programs around the world. Furthermore, the number of international conferences dedicated to the field of digital forensics continues to see increased attendance rates as the integration of digital forensics with other professions evolves.

During this time, the American Academy of Forensic Sciences, one of the most widely recognized professional organizations for establishing the forensic disciplines, created a new section specific to digital and multimedia sciences. This development led to a major advancement in recognizing digital forensics as a scientific discipline by providing a common foundation for specialized groups of people who can share knowledge and address current forensic challenges.

Technology has now reached a point in its evolution where almost every device has some type of storage medium and can, in some fashion, be connected to the Internet. Naturally this has driven the development of systems and applications that are increasingly adaptive and accessible from virtually anywhere and, if not secured properly, by anyone. Capitalizing on technology's modern pervasiveness, cyber-criminals once again expanding their portfolio to incorporate new and sophisticated attacks, such as varying levels of phishing campaigns (ie, spear, whaling, cloning), Advanced Persistent Threats (APTs) or even cyberespionage.

With the change in cyberattacks comes new way that digital evidence is created, gathered, and processed. Adapting to the new wave of digital evidence sources, commercial software suites began to transform from offering functionality specific to digital forensics and into other professions where digital forensics is used. Inclusive to professions like cybersecurity, electronic discovery (e-discovery), or incident response, digital forensics has become an underlying foundation driving several information security disciplines.

THE FUTURE (2015 AND BEYOND)

The digital forensic community has come a long way since the 1960's. Starting out as a hobby made up mostly of homegrown tools and quite often insufficient processes, we have arrived at a convergence of various law enforcement, organizations, and intelligence agencies where everybody is following the same consistent principles, methodologies, and techniques.

Predicting what the future holds for digital forensics is a crapshoot. Rather, if history has taught us anything about how the past has shaped what digital forensics is today, the most realistic and accurate prediction that can be made is this: every person and/or group involved with digital forensics today will have some type of influence on what the future brings.

For the most part, digital forensics has become what it is today because of the tactical influences that have consistently driven its development and maturity, such as technology advancements, creation of commercial tools, or the integration with other professions. On the other hand, while the list of strategic influences might be somewhat smaller, the alignment to forensic science and subsequent creation of principles, methodologies, and techniques to abide by has brought about a standardization and formality to the structure of digital forensics. There are also influences that exist as both tactical and strategic realms that should be considered for the future of digital forensics, such as:

- The continued development of the common body of knowledge (CBK) based on research, knowledge, and experiences of the digital forensic community. At the end of the day, the digital forensic investigators of the future will be better trained and educated because the CBK that was established before them will be extensive and readily available. Organizations will need to ensure that they employ digital forensic professionals who are not only accredited to conduct digital forensic investigations but also have strong business and technical qualities.

- Historically, modern advancements that introduced new ways for technology to be used as either the fruit of crime[3] or tool of crime[4] will subsequently lead to an evolution of how digital forensics is used to investigate these crimes. Until recently, cybercrime was traditionally committed with a focus primarily on content (ie, data exfiltration) and done so with little context (ie, where attacks are being perpetrated). Naturally, Cybercriminals of the future will also be better trained, funded, and organized where the value of their collective efforts will be realized resulting in heightened situational awareness involving their attacks.

- To counter the evolving threat landscape, commercial digital forensic tools will need to evolve to where they can:
  - easily adapt with the ever growing volumes of data that needs to be analyzed
  - further automate known, verified, and validated analytic functions to alleviate manual processing time and reduce error probability
  - understand and interpret both the content and context of human language and communications for better analytical results

- Given the fact that some investigations encompass an international scope, such as data residing under multiple jurisdictions, laws and regulations must evolve to enable a global standard for digital forensics.

DIGITAL FORENSICS OVERVIEW

Since the 1960's the threat landscape has evolved significantly from what is now considered simple cybercrimes (ie, sabotage) to much more sophisticated attacks (ie, APT). From the evolution of cybercrime, digital forensics was born from the ideas of pioneers that continued to develop and expand their interests into a now well-established and recognized profession.

What is currently known as *Digital Forensics* is a discipline that adheres to the forensic science discipline and has been well established as a result of an extensive CBK of proven methodologies, techniques, and principles. In other words, digital forensics is the application of science to law where scientific principles, methodologies, and/or techniques are used during a digital forensic investigation.

WHY IS IT IMPORTANT?

According to Locard's exchange principle, illustrated in Figure 1.1 below, every perpetrator of a crime will bring something into the crime scene and takes something of the crime scene with them. In the digital realm, both of these occurrences can be used as digital evidence in a forensic investigation.

The capability of practicing forensically sound principles, methodologies, or techniques within any organization provides an additional "defense-in-depth" layer to

FIGURE 1.1

Locard's exchange principle triad.

ensure that potential digital evidence is (1) acquired in a manner that preserves its integrity, (2) authenticated to validate that it is identical to the original source data, and (3) analyzed using techniques and processed that maintain the evidence's integrity.

Organizations that have a good understanding of the technical requirements for practicing digital forensics will be better equipped to gather and process digital evidence in line with the legal requirements for prosecuting intruders. But what happens when the technical and/or legal requirements for practicing digital forensics are ignored or not followed properly? The reality is, organizations that do not practice forensically sound principles, methodologies, or techniques run the risk of:

• potential digital evidence being compromised, lost, or overlooked
• digital evidence not being admissible in a court of law due to integrity and/or authenticity issues
• being noncompliant with laws and/or regulations

LEGAL ASPECTS

Even if legal prosecution is not the end-goal of the investigation, such as a corporate policy violation, there may be some form of legal action, such as employee termination. It is important that the forensic science principles, methodologies, and techniques are consistently followed because the investigation may wind up in a court of law at some point. Regardless of criminal proceedings, every digital forensic investigation must ensure that:

• an exact copy of digital data is created to ensure no information is lost or overlooked
• the authenticity of digital data is preserved through the use of cryptographic algorithms

- a chain of custody is established to maintain integrity through the evidence's life cycle
- actions taken by people through the different investigative phases are recorded

COLLECTING DIGITAL EVIDENCE

From the traditional computer system to modern devices such as mobile phones, game consoles, or virtualized environments, the field of digital forensics encompasses a wide range of technologies that serve as potential evidence sources. While the design and functionality of these technologies is uniquely different, the application of digital forensics involves ensuring the integrity and authenticity are upheld throughout the evidence's life cycle. Two basic types of potential digital evidence that can be gathered from these technologies include *nonvolatile* or *volatile* data.

VOLATILE DATA

Volatile data is a type of digital information that is stored within some form of temporary medium that is lost when power is removed. This type of information is an excellent starting point for a forensic investigation because it contains residual data that may be relevant to the processing and analysis of digital evidence that is gathered from nonvolatile data sources.

The primary source of volatile data can be found inside of random access memory (RAM). Most often, the contents of RAM will contain information relating to frequently used applications, content of recently accessed files, or account information such as usernames and passwords (cleartext or hashed).

While the type of files containing potential digital evidence can be extensive, depending on the technology, examples of volatile data that are commonly included within the scope of a typical forensic investigation are as follows:

- *Network configurations* used by the OS are retrieved from nonvolatile data stored on the file system and loaded into RAM for quick and dynamic access, such as Internet protocol (IP) addresses and active network interfaces.
- *Network connections* between the local system and remote systems, in any state (ie, established, listening), listing incoming and outgoing connection properties, such as IP address and local/remote port.
- *Running processes* that are currently executing system commands, supporting operational services, or providing user interfaces, such as applications, scripts, or executables.
- *Open files* from nonvolatile data sources that are actively being accessed by either the system or a user, such as word processing documents, executables, log files.
- *Login sessions* containing information about user and/or service accounts currently logged in the system, such as login time, session duration, and authentication attempts (ie, success, failure).

- *System date/time* maintains the current date and time information, including time zone and day-light savings properties, that can be used when building a chronology of system events or when correlating the local system events to other system events. Special attention must be given to date/time values stored in a system's Basic Input/Output System (BIOS) because it can be different than the values contained within the OS configurations.

NONVOLATILE DATA

Nonvolatile data is a type of digital information that is persistently stored within a file system on some form of electronic medium that is preserved in a specific state when power is removed. Contained within a file system is commonly the largest and richest source of potential digital evidence that can be analyzed during a forensic investigation. While the type of files containing potential digital evidence can be extensive, depending on the technology, examples of nonvolatile data that are commonly included within the scope of a typical forensic investigation are as follows:

- *Account information* belonging to users or system processes including the account name, owner, entitlements, group membership, status, and passwords (either in cleartext[5] or as a hash value[6])
- *Configuration/log files* are used to store various types of system or user settings as well as outputs of auditing information, such as:
  - Audit records containing records of successful and failed authentication attempts within the system
  - System event logs used to track the operational actions performed by OS components, such as when the system is booted
  - Application events used to track the operational actions performed by application, such as when a process is executed
- *Data files* are used to store information for applications that can be either system-generated or user-generated, such as text files, word processing documents, spreadsheets, databases, audio files, or graphics.
- *Paging/swap files* are logical files located on a file system that are used by the OS, in combination within RAM, to extend the amount of temporary storage space available on a system so additional data can be dynamically available, such as usernames or password (cleartext or hashed). While the contents of these files may resemble or originate from volatile data, the page/swap file is nonvolatile and is preserved in its last operating state when power is removed.
- *Dump files* are used by the OS to automatically store the active contents of RAM when an error condition occurs to assist system administrator in troubleshooting. The resulting files will contain the stored RAM content that is preserved when power is removed.
- *Temporary/cache files* are files created by either the OS or applications during activities such as installation, upgrades, or normal operations, such as scripts, executables, or web browsing pages. Although such files can be typically

deleted at the completion of these activities, this does not always occur resulting in this data being preserved in its last operating state when power is removed.

- *Hibernation files* are created by the OS to record the contents of RAM, running applications, and open files before the system is shut down; so the system state can be restored the next time it boots.
- *Slack space* is unused area in between the end of an actual file and the end of the defined storage space, also known as a cluster,[7] available in a file system. When being written to a file system, depending on the volume of data, a file might not occupy the entire cluster resulting in remaining space otherwise referred to as slack space. In this space, data belonging to other files, that previous occupied the cluster but have since been overwritten by a new smaller file, are still accessible and can be recovered during a forensic investigation.
- *Registry* is a database, specific to the Microsoft Windows platform, which contains important information about the system including, but not limited to, hardware components, installed applications, OS configurations, and account information. While caution should be taken to not make manual changes to the registry because one wrong move can render a system inoperable, the information and potential evidence that reside in the registry make it a significant forensic resource, such as most recently used files, applications configured to automatically run at startup, network shares.

ORDER OF VOLATILITY

Generally, the more volatile data within a system the more challenging it is to gather in a forensically sound manner because it is only available for a specific amount of time. Considering the volatile data types listed above, this information can only be gathered from a live system that has not been rebooted or shut down since the incident originally occurred.

Therefore, it is critical that investigators are equipped with adequate knowledge of the incident to make an educated decision on whether volatile data should be preserved as part of the forensic investigation. Ideally, the criteria for making this decision should be documented in advance, as part of the organization's standard operating procedures, so investigators can make act quickly to preserve the volatile data.

The ability to make a decision comes with the inherent risk that the longer it takes to make the decision the greater the risk that the volatile data will be lost. For instance, every action performed on the system, whether by the system or person, will most certainly alter (in some way) the current state of volatile data available to the investigator.

When deciding to preserve volatile data, it is important to keep in mind that the more volatile the data is the greater there is a need to use specialized individuals and tools to guarantee the data is preserved in a forensically sound manner. Illustrated in Table 1.1 below is the order of volatility for digital evidence, ordered from most volatile to least volatile, including its life span and relevance to the forensic investigation.

Table 1.1 Order of Volatility

Life Span	Storage Type	Data Type
As short as a single clock cycle	CPU storage	Registers
		Caches
	Video	RAM
Until host is shut down	System storage	RAM
	Kernel tables	Network connections
		Login sessions
		Running processes
		Open files
		Network configurations
		System date/time
Until overwritten or erased	Nonvolatile data	Paging/swap files
		Temporary/cache files
		Configuration/log files
		Hibernation files
		Dump files
		Registry
		Account information
		Data files
		Slack space
	Removable media	Floppy disks
		Tapes
		Optical disc (read/write only)
Until physically destroyed		Optical disc (write only)
	Outputs	Paper printouts

TYPES OF FORENSIC INVESTIGATIONS

Traditionally, digital forensics is performed in response to an incident and focuses on determining the root cause for what prompted the incident. The purpose of performing a digital forensic investigation is to establish evidence and facts from digital information existing on any number of different technologies (eg, game consoles, mobile devices, computer systems), across dissimilar network architectures (eg, private, public, cloud), or in varying states (eg, volatile, static).

Since the birth of computer forensics in the 1980s, the application of forensic science has become an underlying foundation that has seen an integration of the consistent principles that support repeatable methodologies and techniques within several other information security disciplines. The application of digital forensic science in other disciplines provides organizations with an acceptable level of assurance that validated and verified processes are being followed to gather, process, and safeguard digital evidence. Examples of disciplines where digital forensic science is used include the following:

- *Computer forensics* which relates to the gathering and analysis of digital information as digital evidence on computer systems and electronic storage medium.
- *Network forensics* which relates to the monitoring and analysis of network traffic for the purposes of information gathering, gathering of digital evidence, or intrusion detection.
- *Incident response* which relates to reducing business impact by managing the occurrence of computer security events.
- *Memory forensics* which relates to the gathering and analysis of digital information as digital evidence contained within a system's RAM.
- *Electronic discovery (e-discovery)* which relates to the discovery, preservation, processing, and production of electronically stored information (ESI) in support of legal or regulatory litigation matters.
- *Cloud forensics* which relates to the gathering and analysis of digital information as digital evidence from cloud computing systems.

As digital forensics continues to evolve alongside of technology advancements, one of the most challenging activities is to ensure that the fundamental principles, methodologies, and techniques are upheld. There is a constant struggle to maintain a balance between collecting digital evidence as efficiently as possible without modifying the integrity of the data in the process. Fortunately, the principles and methodologies of forensic science have been clearly defined and well established allowing them to be applied relatively seamlessly to any form of digital evidence.

DIGITAL FORENSIC RESOURCES

This book is written from a nontechnical, business perspective and is intended for use as an implementation guide to prepare any organization to enhance its digital forensic readiness by moving away from reacting to an incident and becoming proactive with their investigative capabilities.

While the basic principles, methodologies, and techniques of digital forensics are covered, this book focuses on outlining—in detail—the where, what, and how an organization can enhance its knowledge, processes, and technologies to implement effective and proactive digital forensic readiness.

There are countless resources available today that are designed specifically to teach different basics or specializations contained within the digital forensic discipline. The volume of reference material on digital forensic topics is beyond the intention to identify and include them as a reference in this book. While there might be some absent from the list below, the following are recent publications that can be used as a learning tool for digital forensics.

Digital Forensics with the Access Data Forensic Toolkit (FTK). McGraw-Hill Osborne Media, September 05, 2015. ISBN: 9780071845021.

Handbook of Digital Forensics of Multimedia Data and Devices. Wiley-IEEE Press, August 31, 2015. ISBN: 9781118640500.

Hacking Exposed Computer Forensics Third Edition: Secrets & Solutions. McGraw-Hill Osborne Media, July 06, 2015. ISBN: 978-0071817745.

Operating System Forensics 1st Edition. Syngress, July 01, 2015. ISBN: 9780128019498.

Cybercrime and Digital Forensics: An Introduction. Routledge, February 12, 2015. ISBN: 978-1138021303.

The Basics of Digital Forensics 2nd Edition. Syngress, December 15, 2014. ISBN: 9780128016350.

Computer Forensics and Digital Investigation with EnCase Forensic v7. McGraw-Hill Osborne Media, May 28, 2014. ISBN: 978-0071807913.

Windows Forensic Analysis Toolkit 4th Edition: Advanced Analysis Techniques for Windows 8. Syngress, April 10, 2014. ISBN: 9780124171572.

Computer Incident Response and Forensics Team Management 1st Edition. Syngress, November 22, 2013. ISBN: 9781597499965.

Digital Forensics Processing and Procedures 1st Edition. Syngress, September 17, 2013. ISBN: 9781597497428.

Computer Forensics InfoSec Pro Guide. McGraw-Hill Osborne Media, April 09, 2013. ASIN: B00BPO7AP8.

Malware Forensics Field Guide for Windows Systems 1st Edition. Syngress, June 13, 2012. ISBN: 9781597494724.

Digital Forensics with Open Source Tools. Syngress, April 14, 2011. ISBN: 9781597495868.

Handbook of Digital Forensics and Investigation. Academic Press, October 26, 2009. ISBN: 978-0123742674.

SUMMARY

The rise and continued evolution of cybercrime has made a significant contribution to the formation of what digital forensic science is today. Growing out from the pastime of hobbyists, the establishment of forensically sound principles, methodologies, and techniques has turned it into a respected and authoritative discipline.

TAXONOMY

1 *Phreaking* is a blend of the words *phone and freaking* used to describe the activities performed to reverse engineer telecommunication systems to allow free calls to be made, such as the plain old telephone system.

2 *Common body of knowledge* (CBK) is the complete concepts, terms, and activities that make up a professional domain.
3 *Fruit of crime* applies to material objects that are acquired during a crime.
4 *Tool of crime* applies to material objects used to perpetrate criminal activities.
5 *Cleartext* is a form of message or data which is in a form that can be immediately read, understood, and interpreted by humans without additional processing.
6 *Hash value* is a numerical value of fixed length used to uniquely identify and/or represent large volumes of data.
7 *Cluster* is a fixed number of contiguous and addressable units of storage space on electronic storage medium.

Investigative Process Models

This chapter analyzes different digital forensic process models used to support investigative workflows. You will learn about the phases contained within each process model, the uniqueness and commonalities of tasks performed, and its application toward digital forensic.

INTRODUCTION

From what was discussed in chapter "Understanding Digital Forensics," we know that digital forensics is the application of forensic science to law and is built on the extensive common body of proven scientific principles, methodologies, or techniques that can be applied to any phase of the investigative workflow.

As early as 1984, law enforcement agencies began developing processes and procedures to use as part of their computer forensic investigations. This eventually led to the realization that, as a result of bypassing, switching, or not following correct processes, the digital investigation would result in missed, incomplete, or inadmissible evidence. Since then, several authors have attempted to develop and propose digital forensic process models to address either a specific need, such as law enforcement, or with a generalized scope with the intention that it could be adopted universally.

EXISTING PROCESS MODELS

There have been several digital forensic process models developed over many years to address either a specific need, such as law enforcement, or with a generalized scope with the intention that the process model could be adopted universally. While there might be some process models absent from the table below, Table 2.1 contains a chronological list of process models including a unique identifier, the author(s), the publication year, and the number of phases included in the model. It is important to note that inclusion of the process models in the table does not suggest that these are better or recommended over other models that were not included.

Every digital forensic process model noted in the table below was developed with distinct characteristics and with the purpose of addressing a need within the digital forensic investigative workflow. There are, however, no criteria for stipulating which

Table 2.1 Digital Forensic Process Models

ID	Name	Author(s)	Year	Phases
M01	Computer Forensic Investigative Process	Pollitt	1995	4
M02	Computer Forensic Process Model	U.S. Department of Justice	2001	4
M03	Digital Forensic Research Workshop Investigative Model (Generic Investigation Process)	Palmer	2001	6
M04	Scientific Crime Scene Investigation Model	Lee et al.	2001	4
M05	Abstract Model of the Digital Forensic Procedures	Reith et al.	2002	9
M06	Integrated Digital Investigation Process	Carrier and Spafford	2003	5
M07	End to End Digital Investigation	Stephenson	2003	9
M08	Enhanced Integrated Digital Investigation Process	Baryamureeba and Tushabe	2004	5
M09	Extended Model of Cyber Crime Investigation	Ciardhuáin	2004	13
M10	A hierarchical, Objective-Based Framework for the Digital Investigations Process	Beebe and Clark	2004	6
M11	Event-Based Digital Forensic Investigation Framework	Carrier and Spafford	2004	5
M12	Four Step Forensic Process	Kent et al.	2006	4
M13	Framework for a Digital Forensic Investigation	Kohn et al.	2006	3
M14	Computer Forensic Field Triage Process Model	Rogers et al.	2006	12
M15	FORZA—Digital forensics investigation framework	Ieong	2006	6
M16	Common Process Model for Incident and Computer Forensics	Freiling and Schwittay	2007	3
M17	Dual Data Analysis Process	Bem and Huebner	2007	4
M18	Digital Forensic Model based on Malaysian Investigation Process	Perumal	2009	7
M19	Generic Framework for Network Forensics	Pilli et al.	2010	9
M20	Generic Computer Forensic Investigation Model	Yusoff	2011	5
M21	Systematic Digital Forensic Investigation Model	Agarwal et al.	2011	11

of the identified process models is the one and only right way for conducting a digital forensic investigation.

Depending on the purpose of why the process model was developed, such as law enforcement, there are advantages and disadvantages depending on the investigative scenario, such as, being too rigid, linear, or generalized. Appendix A: Process Models, further dissect the digital forensic process models identified in the table above to understand the tasks performed in phases and better understand the uniqueness and commonalities with investigative workflow phases. Despite the differences noted among these process models, there are still significant commonalities in how some phases are used across multiple process models. These similarities confirm that while the process models address different investigative requirements, the underlying forensic science principles, methodologies, and techniques are applied consistently throughout.

As illustrated in Figure 2.1, we can get a better sense of how some phases are frequently used across multiple digital forensic process models. Without getting caught up on the subtle differences in naming convention, it is quite apparent that there is an opportunity to consolidate all phases identified throughout each process model into these common phases. Of special note, highlighted in the figure below are seven phases that have the highest frequency of reoccurrence:

- *Preparation* includes activities to ensure equipment and personnel are prepared.
- *Identification* involves detection of an incident or event.
- *Collection* of relevant data using approved techniques.
- *Preservation* establishes proper evidence gathering and chain of custody.
- *Examination* evaluates digital evidence to reveal data and reduce volumes.
- *Analysis* examining the context and content of digital evidence to determine relevancy.
- *Presentation* includes preparing reporting documentation.

Process models developed to support the digital forensic investigative workflow are focused on establishing the activities and tasks performed throughout to ensure that processes are not bypassed, switched, or not followed. As outlined above, there are seven common phases of a digital forensic investigation workflow: *preparation, identification, collection, preservation, examination, analysis,* and *presentation.* From the descriptions of each of these phases, we see that there are further commonalities between them that allow for further consolidation of these phases into higher level grouping of workflow categories:

- *Preparation* includes activities to ensure administrative, technical, and physical provisions are in place.
- *Gathering* involves following proven techniques to identify, collect, and preserve evidence.
- *Processing* reveals data and reduces volumes based on the contextual and content relevancy.
- *Presentation* includes preparing reporting documentation.

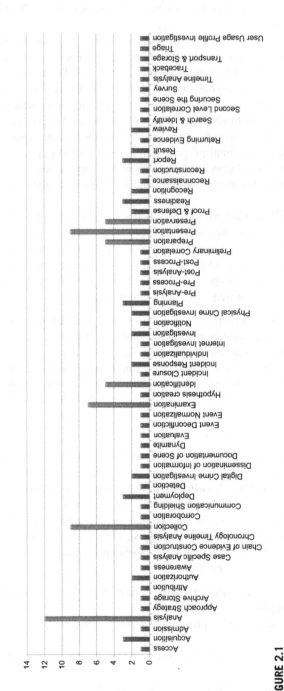

FIGURE 2.1

Process model phase frequency.

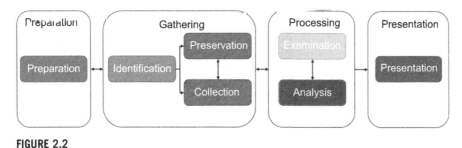

FIGURE 2.2

High-level digital forensic process model.

Illustrated in Figure 2.2, the seven phases have been placed into higher level groupings based on the commonalities of when they are performed during the investigative workflow. The interrelationships between these higher level groupings common phases are illustrated in the order of how they are performed in an investigative workflow; noting the bidirectional interactions between specific phases.

DIGITAL FORENSIC READINESS MODEL

A process model developed to support digital forensic readiness is somewhat different than a process model developed for the digital forensic investigative workflow. Unlike the digital forensic investigative workflow, digital forensic readiness is not a linear process where activities and steps are executed sequentially and there are established "start/end" criteria.

A process model for digital forensic readiness consists of activities and steps within a circular and redundant hierarchy. Initiation of the digital forensic readiness process model can originate from any activity or steps and can subsequently lead to any other phase. The digital forensic readiness process model must establish administrative, technical, and physical foundations to effectively support the activities and tasks performed in all phases of the digital forensic process model by:

- maximizing the potential use of digital evidence.
- minimizing the cost(s) of digital forensic investigations.
- minimizing the interference disruption of business processes.
- preserving and improving the information security posture.

High-level groupings of a digital forensic readiness process model follow the same naming convention as the digital forensic process model. Figure 2.3 illustrates the activities and steps that make up the digital forensic readiness process model. Within this process model, there is a combination of sequential steps within each phase as well as redundant workflows that are dependent on the nature of the investigation at hand. This digital forensic process model serves as the basis for the detailed topics addressed in Section B of this book.

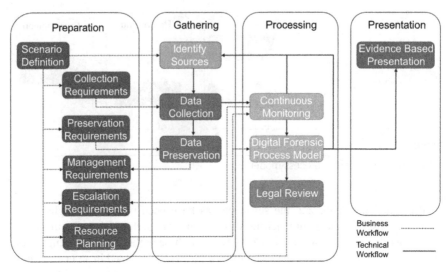

FIGURE 2.3

Digital forensic readiness process model.

SUMMARY

Digital forensics science has long established itself as a discipline that adheres to consistent, repeatable, and defensible processes. Although there have been several models developed to meet the different needs of how digital forensics practices, they are all homogenous in the design methodology. Following a process methodology that is ambiguous to context of its implementation, the digital forensic community adopts a common model as the basis for conducting consistent, repeatable, and defensible processes.

Evidence Management

This chapter follows the high-level digital forensic process model to identify the requirements for properly gathering, processing, and handling digital evidence throughout its lifetime. You will learn about the technical, administrative, and physical controls necessary to safeguard digital evidence in before, during, and after a digital forensic investigation.

INTRODUCTION

Evidence is a critical component of every digital forensic investigation. Whether it is physical or digital, the methodologies and techniques used to gather, process, and handle evidence ultimately affect its meaningfulness, relevancy, and admissibility. Appropriate safeguards must be present during all investigative work to provide an acceptable level of assurance that the life cycle of evidence is forensically sound[1].

Following the high-level digital forensic process model outlined in chapter "Investigative Process Models," each phase of the investigative workflow will be examined to determine and establish the requirements for managing evidence through its lifetime.

Similar to how the CIA triad (confidentiality, integrity, and availability) outlines the most critical components for implementing information security program; the APT triad (administrative, physical, and technical) describes the most critical components for implementing information security controls in support of digital forensic investigations.

EVIDENCE RULES

Rules of evidence govern when, how, and for what purpose, proof of a legal case may be placed before a trier of fact for consideration. Traditionally, the legal system interpreted digital data as hearsay evidence[2] because the contents of this data cannot be proven, beyond a reasonable doubt, to be true. In some jurisdictions, such as under the United States (U.S.) Federal Rules of Evidence 803(6), exceptions to the rule of hearsay evidence exist where digital data is admissible in court if it demonstrates "records of regularly conducted activity" as a business record; such as an act, event, condition, opinion, or diagnosis.

Qualifying business records under this exception requires that the electronically stored information (ESI) can be demonstrated as authentic, reliable, and trustworthy.

As described in U.S. Federal Rules of Evidence 803(6), the requirements for qualifying business record are achieved by proving:

1. the record was made at or near the time by—or information was transmitted by—someone with knowledge[3];
2. the record was kept in the course of a regularly conducted activity of a business, organization, occupation, or calling, whether or not for profit;
3. making the record was a regular practice of that activity;
4. all these conditions are shown by the testimony of the custodian or another qualified witness, or by a certification that complies with Rule 902(11) or (12) or with a statute permitting certification; and
5. neither the source of information nor the method or circumstances of preparation indicate a lack of trustworthiness.

As described in the U.S. Federal Rules of Evidence 902(11), the requirements for certifying domestic records of regularly conducted activity are achieved by:

1. The original or a copy of a domestic record that meets the requirements of Rule 803(6)(A)-(C) as shown by a certification of the custodian or another qualified person that must be signed in a manner that, if falsely made, would subject the signer to criminal penalty under the laws where the certification was signed. Before the trial or hearing, the proponent must give an adverse party reasonable written notice of the intent to offer the record—and must make the record and certification available for inspection—so that the party has a fair opportunity to challenge them.

As described in the U.S. Federal Rules of Evidence 902(12), the requirements for certifying foreign records of regularly conducted activity are achieved by:

2. The original or a copy of a foreign record that meets the requirements of Rule 803(6)(A)-(C) as shown by a certification of the custodian or another qualified person that must be signed in a manner that, if falsely made, would subject the signer to criminal penalty under the laws where the certification was signed. Before the trial or hearing, the proponent must give an adverse party reasonable written notice of the intent to offer the record—and must make the record and certification available for inspection—so that the party has a fair opportunity to challenge them.

Criteria for what type of data constitutes an admissible business record fall within one of the following categories:

- *Technology-generated data* is information that has been created and is being maintained as a result of programmatic processes or algorithms (eg, log files). This type of data can fall within the rules of hearsay exception only when the data is proven to be authentic as a result of properly functioning programmatic processes or algorithms.
- *Technology-stored data* is information that has been created and is being maintained as a result of user input and interactions (eg, word processor document).

This type of data can fall within the rules of hearsay exception only when the individual creating the data is reliable, trustworthy, and has not altered the data it any way.

Business records are commonly challenged on issues of whether data was altered or damaged after its creation (integrity) and the validation and verification of the programmatic processes used (authenticity). As a means of lessening these challenges, Federal Rules of Evidence 1002 describes the need for proving the trustworthiness of digital evidence through the production of the original document. To meet this requirement, organizations must implement a series of safeguards, precautions, and controls to ensure that when digital evidence is admitted into a court of law it can be demonstrably proven as authentic against its original source.

PREPARATION

As the first phase of the investigative workflow, preparation is essential for the activities and steps performed in all other phases of the workflow. Ultimately, if the preparation activities and steps are deficient in any way, whether they are not comprehensive enough or not reviewed regularly for accurateness, there is a greater risk that evidence may be interfered with, altered in some form, or even unavailable when needed (Figure 3.1).

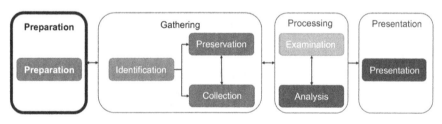

FIGURE 3.1

High-level digital forensic process model - Preparation Phase.

INFORMATION SECURITY MANAGEMENT

The establishment of information security management is a must so that the organization has defined its overall goals. Management, with involvement from key stakeholders such as legal, privacy, security, and human resources, works to define a series of documents that describe exactly how the organization will go about achieving these goals. Figure 3.2 illustrates the hierarchy of the information security management framework and the relationship between these documents in terms of which have direct influence and precedence over others.

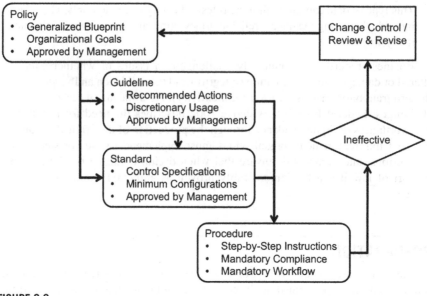

FIGURE 3.2

Information Security Management Framework.

In the context of digital forensics, the implementation of these documents serves as the administrative groundwork for indirectly supporting the subsequent phases where digital evidence is involved. The sections to follow explore these documents individually and provide specifics on the types that contribute to digital forensic readiness.

Policies

At the highest level of documentation, policies are created as formalized blueprint used to describe the organizations goals. These documents address general terms and are not intended to contain the level of detail that are found in standards, guidelines, procedures, or processes. Before writing a policy document, the first step is to define the scope and purpose of why the document is required, what technical and physical evidence is included, and why it is being included. This allows the organization to consider all possibilities and determine what types of policies must be written and even how many policies are required.

A common mistake organizations face is writing a single policy document that encompasses a broad scope which is not easily understood and is difficult to distribute. Instead of having one large document to support all digital forensics requirements, multiple policies should be written to focus on specific evidence sources.

The type of policies to be written is subjective to the organization and its requirements for gathering and maintaining evidence. While there might be a specific type of policy documents not included below, Table 3.1 contains a list of common policies your organization must have in place to support digital forensics.

Table 3.1 Common Policies

Policy	Scope
Acceptable use	Defines acceptable use of equipment and computing services and the appropriate end user controls to protect the organization's resources and proprietary information
Business conduct	Defines the guidelines and expectations of individuals within the organization to demonstrate fair business practices and encourage a culture of openness and trust
Information security	Defines the organization's commitment to globally manage information security risks effectively and efficiently and in compliance with applicable regulations wherever it conducts business
Internet and e-mail	Defines the requirements for proper use of the organization's Internet and electronic mail systems to make users aware of what is considered acceptable and unacceptable use

Guidelines

Following the implementation of a policy, guidelines provide recommendations for how the generalized policy blueprints can be implemented. In certain cases, security cannot be described through the implementation of specific controls, minimum configuration requirements, or other mechanisms. Unlike standards, these documents are created to contain guidelines for end users to use as a reference to follow proper security.

Consider how a policy requires a risk assessment to be routinely completed against a specific system. Instead of developing standards or procedures to perform this task, a guideline document is used to determine the methodologies that must be followed, allowing the teams to fill in the details as needed.

The type of guidelines to be written is subjective to the organization and its requirements for gathering and maintaining evidence. While there might be a specific type of guideline documents not included below, Table 3.2 contains a list of common guidelines your organization must have in place to support digital forensics.

Table 3.2 Common Guidelines

Guideline	Scope
Data loss prevention	Awareness for end users on how to safeguard organizational data from unintentional or accidental loss or theft.
Mobile/portable devices	Recommendations for end users to protect organization's data stored on mobile and/or portable devices.
Passcode selection	Considerations for end users to select strong passcodes for access into organizational systems.
Risk assessments	Direction for assessors to use documented methodologies and proven techniques for assessing organizational systems.

Standards

After policies are in places, or as a result of a guideline, a series of standards can be developed to define more specific rules used to support the implemented governance documentation. Standards are used as the drivers for policies, and by setting standards, policies that are difficult to implement—or that encompass the entire organization—are guaranteed to work in all environments. For example, if the information security policy requires all users to be authenticated to the organization, the standard for using a particular solution is established here.

Standards can be used to create a minimum level of security necessary to meet the predetermined policy requirements. Standard documents can contain configurations, architectures, or design specifications that are specific to the systems or solutions they directly represent, such as firewalls or logical access. While standards might not reflect existing business processes, they represent a minimum requirement that must be adaptable and changeable to meet evolving business requirements.

The type of standard to be written is subjective to the organization and its requirements for gathering and maintaining evidence. While there might be a specific type of standard documents not included below, Table 3.3 contains a list of common standards your organization must have in place to support digital forensics.

Table 3.3 Common Standards

Standard	Scope
Backup, retention, and recovery	Defines the means and materials required to recover from an undesirable event, timely and reliably, that causes systems and/or data to become unavailable.
E-mail systems	Define the configurations necessary to minimize business risk and maximize use of e-mail content as a result of the available and continuity of the supporting infrastructure
Firewall management	Defines the configurations necessary to ensure the integrity and confidentiality of the organization's systems and/or data is protected as a result of the available and continuity of the supporting infrastructure
Logical access	Defines the requirements for authenticating and authorizing user access to mitigate exposure of the organizations systems and/or data.
Malware detection	Defines the configurations necessary to ensure the attack surface of vulnerable systems is mitigated against known malicious software.
Network security	Defines the requirements for controlling external, remote, and/or internal access to the organizations systems and/or data
Platform configurations	Defines the minimum security configurations necessary to ensure the organization's system mitigates unauthorized access or unintended exposure of data.
Physical access	Defines the methods used to ensure adequate controls exist to mitigate unauthorized access to the organization's premise.

Procedures

From the guidelines and standards that have been implemented, the last type of documents to be created is the procedures used by administrators, operations personnel, analysts, etc., to follow as they perform their job functions.

Policies, standards, and guidance documents all have a relationship with digital evidence whereby they do not have direct interactions with the systems or data. On the other hand, procedures are documents whereby interactions with digital evidence is directly associated with the clearly defined activities and steps.

To better understand the different procedures involved with digital evidence management, each procedure will be explored throughout the remainder of this chapter as they apply to the different phases in the high-level digital forensic process model.

Essentially, the culture and structure of each organization influences how these governance documents are created. Regardless of where (internationally) business is conducted or the size of the organization, there are five simple principles that should be followed as generic guidance for achieving a successful governance framework:

- *Keep it simple*: All documentation should be as clear and concise as possible. The information contained within each document should be stated as briefly as possible without omitting any critical pieces of information. Where documentation is drawn out and wordy they are typically more difficult to understand, are less likely to be read, and harder to interpret and implement.
- *Keep it understandable*: Documentation should be developed in a language that is commonly known throughout the organization. Leveraging a taxonomy, as discussed in Appendix F: Building a Taxonomy, organizations can avoid the complication of using unrecognized terms and/or jargon.
- *Keep it practicable*: Regardless of how precise and clear the documentation might be, if it cannot be practiced then it is useless. An example of unrealistic documentation would be a statement indicating that incident response personnel is to be available 24 hours a day; even though there is no adequate means of contacting them when they are not in the office. For this reason, documentation that is not practicable is not effective and will be quickly ignored.
- *Keep it cooperative*: Good governance documentation is developed through the collaborative effort of all relevant stakeholders, such as legal, privacy, security, and human resources. If key stakeholder has not been involved in the development of these documents, it is more likely that problems will arise during its implementation.
- *Keep it dynamic*: Useful governance document should be, by design, flexible enough to adapt with organizational changes and growth. It would be impractical to develop documentation that is focused on serving the current needs and desires of the organization without considering what could come in the future.

DIGITAL FORENSIC TEAM

Depending on the organization, a digital forensic team will vary greatly in terms of size, roles, and procedures. Regardless, there should be consistency in the requirement for all people involved in executing digital forensics activities and steps understanding the fundamental principles, methodologies, and techniques used during an investigation.

Roles and Responsibilities

Illustrated in Figure 3.3, the *FORZA—Digital Forensic Investigation Framework* was developed as a means of linking the multiple practitioner roles with the procedures they are responsible for throughout the investigative workflow. Details on the roles described in the FORZA process model have been described in detail as found in Appendix A: Process Models.

Regardless of an individual's role in the investigative workflow, there are different activities and steps performed that require either general or specialized knowledge in order to maintain digital evidence integrity. It is essential that all persons involved, at any phases of the investigative workflow, diligently follow the rules of evidence and thoroughly apply digital forensic principles, methodologies, and techniques to all aspects of their work.

Illustrated in the FORZA process model, the need for distinct roles and people is subjective to the overall size of the organization and the arrangement of the digital forensic team. For example, organizations that are smaller or localized to a specific geographic location might only employ a few individuals that are responsible for all aspects of digital forensics. Alternatively, organizations that are larger, distributed in geographic location, or have clearly defined structures might employ multiple individuals who are each responsible for a particular aspect of digital forensics.

Regardless of these factors, what remains consistent is the need for individuals who have strong information technology knowledge as well as formalized training of digital forensic principles, methodologies, techniques, and tools. These are essential and fundamental to ensuring that the integrity, relevancy, and admissibility of digital evidence are maintained. While not a comprehensive list, the following roles are commonly employed in support of digital forensics:

- *Forensic technicians* gather, process, and handle evidence at the crime scene. These individuals need to be trained in proper handling techniques, such as the order of volatility discussed in chapter "Understanding Digital Forensics," to ensure the authenticity and integrity of evidence is preserved for potential admissibility in a court of law.
- *Forensic analysts, or examiners,* use forensics tools and investigative techniques to identify and, where needed, recover specific electronic stored information (ESI). Leveraging their technical skills, these individuals most often are the ones who are performing the work to process and analyze electronically stored information as part of an investigation.

	Why (Motivation)	What (data)	How (Function)	Where (Network)	Who (People)	When (Time)
Case leader (contextual investigation layer)	Investigation Objective	Event Nature	Requested Initial Investigation	Investigation Geography	Initial Participants	Investigation Timeline
System owner (if any) (contextual layer)	Business Objective	Business and Event Nature	Business and System Process Model	Business Geography	Organization and Participants Relationship	Business and Incident Timeline
Legal advisor (legal advisory layer)	Legal Objective	Legal Background and Preliminary Issues	Legal Procedures for Further Investigation	Legal Geography	Legal Entities and Participants	Legal Timeframe
Security/system architect/auditor (conceptual security layer)	System/Security Control Objective	System Information and Security Control Model	Security Mechanisms	Security Domain and Network Infrastructure	Users and Security Entity Model	Security Timing and Sequencing
Digital forensics specialists (technical preparation layer)	Forensic Investigation Strategy Objectives	Forensic Data Model	Forensic Strategy Design	Forensics Data Geography	Forensics Entity Model	Hypothetical Forensics Event Timeline
Forensics investigators/system administrator/operator (data acquisition layer)	Forensic Acquisition Objectives	On-site Forensics Data Observation	Forensics Acquisition / Seizure Procedures	Site Network Forensics Data Acquisition	Participants Interviewing and Hearing	Forensics Acquisition Timeline
Forensics investigators/forensics analysts (data analysis layer)	Forensic Examination Objectives	Event Data Reconstrucion	Forensics Analysis Procedures	Network Address Extraction and Analysis	Entity and Evidence Relationship Analysis	Event Timeline Reconstruction
Legal prosecutor (legal presentation layer)	Legal Presentation Objectives	Legal Presentation Attributes	Legal Presentation Procedures	Legal Jurisdiction Location	Entities in Litigation Procedures	Timeline of the Entire Event for Presentation

FIGURE 3.3

FORZA—Digital Forensic Investigation Framework.

- *Forensic investigators* work with internal (ie, IT support teams) and external (ie, law enforcement agencies) entities to retrieve evidence relevant to the investigation. In some environments, these individuals might also perform the duties of both the forensic technician and the forensic analyst. It is important to note that in some jurisdiction, use of the term "investigator" requires individuals to hold a private investigator license that involves meeting a minimum requirement for both education and experience.
- *Forensics managers* oversee all actions and activities involving digital forensics. Within the scope of their organization's digital forensic discipline, these individuals can be accountable for ensuring their organizations digital forensic program continues to operate through activities such as leading a team, coordinating investigations and reporting, and oversee the execution of daily operations. While these individuals do not perform hands-on activities, it is expected that they are educated and knowledgeable of how digital forensic principles, methodologies, and techniques must be applied and followed.

While not typically a role within the digital forensic discipline, the terms forensic specialist and forensic professional are commonly used to describe individuals who have been extensively trained, gained significant amounts of experience, and are recognized for their skills.

Education and Certification

Dating back to the early 2000's there has been a growth in the number of higher education and postsecondary institutes that offer education programs focusing specifically on digital forensic. While each education programs might be slightly different in the curriculum offered, they are all designed to cover the fundamental principles, methodologies, and techniques of digital forensics as required when directly involved in the investigative workflow.

Following the completion of formalized education, there are several recognized industry associations that offer professional certifications in digital forensics. It is important to keep in mind that on their own, these professional certifications do not provide the in-depth level of education and training on digital forensics and information technology that formalized education provides. Professional certifications, or professional designations, provide assurance that an individual is qualified to perform digital forensics.

Appendix B: Education and Professional Certifications provides a list of higher/postsecondary institutes that offer formal digital forensic education programs as well as recognized industry associations offering digital forensic professional certifications.

LAB ENVIRONMENT

A digital forensic lab is where digital evidence is stored. This lab environment must be both physically and logically secure so that evidence contained within is not lost, corrupted, or destroyed. When building a lab, there are common data center characteristics—including, but not limited to, power supply, raised flooring, and lighting—that must be factored into the construction of this controlled and secure environment.

In addition to data center characteristics, there are other attributes that must be considered to protect digital evidence from being lost, corrupted, or destroyed. The following items, in no particular order, provide additional protections against potential impact to digital evidence being stored within the lab environment:

- Labs must be built in an enclosed room, with true floor to ceiling walls, located in the interior of the building.
- To prevent unauthorized access, entrance door must have internal facing hinges, walls must be constructed using permanent materials, and windows must be reinforced with wire mesh material.
- Labs must follow the principle of least-privileged access and only permit access to those individuals who have been approved for entry.
- Physical access to the lab must be provisioned using multifactor authentication including something you know (ie, passcode), something you have (ie, smart-card), and something you are (ie, manager).
- Visitor access must be logged and escorted, at all time, inside the lab.
- Evidence lockers or safes must remain locked at all times with chain of custody logs tracking evidence ownership.
- Control mechanisms need to be created as parallel structures to track and maintain a complete, accurate, and up-to-date inventory of all major hardware and software items.
- Process and procedures must be in place to track access in and out of the lab, hardware and software inventory, and lab maintenance (ie, software currency, evidence lockers).
- Assignment of a custodian responsible for safeguarding digital evidence when it is not in use for processing by investigators.

Lab inspections must be performed consistently to provide assurance that the lab environment continues to operate with the established level of security controls in place. These reviews should be performed by independent parties and not by the digital forensic team to:

- determine if structural issues are present within the walls, door, windows, floor, and ceiling
- inspect all access control mechanisms to ensure they are not damaged and continue to function as expected
- review logs for physical access into the lab environment by both approved individuals and visitors
- analyze tracking logs to identify issues with continuity and integrity of evidence

HARDWARE AND SOFTWARE

With the digital forensic lab built, the team should begin to acquire a series of hardware equipment and software tools that will be needed to conduct investigations in a forensically sound manner. When acquiring forensic tools, it is important for the digital forensic team to keep in mind that each investigation is unique and may require a variety of different tools and equipment to maintain evidence integrity.

To identify and select the proper tools and equipment to perform their investigative activities and steps, the digital forensic team has to have a good understanding of how different business environments function respective to the hardware and operating system(s) they use. This assessment will determine what tools and equipment are required to gather and process evidence from the organizations data sources. While there might be some tools or equipment absent due to new ones being constantly developed, the websites included in the "Resources" section at the end of this chapter list some companies that have commercial offerings for digital forensic tools and equipment.

All digital forensic tools and equipment work differently, and may behave differently, when used on different evidence sources. Before using any tools or equipment to gather or process evidence, investigators have to be familiar with how to operate these technologies by practicing on a variety of evidence sources. This testing must demonstrate that the tools and equipment used during a forensic investigation generate repeatable[4] and reproducible[5] results. This process of testing introduces a level of assurance that the tools and equipment being used by investigators are forensically sound and will not introduce doubt into the evidence's integrity. Appendix C: Tool and Equipment Validation Program outlines guidance for digital forensic professional to follow when performing testing of their tools and equipment.

GATHERING

As the second phase of the investigative workflow, gathering is made up of the activities and steps performed to identify, collect, and preserve evidence. These activities and steps are critical in maintaining the meaningfulness, relevancy, and admissibility of evidence for the remainder of its life cycle (Figure 3.4).

OPERATING PROCEDURES

Prior to gathering evidence, there must be a series of written and approved standard operating procedures (SOP) to assist the forensic team when performing evidence

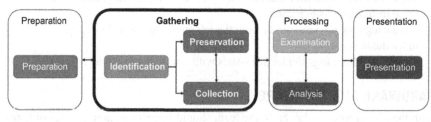

FIGURE 3.4

High-level digital forensic process model - Gathering Phase.

gathering activities and steps. The combination of governance that was developed through the information security management program, along with the validation and verification results from tool and equipment testing, operating procedures are the backbone for investigators to follow as they work through the investigation.

Identification

Identification of evidence involves a series of activities and steps that must be performed in sequence. It is important to know what data sources, such as systems, peripherals, removable media, etc., are associated or have an impacting role to the investigation.

When a data source has been identified, proper evidence handling must be followed at all times. If the evidence is handled incorrectly, there is high probability that the evidence will no longer be meaningful, relevant, or admissible. SOPs are required to support the investigative workflow and provide investigators with direction on how to execute their tasks in a repeatable and reproducible way.

Securing the Scene

Even though the main focus of digital forensics is about digital evidence, it is critical that digital forensic professional include both digital and physical evidence within the scope of every investigation. Similar to how the first step law enforcement takes is to establish a perimeter around a crime scene to secure evidence, the same first step must be done during a digital forensic investigation. Whoever is responsible for securing the scene must be trained and knowledgeable of the accepted activities, steps, and procedures to be followed.

Securing the physical environment, the current state of evidence can be documented and a level of assurance establishes that evidence will be protected against tampering or corruption. While the activities, steps, and procedures used will vary and are subjective depending on the environment, it is critical that they are followed to minimize the potential for errors, oversights, or injuries.

An important rule to remember in all crime scenes is that everyone who enters or leaves a crime scene will either deposit something or take something with them. It is crucial that no unauthorized individuals are within a reasonable distance of the secured environment as these persons can interfere with evidence and potentially disrupt the investigation.

At this phase, the information and details collected about the state of the scene is done so at the highest level. Proper planning must take place to develop and implement operating procedures that address the different scenarios for how to physically and logically secure crime scenes.

Documenting the Scene

Having secured the physical environment, the next step is to document the scene and answer questions around what is present, where it is located, and how it is connected.

The most effective way to answer these questions is by videotaping, photographing, or sketching the secured environment before any evidence is handled. When capturing images of the physical environment, the following aspects of the scene must be documented:

- A complete view of the physical environment (eg, floor location, department, workspace);
- Individual views of specific work areas as needed (eg, book shelves, systems, open cabinets, garbage cans);
- Hard wire connections to systems and where they lead (eg, USB drives, printers, cameras);
- Empty slots or connects not in use on the system as evidence that no connection existed;
- Without pressing mouse or keypad buttons, what is visible on the monitor (eg, running processes, open files, wallpaper).

Just like police officers record events in their notebooks, forensic investigators must maintain documentation for every interaction on the presumption that the investigation could end up in a court of law. The investigator's notes must include (at a minimum) date, time, and investigator's full name, and thorough details about all interactions. The notes should also illustrate page number/sequence and have no white space available—fill that space with a solid line to prevent supplementary comments from being inserted. A logbook template has been provided as a reference in the Templates section of this book.

Search and Seizure

Once the scene is secured and thoroughly documented, investigators work to seize evidence. But the goal of seizing evidence is not to seize everything at the scene. Through the knowledge and experience of trained investigators, educated decisions can be made about what evidence need to be seized and then documenting the justifications for doing so.

Digital evidence comes in many forms, such as application logs, network device configurations, badge reader logs, or audit trails. Given that these are only examples and depending on the scope of the investigation, there are potentially significantly more relevant evidence forms. Identifying and seizing all evidence can prove to be a challenging task to which technical operating procedures will provide guidance and support. However, from time to time, investigators might encounter situations where these technical operating procedures do not address collecting a specific evidence source. In these situations, the importance of having trained digital forensic professional is essential in having the knowledge and skills necessary to apply the fundamental principles, methodologies, and techniques of forensic science in seizing the evidence.

Documentation is at the center of the investigative workflow and is equally important when it comes to seizing evidence. When a physical (ie, computer) or logical (ie, text file) artifact has been identified as relevant to an investigation, the act of seizing it as evidence initiates the chain of custody to establish authenticity by tracking where it came from, where it went after it was seized, and who handled it for what purpose. Custody tracking must accompany the evidence and be maintained throughout the lifetime of the evidence. A chain of custody template has been provided as a reference in the *Templates* section of this book.

All digital evidence is subject to the same rules and laws that apply to physical evidence where prosecutors must demonstrate, without doubt, that evidence is in the exact and unchanged state as it was when the investigator seized it. The Good Practices Guide for Computer-Based Electronic Evidence was developed by the Association of Chief of Police Officers (ACPO) in the United Kingdom to address evidence handling steps for the types of technologies commonly seized during an investigation. Within this document, there are four overarching principles that investigators must follow when handling evidence in order to maintain evidence authenticity:

- *Principle #1*: No action taken by law enforcement agencies or their agents should change data held on a computer or storage media which may subsequently be relied upon in court.
- *Principle #2*: In circumstances where a person finds it necessary to access original data held on a computer or on storage media, that person must be competent to do so and be able to give evidence explaining the relevance and the implications of their actions.
- *Principle #3*: An audit trail or other record of all processes applied to computer-based electronic evidence should be created and preserved. An independent third party should be able to examine those processes and achieve the same result.
- *Principle #4*: The person in charge of the investigation (the case officer) has overall responsibility for ensuring that the law and these principles are adhered to.

Collection and Preservation

The transition between a physical investigation into digital forensic activities starts with the collection of digital evidence. Digital evidence is volatile by nature, and investigators are responsible for ensuring that the original state of seized evidence is preserved as a result of any tool or equipment used to collect it. Working in a controlled lab environment, investigators must create an exact, bit-level duplicate of original evidence using digital forensic tools and equipment that have been subject to validation and verification testing programs.

Under the Federal Rules of Evidence, Rule 1001 describes that duplicates of digital evidence are admissible in court instead of the original when it is "the product of a method which insures accuracy and genuineness." To guarantee that the bit-level copy is an accurate and genuine duplicate of the original evidence source, one-way cryptographic algorithms such as the message-digest algorithm family (ie, MD5, MD6)[6] or the secure hashing algorithm family (ie, SHA-1,SHA-2,SHA-3)[7] are used to generate hash values of both original and duplicate. Not only does the use of one-way cryptographic hash algorithms provide investigators with assurance that the bit-level copy is an exact duplicate of the original, they also provide investigators with the means of verifying the integrity of the bit-level duplicate throughout the subsequent activities and task of the investigative workflow.

With an exact bit-level duplicate created for use during the processing phase, the original evidence must be placed back into secure lockup; accompanied by an updated chain of custody that documents the evidence interactions. In addition, a new chain of custody for the bit-level duplicate must be created and maintained throughout the remainder of the evidence's lifetime.

Between 2004 and 2005, it was discovered that both MD5 and SHA-1 algorithms contain flaws whereby two different data files or data sets have a cryptographic hash value that are identical even though there are distinctly different properties and characteristics in the data themselves.

Otherwise known as "hash collisions," these flaws created concerns among the forensic community about the potential impact on the admissibility of digital evidence in a court of law. From a digital forensic perspective, this meant that a hash collision could be engineered so that separate pieces of digital evidence return the same hash value.

However, during a forensic investigation, both the MD5 and SHA-1 algorithms are used as a way of demonstrating to the courts that the digital evidence being presented is in the same state as it was when it was obtained and that it has not been altered in any way, demonstrating the authenticity and integrity of digital evidence.

In the 2009 trial of the United States v. Joseph Schmidt III, findings of facts and conclusions of law determined that the SHA-1 digital fingerprint for a file produces a unique digital algorithm that specifically identified the file. Further it was ruled that the chances of a hash collision are not mathematically significant and are not at issue.

Legally, this means that if digital evidence was cryptographically hashed using either MD5 or SHA-1 when it was obtained and then validated at a later time using the same cryptographic algorithm, then the authenticity and integrity of the digital evidence can be relied upon in a court of law.

PROCESSING

As the third phase of the investigative workflow, processing involves the activities and steps performed by the investigator to examine and analyze digital evidence. These activities and steps are used by investigators to examine duplicated evidence in a forensically sound manner to identify meaningful data and subsequently reduce volumes based on the contextual and content relevance (Figure 3.5).

All activities and steps performed during the processing phase should occur inside a secure lab environment where digital evidence can be properly controlled and is not susceptible to access by unauthorized personnel or exposure to contamination. Before performing any examination or analysis of digital evidence, investigators must complete due diligence by proving the integrity of the forensic workstations that will be used, including inspecting for malicious software, verifying wiped media, and certifying the host operating system (eg, time synchronization, secure boot[8]).

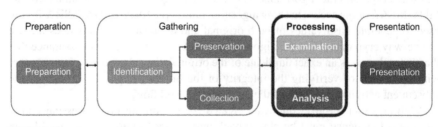

FIGURE 3.5

High-level digital forensic process model - Processing Phase.

Maintaining the integrity of digital evidence during examination and analysis is essential for investigators. By using the one-way cryptographic hash algorithm calculated during the gathering phase, investigators can prove that their interactions do not impact the integrity and authenticity of the evidence. Digital forensic tools and equipment provide investigators with automated capabilities, based on previous professional knowledge and criteria, which can be used to verify and validate the state of evidence.

On occasion, the programmatic processes or algorithms provided through tools and equipment require extended and potentially unattended use of digital evidence. During this time, the investigator remains the active custodian of all digital evidence in use and is responsible for maintaining its authenticity, reliability, and trustworthiness while unattended. Within the controlled lab environment, access to evidence can be restricted from unauthorized access through the use of physical controls, such as individual work areas under lock/key entry, or logical controls, such as use individual credentials for accessing tool and equipment.

PRESENTATION

As the fourth and last phase of the investigative workflow, presentation involves the activities and steps performed to produce evidence-based reports of the investigation. These activities and steps provide investigators with a channel of demonstrating that processes, techniques, tools, equipment, and interactions maintained the authenticity, reliability, and trustworthiness of digital evidence throughout the investigative workflow (Figure 3.6).

Having completed the examination and analysis, all generated case files and evidence must be checked in to secure lockers and the chain of custody updated. Unless otherwise instructed by legal authorities, the criteria for retaining digital evidence must comply with, and not exceed, the timelines established through policies, standards, and procedures. Proper disposal of digital evidence must be done so using the existing chain of custody form.

Documentation is a critical element of an investigation. In alignment with established operating procedures, each phase of the investigative workflow requires

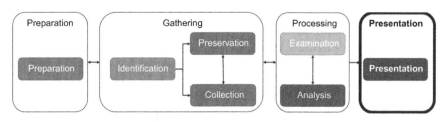

FIGURE 3.6

High-level digital forensic process model - Presentation Phase.

different types of documentation to be maintained that is as complete, accurate, and comprehensive as possible. From the details captured in these documents, investigators can demonstrate for all digital evidence the continuity in custody and interactions with authorized personnel.

Layout and illustration of the final report must clearly articulate to the audience a chronology of events specific to evidence interactions. This chronology should be structured in sequence to the phases of the investigative workflow and accurately communicate through defined section heading the activities and steps performed. A final report template has been provided as a reference in the Templates section of this book.

SUMMARY

A critical component of every forensic investigation is the need for credible digital evidence abides with the legal rules of admissibility. Throughout the entire investigative workflow, there must be a series of administrative, physical, and technical in place to guarantee that the authenticity and integrity of digital evidence is maintained throughout its entire lifecycle.

RESOURCES

Digital Forensic Tools and Equipment Tools, ForensicsWiki. http://www.forensicswiki.org/wiki/Tools, 2015.

List of Digital Forensics Tools, Wikipedia. http://en.wikipedia.org/wiki/List_of_digital_forensics_tools, 2015.

Free Computer Forensic Tools, Forensic Control. https://forensiccontrol.com/resources/free-software/, 2015.

21 Popular Computer Forensics Tools, InfoSec Institute. http://resources.infosecinstitute.com/computer-forensics-tools/, 2014.

TAXONOMY

1   *Forensically Sound* qualifies and, in some cases, justifies the use of a particular forensic technology or methodology.
2   *Hearsay evidence* is second hand or indirect evidence that is offered by a witness of which they do not have direct knowledge but, rather, their testimony is based on what other has said to them.
3   *Someone with knowledge* describes any person who has awareness or familiarity gained through experience or learning.
4   *Repeatable* refers to obtaining the same results when using the same method on identical test items in the same laboratory by the same operator using the same equipment within short intervals of time.

5 *Reproducible* refers to obtaining the same results being obtained when using the same method on identical test items in different laboratories with different operators utilizing different equipment.

6 *Message digest algorithm (MD)* is a family of one-way cryptographic hashing functions commonly used to creation a unique digital fingerprint with hash lengths that vary, depending on version, between 128-bit and 512-bit.

7 *Secure hashing algorithm (SHA)* is a family of one-way cryptographic hashing functions commonly used to create a unique digital fingerprint with hash lengths that vary, depending on version, between 160-bit and 512-bit.

8 *Secure boot* is a security standard to ensure that a system only loads and uses known-good and trusted software.

Digital Forensic Readiness

B

B

Digital Forensic
Readiness

Understanding Forensic Readiness

## 4

This chapter provides an introduction to digital forensic readiness by exploring the purpose and scope behind the program, the high-level goals of the program, the business benefits realized from implementing the program, and codependence on an information security program.

INTRODUCTION

Digital forensic investigations are commonly performed in reaction to an event or incident. During postevent response activities, investigators must work quickly to gather, process, and present digital evidence. Depending on the environment where an investigation is conducted, the evidence necessary to support the investigation may or may not exist leading to complications with arriving at factual and credible conclusions.

Within a business environment the opportunity to proactively gather digital evidence is more prevalent than the ability to gather evidence in a law enforcement setting. If digital evidence has not been gathered to start with, there is a greater chance that it may not be available when needed. Any organization that depends on, or utilizes, technology should have a balanced concern for information security and digital forensic capabilities.

Digital evidence is fundamental in helping organizations to manage the impact of many different business risks; such as validating the impact of an event or incident, supporting litigation matters, or demonstrating compliance. Regardless of the business risk, there are situations where an event or incident can escalate into something much more serious. Digital forensic readiness is the ability of an organization to proactively maximize the prospective use of electronically stored information (ESI) to reduce the cost of the digital forensic investigative workflow.

DIGITAL FORENSICS AND INFORMATION SECURITY

As technology advances to become more and more pervasive within both personal and business uses, so do the opportunities for committing cybercrime. Through evolved, advanced, and perfected techniques, cybercriminals are focused on harvesting the volumes of digital information that is generated from our every interaction, making an effective and efficient information security program essential.

Many organizations have established an information security program, architectures, and strategies in place to mitigate the risk of losing information and information assets. However, an information security program is only as strong as its weakest link and incidents will happen. When they do occur, it is essential that organizations work quickly to contain the business impact recover business functions, and investigate the root cause of the incident.

By default, gaining access to relevant digital evidence during this time is more challenging because there is greater potential it has been damaged, dismissed, or simply overlooked. Organizations commonly develop their information security program and strategies based on industry best practices[1] that, for the most part, do not consider the importance of putting appropriate controls or procedures in place to ensure the investigation is successful. Even though digital forensics and information security are separate and uniquely distinct disciplines, commonalities do exist where specific activities overlap across both.

PROACTIVE ACTIVITIES

Within information security, the primary focus is to reduce the potential for damage or loss to information and information assets. To support this, security controls can be implemented to include, but are not limited to, the following:

- Information security management framework (ie, policies, standards, guidance);
- Administrative, technical, physical control mechanisms (eg, operating procedures, programmatic solutions, specialized technical skills);
- Security awareness training (ie, stakeholder, general user);
- Organizational, regulatory, and legal compliance requirements.

Within digital forensics, the primary focus is to minimize disruption to business functions while maintaining the meaningfulness, relevancy, and admissibility of evidence. To support this, controls that can be implemented include, but are not limited to, the following:

- Evidence management framework (ie, policies, standards, guidance);
- Administrative, technical, physical control mechanisms (eg, operating procedures, tools and equipment, specialized technical skills);
- Digital forensic training (ie, knowledge, skills);
- Organizational, regulatory, and legal compliance requirements.

REACTIVE ACTIVITIES

Within information security, the primary focus is to achieve a level of assurance that the damage or loss to information and/or information assets is minimized and ongoing risk is mitigated. To support this, controls that can be implemented include, but are not limited to, the following:

- Incident response capabilities;
  - Security incident response team (SIRT);
  - Computer (security) incident response team (CIRT/CSIRT).

- Disaster recovery planning (DRP);
- Business continuity planning (BCP);
- Information security gap analysis and recommendations.

Within digital forensics, the primary focus is to perform an investigative root-cause analysis of an incident by gathering and processing digital evidence. To support this, controls that can be implemented include, but are not limited to, the following:

- Incident response capabilities;
  - Security incident response team (SIRT);
  - Computer (security) incident response team (CIRT/CSIRT).
- Disaster recovery planning;
- Business continuity planning;
- Supplemental digital forensic operating procedures.

A proper balance must be made to adapt information security best practices to include all aspects of digital forensics so containment and recovery activities are properly balanced with the gathering and processing of digital evidence. Digital evidence is required wherever it can be used to manage business risk; and organizations require access to digital evidence to demonstrate and support their acceptable risk posture. However, digital information does not become digital evidence until a crime has been committed and the data is needed in an investigation.

WHAT IS FORENSIC READINESS?

The concept of a digital forensic readiness program was first published in 2001 by John Tan. Through a digital forensic readiness program, organizations can make appropriate and informed decisions about business risks to make the most of its ability to proactively gather digital evidence. Tan outlines that the primary objectives for an organization to implement a digital forensic readiness program are to:

1. maximize the ability to collect credible digital evidence and
2. minimize the cost of forensics during an event or incident.

In the 2001 Honeynet Project, John Tan participated as a judge where he discovered the most remarkable finding in this exercise was the cost of the incident.

During e-mail communications with Dave Dittrich, head of the Honeynet Project, John and Dave identified that the time spent by intruders (approximately 2 hours) significantly differed from the time spent to clean up after them (between 3 and 80 hours).

This led to the conclusion that every 2 hours of intruder time resulted in 40 billable hours of forensic investigative time. However, this estimation did not include intrusion detection (human element), disk image acquisition, restoration and hardening of compromised system(s), network scanning for other vulnerable systems, and communications to stakeholders.

Digital forensic readiness places emphasis on the anticipation that an incident will occur by enabling organizations to make the most efficient use of digital evidence; instead of concerning itself with the traditional responsive nature of an incident. It is a business requirement of any organization that requires key stakeholders to serve a broad role in the overall investigative workflow, including, but not limited to:

- The investigative team;
- Senior/executive management;
- Human resources and employee relations;
- Privacy and compliance;
- Corporate Security;
- IT support staff;
- Legal.

By having key stakeholders involved in the overall investigative workflow, digital forensic readiness enables an overall organizational approach to proactively gathering digital evidence. As an overall strategy, the objectives of forensic readiness can be summarized as "the ability to maximize potential use of digital evidence while minimizing investigative costs"; with the purpose of achieving the following goals:

- Legally gather admissible evidence without interrupting business functions;
- Gather evidence required to validate the impact events of incident have on business risks;
- Permit investigations to proceed at a cost that is lower than the cost of an event or incident;
- Minimize the disruption and impact to business functions;
- Ensure evidence maintains positive outcomes for legal proceedings.

COST AND BENEFIT OF FORENSIC READINESS

Management will be cautious of the cost for implementing a digital forensic readiness program. While cost implications will be higher where organizations have immature information security programs and strategies, the cost is lessened for organizations that already have a good handle on their information security posture. In either case, the issues raised by the need for a digital forensic readiness program have to be presented to senior management where a decision can be made.

Cost analysis of a digital forensic readiness program has to be weighed against the value-added benefits that the organization will realize once implemented. To make an educated and informed decision about whether implementing a digital forensic readiness program is practical, organizations must be able to perform an "apples-to-apples" comparison of the tangible and intangible contributors to the program. The starting point of this task is to document the individual security controls that will be aligned to the digital forensic readiness program through a service catalog. Appendix D: Service Catalog further discusses the service catalog to better understand how to hierarchically align individual security controls into the forensic readiness program.

COST ASSESSMENT

Forensic readiness consists of costs involving administrative, technical, and physical information security controls implemented throughout the organization. Through the service catalog, each of these controls will be aligned to a service where all cost elements can be identified and allocated appropriately. While not all controls and services will contribute to digital forensic readiness, the following will have direct influences to the overall cost of the digital forensic readiness program:

- *Governance document maintenance* is the ongoing review and updating to the information security and evidence management frameworks (eg, policies, standards, guidance, procedures);
- *Education and awareness training* provides continued improvements to:
  - information security awareness of staff indirectly involved with the information security discipline;
  - information security training of staff directly involved with the information security discipline;
  - digital forensic training of staff directly involved with the digital forensic discipline.
- *Incident management* involves the activities of identifying, analyzing, and mitigating risks to reduce the likelihood of reoccurrence;
- *Data security* includes the enhanced capability to systematically gather potential evidence and securely preserve it;
- *Legal counsel* provides advice and assurance that methodologies, operating procedures, tools, and equipment used during an investigation will not impede legal proceedings.

The inclusion of a service as a cost contributors to the digital forensic readiness program is subject to the interpretation and appetite of each organization. Knowing which services, where controls are aligned, contribute to the digital forensic readiness program is the starting point for performing the cost assessment. From the service catalog, the breakdown of fixed and variable costs can be used as part of the cost-benefit analysis for demonstrating to manage the value of implementing the program.

BENEFITS

With digital forensic readiness, it is necessary to assume that an incident will occur, even if a thorough assessment has determined that residual risk from defensive information security controls is minor. Depending on the impact from this residual risk, organizations need to implement additional layers of controls to proactively collect evidence to determine the root cause.

When organizations come to the realization that some type of investigative capability is required, the next step is to address this need through efficient and competent capabilities. Digital forensic readiness that is designed to address the residual risk and enhance proactive investigative capabilities offers organization with the following benefits:

- *Minimizing costs*: Operating on the anticipation that an event or incident will occur, organization will minimize the disruption to business functions and support investigative capabilities that are much more efficient, quick, and cost effective. Having precollected digital evidence, the investigative workflow becomes much simpler to navigate through as more focus can be placed on the processing and presentation phases.
- *Control expansion*: In response mode, the capabilities and effectiveness of information security controls provide functionality limited to notification, containment, and remediation. Where proactive monitoring is utilized, organizations are able to expand their implementation of these information security controls to identify and mitigate a much wider range of cyberthreats before they become more serious incidents or events.
- *Crime deterrent*: Proactive evidence gathering, combined with continuous monitoring, of this information increases the opportunity to quickly detect malicious activity. As word of proactive evidence collection become more widely known, individuals will be less likely to commit malicious activities because the probability of being caught is much greater.
- *Governance and Compliance*: With a good information management framework in place, organizations can better demonstrate their ability to conduct incident prevention and response. Showing this maturity not only provides customers with a sense of security and protection when it comes to safeguarding their assets, but investors will also have more confidence in the organizations ability to minimize threats against their investments.
- *Law enforcement*: Ensuring compliance with laws and regulations encourages good working relationships with both law enforcement and regulators. When an incident or event occurs, the job of investigators is much easier because the organization has taken steps to gathering digital evidence before, during, and after an incident or event.
- *Legal preparations:* International laws relating to electronic discovery (e-discovery), such as the Federal Rules of Civil Procedure in the United States, Rules of Civil Procedure in Canada, or the Practice Direction 31B in the United Kingdom, require that digital evidence is provided quickly and in a forensically sound manner. Information management in support of Electronic Discovery (e-discovery) involves activities such as incident response, data retention, disaster recovery, and business continuity policies; all of which are enhanced through a digital forensic readiness program. When an organizations enters into legal proceedings, the need for e-discovery is significantly reduced because digital evidence will already be preserved, increasing the probability of success when used as part of legal defense.
- *Disclosure costs*: Regulatory authorities and law enforcement agencies may require immediate release or disclosure of electronically stored information

$(ESI)^2$ at any time. An organization's failure to produce the requested ESI in an appropriate and timely manner can result in considerable financial penalties for being noncompliant with mandated information management regulations. A digital forensic readiness program also helps to strengthen information management strategies, including data retention, disaster recovery, and business continuity, by having digital evidence proactively gathered in a forensically sound manner makes it possible for organizations to easily process and present ESI when required.

In June 2005, AMD launched a lawsuit against its rival Intel, claiming that Intel engaged in unfair competition by offering rebates to PC manufacturers who agreed to eliminate or limit the purchase of AMD microprocessors.

As part of e-discovery, AMD requested the production of e-mail evidence from Intel to demonstrate this claim. Intel failed to produce the e-mail evidence due to (1) a fault in e-mail retention policy and (2) failing to properly inform employees that their ESI was required as evidence through legal hold.

Due to this failure to produce evidence, in November 2009, Intel agreed to pay AMD $1.25 billion as part of a deal to settle all outstanding legal disputes between the two companies.

Appendix E: Cost-Benefit Analysis further discusses how to perform a cost-benefit analysis to determine if implementing a forensic readiness program is valuable to an organization.

IMPLEMENTING FORENSIC READINESS

Digital forensic readiness provides a "win–win" situation for organizations because it is complementary to, and an enhancement of, the information security program and strategies. Even if not formally acknowledged, many organizations already perform some information security activities, such as proactively gathering and preserving digital information, relative to digital forensic readiness.

Making progress with a digital forensic readiness program requires a risk-based approach that facilitates a practical implementation to manage business risk. The chapters to follow will examine the key activities within information security that are relevant to implementing an effective digital forensic readiness program. Specifically, the inclusion of certain aspects of digital forensic readiness as a component of information security best practices will be discussed in the following steps:

1. Define the business risk scenarios that require digital evidence;
2. Identify available data sources and different types of digital evidence;
3. Determine the requirements for gathering digital evidence;
4. Establishing capabilities for gathering digital evidence in support of evidence rules;
5. Develop a framework to govern digital evidence management;
6. Design targeted security monitoring controls to detect events;

7. Specify the criteria for escalating incidents into formal digital investigations;
8. Conduct ongoing training to educate stakeholder on their organizational role;
9. Document and present evidence-based findings and conclusions;
10. Ensure legal review to facilitate event or incident response actions.

SUMMARY

Digital forensic readiness enables organizations to maximize their proactive investigative capabilities. By completing a proper cost-benefit analysis, the value add of an enhanced level of readiness can be demonstrated through investigative cost reduction and operational efficiencies gains.

TAXONOMY

1 *Best practice* is a method or technique that has consistently shown results superior to those achieved with other means, and that is used as a benchmark.
2 *Electronically stored information (ESI)*, for the purpose of the Federal Rules of Civil Procedure, is information created, manipulated, communicated, stored, and best utilized in digital form, requiring the use of computer hardware and software.

Define Business Risk Scenarios

## 5

This chapter discusses the first step for implementing a digital forensic readiness program as the need to define the business scenarios of why the program is required. By completing a formal business risk assessment, organizations can clearly describe their motives for implementing a digital forensic readiness program.

INTRODUCTION

As the first stage, organizations must clearly understand the "who, where, what, when, why, and how" motives for investing their time, money, and resources into implementing a digital forensics readiness program. To better gain this understanding, a risk assessment is performed to identify the potential impacts on business operation from various types of digital crimes, disputes, incidents, and events.

This risk assessment will be used, from the business perspective, to describe where digital evidence is required and its benefit in reducing impact to business operations, such as alleviating effort to reactively collect digital evidence. Generally, if the identified business risks and the potential benefits of a digital forensic readiness program indicate that the organization will realize a positive return on investment (ROI),[1] then there is a need to consider proactively gathering digital evidence to mitigate the identified business risk scenarios.

WHAT IS BUSINESS RISK?

Business risk implies a level of uncertainty due to unforeseen events that present a threat[2] to an organization. Generally, business risk is the chance of some event happening that will have an impact to the organization. Business risks can directly or indirectly impact an organization but collectively can be grouped as being influenced by two major types of risk contributors:

- *Internal events* are those risks that can be controlled and take place within the boundaries of the organization, including, but not limited to:
    - technology (ie, outages, degradations)
    - workplace health and safety (ie, accidents, ergonomics)
    - information/physical security (ie, theft, data loss, fraud)
    - staffing (ie, human error, conflict management)

- *External events* are those risks that occur outside of the organization's control, including, but not limited to:
  - natural disasters (ie, floods, storms, and drought)
  - global events (ie, pandemics, climate change)
  - regulatory and government policy (ie, taxes, restrictions)
  - suppliers (ie, supply chain, business interruptions)

Internal and external events that have potential to impact an organization are subjective depending on the type of business operations offered by an organization (ie, financial, records management) and should not be treated as universally equivalent. Putting these risks into business context, internal and external events can be grouped into five major types of risk classifications:

- *Strategic risk* is associated with the organization's core business functions and commonly occurs because of:
  - business interactions where goods and services are purchased and sold, varying supply and demand, adjustments to competitive structures, and the emergence of new or innovative technologies.
  - transactions resulting in asset relocation from mergers and acquisitions, spin-offs, alliances, or joint ventures.
  - strategies for investment relations management and communicating with stakeholder who have invested in the organization.
- *Financial risk* is associated with the financial structure, stability, and transactions of the organization.
- *Operational risk* is associated with the organization's business operational and administrative procedures.
- *Legal risk* is associated with the need to comply with the rules and regulations of the governing bodies.
- *Other risks* are associated with indirect, nonbusiness factors such as natural disasters and others as identified based on the subjectivity of the organization.

As part of the overall risk management approach and process, a risk assessment should be completed in order to evaluate:

- vulnerabilities that exist in the environment
- threats targeting organizational assets
- likelihood of threats creating actual impact
- severity of the impact that could be realized
- risk associated with each threat

Without knowing the assets that are most critical and equally what threats, vulnerabilities, or risks can impact the organization, it is not possible for key decision makers to response with appropriate protection strategies. Appendix G: Risk Management further discusses the overall approach and process for how organizations can complete a risk assessment.

FORENSIC READINESS SCENARIOS

Similar to the business risk contributors noted previously, within the context of digital forensic readiness there are also a series of direct and indirect influences that organizations must be identify and develop strategies to manage the exposure to digital evidence. To illustrate the business risks where digital forensic readiness can demonstrate positive benefit, each scenarios will be explained following the "who, where, what, when, why, and how" motives to justify why organizations should invest their time, money, and resources.

SCENARIO #1: REDUCING THE IMPACT OF CYBERCRIME

Having technology play such an integral part of most core business functions increasingly exposes organizations to the potential impact of cybercrime and the constantly evolving threat landscape. Completing a risk assessment for this scenario first requires organizations to understand the security properties of their business functions that they need to safeguard. The list below describes the security properties that organizations have to protect:

- *Confidentiality*: Ensuring that objects[3] and assets[4] are only made available to the subjects[5] it is intended for.
- *Integrity*: Validating that change to objects and assets is done following approved processes and by approved subjects.
- *Availability*: Guaranteeing that objects and assets are accessible when needed and that performance is delivered to the highest possible standards.
- *Continuity*: Ability to recovery the loss of processing capabilities within an acceptable period of time.
- *Authentication*: Establishing that access into objects and assets identifies the requesting subject; or alternatively a risk acceptance is approved to permit alternate means of subject access.
- *Authorization*: Explicitly denying or permitting subjects access into objects and assets.
- *Nonrepudiation*: Protects against falsely denying a subjects ownership over a particular action.

Reducing the impact of cybercrime should be a consideration for all security properties noted in the list above. However it is not enough to only consider the security properties that need to be safeguarded, further analysis needs to be done to understand exactly how individual security threats pose business risk and can potentially impact operational functions.

Using a threat modelling methodology, as discussed in Appendix H: Threat Modelling, allows organizations to become better equipped to identify, quantify, and address security threats that present a risk. Resulting from the threat modelling, a structured representation of the risk(s) can be created into the different ways that threat actors[6] can go about executing attacks and how their tactics, techniques, and procedures[7] can be used to impact the organization.

Table 5.1 Threat Category to Security Property Relationship

Threat Category	Security Property
Spoofing	Authentication
Tampering	Integrity
Repudiation	Nonrepudiation
Information disclosure	Confidentiality
Denial of service	Availability, Continuity
Elevation of privilege	Authorization

Detailed information collected from the threat modelling exercise must now be translated into a business language that aligns with strategies for reducing the impact of cybercrime. Using a series of threat categories, individual security threats can be placed into larger groupings based on commonalities in their tactics, techniques, and procedures. As discussed in Appendix H: Threat Modelling, the STRIDE (Spoofing, Tampering, Repudiation, Information disclosure, Denial of service, Elevation of privilege) threat model describes the six threat categories where individual security threats can be grouped. Illustrated in Table 5.1, the relationships between security properties and threat categories can be correlated to further enhance the alignment of individual security threat into focus areas for reducing the impact of cybercrime.

SCENARIO #2: VALIDATING THE IMPACT OF CYBERCRIME OR DISPUTES

When cybercrime occurs, organizations must be prepared to show the amount of impact the incident had to its business operations, functions, and assets. To do so requires that supporting evidence is gathered and made readily available when an incident is declared, which if necessary preparation have not been taken can lead to delayed validation or insufficient results.

The total cost an incident has on an organization should not be limited to only include those business operations, functions, and assets that were directly impacted. To gain a complete and accurate view of the entire cost of an incident, organizations should consider both indirect and collateral contributors as part of validating the impact of cybercrime or disputes.

Mitigating Control Logs

The constantly evolving threat landscape brings about new and transformed cybercrimes which must be identified and assessed to determine its relevance and potential impact. Using the threat tree workflows, such as the one illustrated in Appendix H: Threat Modelling, organizations can leverage the outputs of "Risk Mitigation Controls" to validate the impact of an incident. Generally, controls can be implemented as either:

- *Preventive*: stop loss, harm, or damage from occurring
- *Detective*: monitor activity to identify errors or irregularities
- *Corrective*: restore objects and information to a known good state

Depending on the type of control there will be different types of log files generated that contain relevant, meaningful, and valuable information for validating the impact of an incident. Regardless of whether the control was implemented as a component (eg, host-based malware prevention) or standalone (eg, network-based firewall) at a minimum the following log file types should be maintained:

- *Application*: records actions, as predetermined by the application, taken by secondary systems components and processes
- *Security*: records actions, as chosen by the organization, taken by nonsystem subjects relating to authorization and authentication activities into the system and contained objects
- *System*: records actions, as predetermined by the system, taken by system components and processes

Overhead Time and Effort

The time it takes to contain and remediate an incident depends on the amount of impact suffered. However, when an incident occurs, the costs associated to the overall business impact are commonly scoped down to the loss, harm, or damage of assets and operations. While these are essential considerations in determining the overall impact of an incident, the overhead cost of managing the incident can sometime be overlooked as a contributor to the overall business impact.

Generally, as a best practice the overhead cost required to run the incident response program should be included in the overall cost of the incident. This requires that organizations maintain accurate time tracking to ensure that the total amount of time invested by resources assigned to the incident response process is recorded. Without tracking overhead costs, organizations cannot effectively demonstrate the resource time and effort required to manage the incident.

Indirect Business Loss

Generally an incident requires a team of specialized resources to participate in one or more of the incident response stages. Additionally, it is not uncommon that resources participating in the incident response process also have daily functions and operations they perform.

Under these circumstances, the time and effort required for these resources to participate in the incident response process creates a cascading effect where other business operations and functions are subsequently impacted by the incident. Through the use of time tracking, the costs associated with the inability to perform normal duties should be taken into consideration as a contributor to the overall impact of the incident.

Recovery and Continuity Expenses

Following the threat tree workflows illustrated in Appendix H: Threat Modelling, the progression from potential threat into a business impact includes technical impact.

Incidents that generate a technical impact where assets are harmed, lost, or damaged require several steps to ensure the organization's recovery time objectives (RTO) are met.

In these circumstances, the overall impact of the incident should include disaster recovery and business continuity costs. While the inclusion of these costs is subjective to each organization, at a minimum it should include:

- the overhead time and effort to restore business operations
- indirect productivity loss due to unavailable systems
- new hardware to replace harmed or damaged hardware (if needed)
- restoration of information lost due to harmed or damaged hardware

SCENARIO #3: PRODUCING EVIDENCE TO SUPPORT ORGANIZATIONAL DISCIPLINARY ISSUES

For the most part, organizations have a requirement that employees comply with their business code of conduct policy. The organizational goal for having a business code of conduct document is to promote a positive work environment that strengthens the confidence of employees and stakeholders alike.

By signing this document and agreeing to comply, employees will be held to the organization's level of expectation in how they behave ethically either in the work environment, when performing their operational duties, or as part of their relationship with external stakeholders. Where employees have violated the guidelines set out in the business code of conduct, they could be subject to appropriate disciplinary actions where supporting digital evidence may need to be gathered and processed.

With any disciplinary actions, there is potential that the employee could decide to escalate the situation into a legal matter. To prevent this from happening, the organization must approach the situation fairly and reasonably using consistent procedures that, at a minimum:

- are in writing;
- are specific and clear;
- do not discriminate;
- allow the matter to be dealt with quickly;
- ensure gathered evidence is kept confidential;
- inform the employee(s) of what disciplinary actions might be taken;
- indicate what authority each level of management has to take different disciplinary actions;
- inform the employee(s) of the complaints against them with supporting evidence;
- provide the employee(s) with an opportunity to appeal before a decision is made;
- allow the employee(s) to be accompanied (ie, human resources);
- assure no employee(s) will be dismissed for first offenses, except in the circumstance of gross misconduct;
- require a complete investigation is performed before disciplinary action is taken.

SCENARIO #4: DEMONSTRATING COMPLIANCE WITH REGULATORY OR LEGAL REQUIREMENTS

The need for regulatory or legal compliance can be business-centric depending on several factors, such as the industry the organization operates within (ie, financial), or the countries where business operations are conducted (ie, Unites States, India, Great Britain). Laws and regulations can also be enforced by different entities having different requirements for managing compliance and identifying noncompliance, such as:

- self-policed by a community (ie, "peer regulation");
- unilaterally by those in power (ie, "fiat regulation"); or
- delegated to an independent third-party authority (ie, "statutory regulation").

The importance of how these governing laws and regulations directly influence the way organizations operate must be clearly understood. Despite the grumblings of ensuring business operations follow the "red tape" of regulations, they are generally necessary to provide evidence of controls and show due care in circumstances where there is potential for negligence. While the types of regulations listed below may not be complete, it provides an understanding of the categories that can be applicable to organizations:

- *Economic regulations* are a form of government regulation that adjusts prices and conditions of the economy (ie, professional licenses to conduct business, telephony service fees)
- *Social regulations* are a form of government regulation that protects the interest of the public from economic activity such as health and the environment (ie, accidental release of chemical into air/water)
- *Arbitrary regulations* mandate the use of one out of several equally valid options (ie, driving on the left or right side of the road)
- *Good faith regulations* establish a baseline of behavior for a particular area (ie, restaurant health checks)
- *Good conflict regulations* recognize an inherent conflict between two goals and take control for the greater good (ie, wearing seat belts in vehicles)
- *Process regulations* dictates explicitly how tasks are to be completed (ie, call center scripts)

SCENARIO #5: EFFECTIVELY MANAGING THE RELEASE OF COURT ORDERED DATA

No matter how diligent an organization, there are times when a dispute will end up before a court of law. When this happens, organization must be able to quickly produce credible evidence that supports their case and will not be called into question during legal proceedings.

For the most part, all organizations have common types of electronically stored information (ESI)[8] that are considered discoverable as digital evidence, such as e-mail messages. However, the likelihood that the courts will require discovery of different ESI will vary depending on the nature of the dispute or the business performed by the organization.

With adequate preparation, routine follow-ups, and a thorough understanding of what is considered reasonable in a court of law, organizations can effectively manage this risk. The most critical aspect of managing this risk to the court's expectations is to be diligent with validating and verifying the integrity of ESI and avoid any interaction or activity that will be viewed as practicing bad faith.[9]

Discussed in chapter "Evidence Management," the Federal Rules of Evidence 803(6) describes that ESI is admissible as digital evidence in court if it demonstrates "records of regularly conducted activity" as a business record; such as an act, event, condition, opinion, or diagnosis. Ensuring compliance with this ruling requires organizations to implement a series of safeguards, precautions, and controls to ensure ESI is admissible in court and that it is authenticated to its original source.

SCENARIO #6: SUPPORTING CONTRACTUAL AND/OR COMMERCIAL AGREEMENTS

Depending on the nature of business performed, organizations can face disagreements that extend beyond disputes that commonly involve internal staff. Resulting in a various actions from breach of contract terms, improper termination of contracts, or large-scale class action lawsuits, these disputes can involve external entities such as business partners, competitors, shareholders, suppliers, or customers.

The majority of the interactions involved with contractual and commercial agreements can take place electronically. With these interactions being largely electronic, organization must ensure they capture and electronically preserve critical metadata about the agreements, such as details about the terms and conditions or the date the agreement was cosigned. Having this information available when needed can be extremely useful when it comes to preventing any type of loss (ie, financial, productivity, etc.) or when using arbitration as an alternative resolution path.

ESI needed to support contractual and commercial disputes may require detailed documentary evidence that thoroughly describes the relationship between the organization and the external entities. To ensure information regarding contractual and commercial agreements is accurately captured, a contract management system can be used to standardize and preserve on the metadata needed to provide sufficient grounds for supporting a dispute.

SCENARIO ASSESSMENT

Of the six digital forensic readiness scenarios discussed in this chapter not all of them might be relevant to every organization. Determining which scenarios are applicable requires that a thorough risk assessment of each scenario is completed.

Determination of whether any of these scenarios applies to an organization requires that both the qualitative and quantitative assessment, discussed further in Appendix G: Risk Assessment, is performed to ensure that a thorough understanding of the potential risks is achieved. Following the completion of these assessments, organizations will have a complete picture of all potential risks which can then be used to perform a cost-benefit analysis, discussed further in Appendix E: Cost-Benefit Analysis, to determine the likely benefits of being able to use digital evidence.

Generally, if risks exists in a specific scenario and it has been identified that there is an ROI for digital forensic readiness, then the organization needs to consider what evidence sources need to be gathered.

SUMMARY

Defining the business risk scenarios that are the primary driver for establishing proactive investigative capabilities is the most critical aspect of practicing digital forensic readiness. Although each business risk scenario contains a series of unique use cases and requirements for proactively gathering digital evidence, there remains a degree of commonalities in the justifications for why these data sources need to be readily available.

TAXONOMY

1 *Return on investment (ROI)* is the benefit to the investor resulting from an investment of some resource.
2 *Threats* are any intentional (ie, cybercrime) or accidental (ie, natural disaster) course of action with the potential to adversely impact people, processes, or technology.
3 *Objects* are passive elements that contain or receive information.
4 *Assets* are any resource of value such as people, information, or systems.
5 *Subject* is an active element that operates on information or the system state.
6 *Threat actors* describe the identification and/or characterization of the adversary or attacker.
7 *Tactics, techniques, and procedures* describe the attack patterns, tools, exploits, infrastructure, victim targeting, and other methods used by the adversary or attacker.
8 *Electronically stored information (ESI)*, for the purpose of the Federal Rules of Civil Procedure (FRCP), is information created, manipulated, communicated, stored, and best utilized in digital form, requiring the use of computer hardware and software.
9 *Bad faith* is the intentional dishonest act by not fulfilling legal or contractual obligations, misleading another, entering into an agreement without the intention or means to fulfill it, or violating basic standards of honesty in dealing with others.

Identify Potential Data Sources

## 6

This chapter discusses the second stage for implementing a digital forensic readiness program as the need to identify and document data sources. From establishing an inventory of the systems and applications where data is readily available, organizations can not only better determine where data relevant to digital forensic readiness program is located but also identify potential gaps in data availability.

INTRODUCTION

As the second stage, organizations must work from the risk scenarios they identified as relevant to their business operations. With each business scenario, work needs to be done to determine what sources of potential digital evidence exist, or could be generated, and what happens to the potential evidence in terms of authenticity and integrity.

Generally, the purpose of completing this stage is to create an inventory of data sources where digital evidence is readily available throughout the organization. This inventory not only supports the proactive gathering of digital evidence to support digital forensic readiness, but also allows the organization to identify systems and applications that are deficient in their data collection requirements.

WHAT IS A DATA SOURCE?

Perhaps the most familiar technology where potential digital evidence is located comes from traditional computing systems such as desktops, laptops, and servers. Typically, with these technologies digital evidence will be located directly on the internal storage medium, such as the internal hard drive(s), or indirectly on external storage medium, such as optical discs or universal serial bus (USB) devices.

However, organizations should also consider the possibility that data source exists beyond the more traditional computing systems. With the widespread use of technology in business operations, every organization will have electronically stored information[1] that is considered potential digital evidence generated across many different sources.

Careful consideration must be given when determining what potential digital evidence should be gathered from data sources. When identifying data sources, organizations should consider placing the potential digital evidence into either of the following categories.

BACKGROUND EVIDENCE

Background evidence is data that has been gathered and stored as part of normal business operations according to the organization's policies and standard governance framework. The gathering of this type of evidence includes, but is not limited to:

- Network devices such as routers/switches, firewalls, domain name system (DNS) servers, dynamic host configuration protocol (DHCP) servers
- Authentication records such as directory service logs, physical access logs, employee profile database
- Electronic communication channels such as e-mail, text, chat, instant messaging
- Data management solutions such as backups, archives, classification engines, integrity checkers, transaction registers
- Other sources such as Internet service providers (ISP) and cloud service providers (CSP)

FOREGROUND EVIDENCE

Foreground evidence is data that has been specifically gathered and stored to support an investigation or identify perpetrators. The action of gathering this type of evidence can also be referred to as "monitoring" because it typically involves analyzing—in real time—the activities of subjects.[2] Depending on regulations and laws concerning privacy and rights, organizations should consult with their legal teams to ensure that the active monitoring of employees is done correctly. The gathering of this type of evidence includes, but is not limited to:

- Network monitoring systems such as intrusion prevention systems (IPS), packet sniffers, Anti-Malware
- Application software such as Anti-Malware, data loss prevention (DLP)
- Business process systems such as fraud monitoring

While the above sample of data sources is by no means a complete representation of potential digital evidence, every organization has different requirements and will need to determine the relevance and usefulness of each data source as it is identified.

CATALOGING DATA SOURCES

Similar to how a service catalog provides organizations with a better understanding of how to hierarchically align individual security controls into the forensic readiness program, discussed further in *Appendix D: Service Catalog*, each data source must be placed into a similar hierarchical structure.

The methodology for successfully creating a data source inventory includes activities that have been completed previously, as discussed in chapter "Define Business Risk Scenarios" of this book, and as well as activities that will be completed afterward, as discussed in subsequent chapters of this book. Specific to the scope of this chapter, creating a data source inventory includes the following phases.

PHASE #1: PREPARATION

An action plan is an excellent tool for making sure the strategies used by the organization when developing the data source inventory to achieve the desired final vision. The action plan consists of four steps that must be completed to deliver a complete and accurate inventory:

- Step 1: Determine what tasks and activities are required in order to identify data sources.
- Step 2: Identify who will be responsible and accountable for ensuring these tasks and activities are completed.
- Step 3: Document when these tasks and activities will take place, in what order, and for how long.
- Step 4: Establish what resources (ie, funding, people, etc) are needed in order to complete the tasks and activities.

At this point, there are several questions that organizations need to answer so that when it comes time to identifying and documenting data sources, they will be able to thoroughly and accurately collect the information needed to produce the inventory. In no particular order, these questions include:

- *Where is the data generated?*—Have the systems or applications that are creating this data been identified and documented in the organization's service catalog?
- *What format it is in?*—Is the data in a structure that can be interpreted and processed by existing tools and processes; or are new tools or processes required?
- *How long is it stored for?*—Will the data be retained for a duration that will ensure availability for investigative needs
- *How it is controlled, secured, and managed?*—Is the authenticity, integrity, and custody of the data maintained throughout its entire life cycle?
- *Who has access to it?*—Are adequate authentication and authorization mechanisms in place to limit access to only those who require it?
- *How much data is produced at a given interval?*—what volume of relevant data is created that needs to be stored?
- *How, where, and for how long is the data archived?*—Is there sufficient resources (ie, network bandwidth, long-term storage, etc.) available to store it?
- *How much data is currently being reviewed?*—What percentage of the data is currently being analyzed using what tools and processes.
- *Who is responsible for this data?*—What business line within the organization manages and is responsible for each aspect of the data's life cycle?
- *Who is the data owner?*—Identify the specific individual that is responsible for the data.
- *How can it be made available for investigations?*—What processes, tools, or techniques exist that allow this data to be gathered for investigative needs?
- *What business processes does this data relate to?*—What are the business or operational workflows where this data is created, used, stored?
- *Does it contain any personally identifiable information?*—Does the data contain any properties that can be used to reveal confidential or sensitive personal information?

PHASE #2: IDENTIFICATION

Following the direction established in the action plan, organization will be better equipped to identify data sources throughout their environment where potential digital evidence persists. As data sources are identified, each must be cataloged and recorded in a centralized inventory matrix.

There are no predefined requirements indicating what specific elements must be included in the inventory matrix; leaving the decision to include or exclude elements entirely up to the subjectivity of the organization. The most common descriptive elements that organizations should use in the data source inventory matrix, as provided as a reference in the *Templates* section of this book, should include:

- *Overall status* provides a visual representation of the organization's progress related to the gathering of digital evidence for the overall business scenario, including the following labels:
  - *Green (dark gray in print versions)* = fully implemented
  - *Blue (black in print versions)* = partially implemented
  - *Orange (gray in print versions)* = in progress
  - *Yellow (white in print versions)* = plan in place
  - *Red (light gray in print versions)* = not implemented
- *Business scenario* indicates which of the business scenarios, as discussed in chapter "Define Business Risk Scenarios," the data source contributes as digital evidence.
- *Operational service* aligns the data source to the operational service it is associated with as documented in the organization's service catalog, discussed further in *Appendix D: Service Catalog*, such as digital investigations, litigation support.
- *Data format* describes the high-level grouping of how the information is arranged in this data source; such as structured[3] or snstructured.[4]
- *Data origin* identifies the system or application where the information is generated; such as e-mail archive, end-user system, network share, CSP.
- *Data category* illustrates the exact type of information available in this data source; such as multimedia, e-mail messages, productivity suite documents.
- *Data location* determines how the information persists within the data source; such as at-rest, in-transit, in-use.
- *Data owner* documents the specific individual who is responsible for the data.
- *Business use case* identifies the high-level grouping representing the motive for why this information exists; such as DLP, data classification, intrusion prevention.
- *Technology name* documents the organization which created and provides ongoing support of the solution where the data source persists.
- *Technology vendor* documents the organization which created and provides ongoing support of the solution where the data source persists.
- *Technology owner* documents the specific individual who is responsible for the solution where the data source persists.

- *Status* provides a visual representation of the organization's progress related to the gathering of digital evidence for the specific data source; including the following labels:
  - *Green (dark gray in print versions)* = fully implemented
  - *Blue (black in print versions)* = partially implemented
  - *Orange (gray in print versions)* = in progress
  - *Yellow (white in print versions)* = plan in place
  - *Red (light gray in print versions)* = not implemented
- *Status details* provide a justification for the status assigned to the status progress rating for the specific data source.
- *Action plan* describes the activities required for the organization to improve the maturity rating for the specific data source.

PHASE #3: DEFICIENCIES

As the inventory matrix is being developed, the organizations might encounter instances where there is insufficient information currently available in a data source or gaps in the availability of information from unidentified data sources. Resolving these findings should be done separately because the activities that need to be performed are somewhat different in scope.

Insufficient Data Availability

Although a data source has been identified and included in the inventory matrix does not mean that it contains relevant and useful information to support forensic readiness. Generally, determining whether a data source provides an acceptable level of digital evidence requires that organizations ensure that the information contained within supports the investigation with either content or context.

Content Awareness

Content is the elements that exist within data that describes the details about an investigation. Information that can be used as digital evidence during an investigation must provide the organization with sufficient details that allows them to arrive at credible and factual evidence-based conclusions.

Commonly categorized as foreground evidence, information gathered from data sources should contain enough content to support the "who, where, what, when, how" aspects of an investigation. This requires that, at a minimum, all information within data sources that will be used as digital evidence must include the following metadata[5] properties:

- *Time stamp* of when the event or incident occurred; including full date and time fields with time zone offset
- *Source* of where the event or incident originated; including an identifier such as host name or Internet Protocol (IP) address

- *Destination* of where the event or incident was targeted; including an identifier such as host name or IP address
- *Description* provides an unstructured, textual description of the event or incident

In addition to these minimum requirements, organizations must recognize that every data source is different and depending on the system or application that created it the information contained within will provide varying types of additional details. By assessing the content of a data source, organizations will be able to determine if it contains information that is relevant and useful as digital evidence.

Context Awareness

Context is the circumstances whereby supplemental information can be used to further describe an event or incident. Commonly categorized as background evidence, supplemental information gathered from data sources can enhance the "who, where, what, when, how" aspects of an investigation.

Consider a layered stack model, similar to that of the open systems interconnection (OSI) model,[6] where each layer serves both the layer above and below it. The model for how context is used to enhance digital evidence can also be grouped into distinct categories that each provides its own supplemental benefit to the data source information.

A layered context model follows the same methodology as the OSI model where each layer brings supplemental information that can be applied as an additional layer onto the existing digital evidence. Illustrated in Figure 6.1, the attributes comprised within a layered context model includes the following:

- *Network*—Any arrangement of interconnected hardware that support the exchange of information.
- *Device*—Combination of hardware components adapted specifically to execute software-based systems.
- *Operating system*—Variations of software-based systems that manage the underlying hardware components to provide a common set of processes, services, applications, etc.
- *Identity*—Characteristics that define subjects[6] interacting with software-based systems, processes, services, applications, etc.
- *Application*—Software-based processes, services, applications, etc. that allow subjects to interface (read, write, execute) with the data layer.
- *Data*—Structured and/or unstructured content that is gathered as foreground digital evidence in support of an investigation.

By applying meaningful contextual information to digital evidence, credible, and factual evidence-based conclusions can be reached in a much quicker rate because the team is capable of answering the "who, where, what, when, why, how" questions with a higher level of confidence and assurance.

In 2013, Target retailers were the victims of a sophisticated cyber attack that lead to an eventual data breach where cyber criminals stole approximately 40 million credit cards, debit cards, and approximately 70 million personal records of customers (ie, name, address, e-mail, phone).

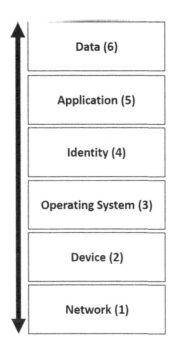

FIGURE 6.1

Context awareness model.

In a statement made by Target's spokesperson, it was indicated that:

Like any large company, each week at Target there are a vast number of technical events that take place and are logged.

Krebs, 2014

Furthermore, the Target spokesperson stated that:

Through our investigation, we learned that after these criminals entered our network, a small amount of their activity was logged and surfaced to our team. That activity was evaluated and acted upon.

Harris and Perlroth, 2014

However, the Target spokesperson continued on to say that:

Based on their interpretation and evaluation of that activity, the team determined that it did not warrant immediate follow up… With the benefit of hindsight, we are investigating whether if different judgments had been made the outcome may have been different.

Finkle and Heavey, 2014

From the statements made by Target's spokesperson, it is recognized that the company was well equipped with proper information security defenses that ultimately identified and alerted their security team of the ongoing attack. However, Target indicated that the ability of their security team to make an informed decision was due to the absence of context about the alert.

Unidentified Data Sources

Before a decision is made to include these data sources in the inventory matrix, organization must first determine the relevance and usefulness of the data during an investigation. When assessing additional data sources, the business scenarios aligned to the digital forensic readiness program must be used as the foundation for the final decision to include or exclude the data source.

If a decision is made to include the data source into the inventory matrix, the organization will need to start back at *Phase #1: Preparation* discussed previously to ensure that the action plan is followed and all prerequisite questions have been answered.

EXTERNAL DATA CONSIDERATIONS

Retrieving digital evidence from data sources owned by the organization can be relatively straightforward. However, with the continuous growth in using CSP[7] there is a new level of complexity when it comes to gathering digital evidence from this type of data source.

For the most part, with these cloud environments, organizations do not have direct access to or ownership over the physical systems where their digital evidence can persist. This requires that in order to make sure that digital evidence will be readily available in an acceptable state (ie, integrity, authenticity), organizations need to ensure that a service agreement contract is established with the CSP where service-level objectives (SLO)[8] for incident response are outlined.

Where a CSP has been contracted to manage and offer computing services, organizations must ensure that the service agreement between both parties includes terms and conditions specific to incident response and investigation support. Generally, the CSP must become an extension of the organization's incident response team and ensure that they follow forensically sound processes to preserve digital evidence in their environment(s).

Organizations have to first obtain a reasonable level of assurance that the CSP will protect their data and respond within an acceptable SLO. The terms and conditions for how this assurance is achieved should be included as part of the services agreement established between both parties. Once the terms and conditions have been agreed by both parties, the roles and responsibilities of the CSP during an incident or investigation must be defined so that the organization knows who will be involved and what roles they will play.

Having established the terms and conditions specific to incident response and investigative support, it is essential that organizations involve the CSP when practicing their computer incident response program.

DATA EXPOSURE CONCERNS

The aggregation of data from multiple data source into a single repository will ensure that digital evidence is proactively gathered and is readily available during an investigation. However, the security posture of the aggregated digital evidence from the multiple data sources is extremely critical and should be subject to stringent requirements for technical, administrative, and physical security controls.

Essentially, the collection of this digital evidence into a common repository has the potential to become a single point of vulnerability for the organization. Completion of a risk assessment on this common data repository, as discussed further in *Appendix G: Risk Management,* will identify the organization's requirements for implementing necessary countermeasures to effectively secure and protect the digital evidence.

FORENSICS IN THE SYSTEM DEVELOPMENT LIFE CYCLE

Output from phase three of creating the data source inventory might lead to the identification of deficiencies in digital evidence availability (ie, insufficient log information) or additional relevant data sources that need to be gathered. In either case, organizations should consider the opportunity of integrating the requirements to support digital forensic readiness into their system development life cycle (SDLC). Examples of how digital forensic requirements that should be integrating into the SDLC include the following:

- Regularly performing system and application backups and maintaining it for the period of time as defined in organizational policies and/or standards.
- Enabling auditing of activities and events (ie, security, informational, etc.) of systems and applications (ie, end-user systems, servers, network devices, etc.) to a centralized repository.
- Maintaining a record of know-good and known-bad hash values of common systems and applications deployments.
- Maintaining accurate and complete records of network, system, and application configurations.
- Establishing an evidence management framework to address the control of data throughout its life cycle.

SUMMARY

Digital evidence that is beneficial in supporting proactive investigations can be identified from a broad range data sources. When information from these data sources is being gathered, it must not only provide details about the incident or event, but also provide investigators with the contextual information necessary to make credible and factual conclusions. Furthermore, incorporating forensic requirements during the SDLC will enhance an organizations ability to gather digital evidence from data sources that is meaningful and relevant.

TAXONOMY

1 *Electronically stored information (ESI)*, for the purpose of the Federal Rules of Civil Procedure , is information created, manipulated, communicated, stored, and best utilized in digital form, requiring the use of computer hardware and software.
2 *Subject* is an active element that operates on information or the system state.
3 *Structured* data is information that resides in a fixed field within a record or file (ie, databases, spreadsheets).
4 *Unstructured* data is information that does not resides in a traditional row–column arrangement (ie, e-mail, productivity documents).
5 *Metadata* is data about data that is used to describe how and when and by whom a particular set of information was collected, and how the data is formatted.
6 *Open systems interconnection (OSI)* model is a conceptual model that characterizes and standardizes the communication function of a telecommunication or computer system.
7 *Cloud service providers (CSP)* are companies that offer and manage components of distributed computing services over the Internet.
8 *Service-level objectives (SLO)* are specific quantitative characteristics used to measure service delivery in terms of availability, throughput, frequency, response time, or quality.

Determine Collection Requirements

This chapter discusses the third stage for implementing a digital forensic readiness program as the need to establish the requirements for gathering digital evidence. By establishing collection requirements, stakeholders throughout the organization who are responsible for managing the business risk scenarios can effectively communicate the requirements for gathering digital evidence to the necessary support teams.

INTRODUCTION

As the third stage, organizations must produce a collection requirements statement so that stakeholders responsible for managing business risk scenarios, as discussed in chapter "Define Business Risk Scenarios," can effectively communicate to those who are responsible for operating and monitoring the systems where digital evidence will be sources, as discussed in chapter "Identify Potential Data Sources."

However, in addition to the need for defining business risk scenarios and identifying data sources, before an organization can establish a statement around the proactive gathering of digital evidence they have to ensure that a thorough assessment is performed to ensure the requirements for collecting any digital evidence is justified.

PRECOLLECTION QUESTIONS

Deciding on what the organization's requirements are for proactively gathering digital evidence requires some preliminary activities to be completed before work can begin on creating an overall statement describing exactly what these requirements are. As the moderating factor to producing a requirements statement comes the need to complete a cost–benefit analysis (CBA).

Similar to how a CBA is used to determine if implementing a digital forensic readiness program is valuable to an organization, as discussed in chapter "Understanding Forensic Readiness," this time around it is used to help organizations determine factors such as how much it will cost to gather the digital evidence and what benefit there is in collecting it. To determine if creating a requirements statement is beneficial, organizations have to answer several questions that focus on whether it can be done in a cost-effective manner.

Question #1: Can a forensic investigation proceed at a cost in comparison to the cost of an incident?

To get an accurate comparison, organizations have to factor in all monetary aspects associated with conducting an investigation in reaction to an incident against the resulting impact of an incident. As a starting point, organizations can pull cost elements from their service catalog, discussed further in Appendix D: Service Catalog, to understand how administrative, technical, and physical security controls contribute to conducting a forensic investigation. Examples of cost elements that organizations must consider to be included as part of this comparison includes ongoing maintenance of governance documentation (ie, standard operating procedures (SOP)); resource allocation to facilitate both the incident management and continuous improvement activities; and the operational cost for all tools and technologies used to manage the business risk. With this initial analysis complete, a secondary comparison must be complete including all monetary aspects, tangible and intangible, associated with conducting an investigation having proactively gathered digital evidence against the resulting impact of an incident. Using results from the two comparative analyses, organizations can determine quantitative benefits of creating a requirements statement.

Question #2: Can the digital evidence be gathered without interfering with business functions and operations?

When conducted in reaction to an event, forensic investigations can require that organizations temporarily assigned several support resources to assist in the gathering of digital evidence. In some instances, the organization might realize that their ability to effectively and efficiently gather digital evidence in reaction to an incident is challenged by some type of roadblock (ie, restoration time delay). Where potential digital evidence can be proactively gathered, organizations can benefit from having digital evidence readily available when needed and not having to re-allocate resources away from their day-to-day business operations to assist. This improvement in operational efficiencies can reduce the need for resources to be temporarily removed from their normal duties and avoid any lost productivity or degradation in service availability.

Question #3: Can a forensic investigation minimize the impact or interruption to business functions and operations?

The potential for an incident to result in the loss or degradation of day-to-day business operations is a realistic scenario that most organizations face. In reaction to these events, the organization's ability to manage the incident has a direct dependency on their capability to quickly gather and process digital evidence to understand the content and context of the incident. Having digital evidence gathered and made readily available, not only can the organization improve on the amount of time needed to investigate but they can also enable the ability to conduct proactive investigations. In addition to supporting forensic investigations, the capability to perform proactive investigations in support of security control assessments or user behavior analytics can reduce the likelihood of an event resulting in impact or interruption to the business.

Question #4· Can the digital evidence make a positive impact on the likely success of any formal legal actions?

Producing digital evidence in support of legal matters requires that organizations ensure their electronically stored information (ESI)[1] is admissible in a court of law. As discussed in chapter "Evidence Management," the US Federal Rules of Evidence 803(6) describes that ESI is admissible as digital evidence in a court of law if it demonstrates business "records of regularly conducted activity"; such as an act, event, condition, opinion, or diagnosis. Determining the relevance and usefulness of ESI as digital evidence before creating a collection requirements statement ensures that organizations will not give way to overcollecting resulting in unnecessary downstream processing and review expenses.

Question #5: Can the digital evidence be gathered in a manner that does not breach the compliance with legal or regulatory requirements?

Laws and regulations can be imposed against organizations depending on several factors such as the industry they operate within (ie, financial) or the countries they conduct business (ie, the Unites States, India, Great Britain). Organizations must have a good understanding of how these governing laws and regulations influence the way they conduct their business operations. To provide reasonable assurance there is adherence to these requirements, organizations may need to produce digital evidence of controls that demonstrate they are practicing a reasonable level of due care. Consideration must be given on how background and foreground digital evidence, as discussed in chapter "Identify Potential Data Sources," will be proactively gathered and preserved in accordance with the compliance requirements.

Assessing the quantitative and qualitative implications of creating a collection requirements statement in advance helps organizations to determine if proactively gathering digital evidence will reduce investigative costs; such as selecting storage options, purchasing technologies, and developing SOPs. Appendix E: Cost-Benefit Analysis, further discusses how to perform a CBA in support of producing the digital evidence collection requirements statement.

EVIDENCE COLLECTION FACTORS

Traditionally, the majority of digital evidence is gathered from sources that contain the actual data content used to describe the "who, where, what, when, how" elements of a forensic investigation. In addition to the actual data content, there are several other factors that can be used to supplement the details about an event/incident and influence its meaningfulness, usefulness, and relevance during a forensic investigation.

TIME

When collecting digital evidence from multiple data sources, time synchronization is a huge concern. Essentially, the higher the number of devices that are connected to a networked environment can result in the less chance they will all hold the exact same time; which will create increased confusion when it comes to analyzing digital evidence from across these sources.

Using a centralized logging solution, such as an enterprise data warehouse (EDW),[2] time stamps can be generated and recorded as data is collected. Additionally, using a consistent and verifiable time stamp unanimously across all distributed data sources will ensure that digital evidence collected will be much easier to correlate and corroborate during the analysis phase.

There are a number of mechanisms that can be used across many different platforms but are still considered a decentralized means of establishing time synchronization across distributed data sources. Alternatively using the network time protocol (NTP) set to Greenwich Mean Time (GMT), with time zone offsets configured on the local systems, is the best practice for establishing consistent time stamps in support of a forensic investigation. While NTP addresses the issue of centralized time synchronization, it does not account for the accuracy of time being published to connected data sources.

Originally developed for military use, global positioning system (GPS) provides accurate data about current position, elevation, and time. GPS receivers have a high rate of accuracy and are relatively simple to install because they only need an antenna with unobstructed line of sight to several satellites in order for them to work correctly. Connecting a GPS receiver to the NTP device is a cost-effective way of ensuring accurate time signals are being received.

Although organizations might only conduct business in a single time zone, an incident will most often produce digital evidence in data sources that span across several time zones. Having a centralized solution to provide these distributed data sources with accurate time synchronization is not something traditionally easy to challenge in a court of law.

METADATA

On its own, the data content of digital evidence can be challenging for investigators to use because it lacks contextual awareness; discussed further in chapter "Identify Potential Data Sources." Metadata, which is essentially "data about data," is used to add a supplemental layer of contextual information to data content. It gives digital evidence meaning and relevance by providing corroborating information about the data itself, revealing information that was either hidden, deleted, or obscured, and also helps to automate the correlation of data from different data sources.

One of the most common use of metadata during an investigation is to reduce the volume of ESI by adding meaning to the data content so that relevant digital evidence can be more accurately located. Additional, metadata can also be used to provide forensic investigators with the ability to identify additional evidence, associate different pieces of evidence, distinguish different pieces of evidence, and provide location details. Some of the most common types of metadata used during a forensic investigation include, but is not limited to, the following:

- Date and time when a file was modified, accessed, or created
- Location where a file is stored on an electronic storage medium

- Identity and profile information of user accounts
- Digital image properties such as number of colors or the originating camera model
- Document properties such as author or the last saved/printed time stamp

Regardless of its application within digital forensics, metadata can be distinguished in the following distinct categories:

- *Structural metadata* is used to describe the organization and arrangement of information and objects,[3] such as database tables, columns, keys, and indexes.
- *Guide metadata* is used to assist with locating and identifying information and objects, such as a document title, author, or keywords.

However, because metadata is fundamentally just data it is also susceptible to the same evidence management requirements imposed on digital evidence; discussed further in chapter "Evidence Management." Safeguards must be taken to ensure that the authenticity and integrity of metadata is upheld so that it can be used effectively during a forensic investigation and meets the legal requirements for admissibility in a court of law.

Nevertheless, because metadata is not generally accessible or visible there is a need for greater skills and the use of specialized tools to properly gather, process, and preserve it. An organization's capability to use metadata to contextualize a forensic investigation will significantly reduce the amount of resources spent manually analyzing digital evidence by improving its meaningfulness, usefulness, and relevance.

CAUSE AND EFFECT

The "Pareto Principle," also referred to as the "80/20 Rule," states that approximately 80% of all effects come from roughly 20% of the causes. As a rule of thumb, for example, this rule can be used as a representation of the information security industry where 80% of security risks can be effectively managed by prioritizing the implementation of 20% of available security controls; reinforcing a very powerful point that distributions are very rarely equal in any scenario.

In 2002, Microsoft announced they had made initial progress on the Trustworthy Computing initiative which focused on improving the reliability, security, and privacy of their software.

As the initiative continued to develop over the year, Microsoft quickly realized that among all the bugs reported in their software a relative small quantity of them resulting in some type of error.

Through further analysis, Microsoft learned that approximately 80% of the errors and crashes in their software were caused by 20% of all bugs detected.

A common challenge with any forensic investigation is to identify the cause of an event because the effect can very well be different depending on the context; such as the type of storage media it occurred on, the user/process that generated the event, etc. For example, one of the most common scenarios is when a user or process modifies a file which will result in a change to its metadata properties; specifically the file's time stamp. While this scenario is common across the majority of file systems, regardless of the underlying electronic storage medium, an event where a file has been deleted has a much different effect. Depending on the file system, and the way in which the file was deleted, the activities to identify and recover the data can vary in terms of complexity and effort (ie, soft-delete[4] vs. hard-delete[5]).

It is not realistic for an organization to identify and understand every combination of cause and effect that are possible. Instead, by referring back to the business risk scenarios outlined in chapter "Define Business Risk Scenarios," organizations can reduce the scope of which cause and effect events need to be considered based on its application to the organization and the business risk scenarios. From narrowing the scope cause and effect down to only those that are relevant to the organization, supplementary data sources can be identified and considered for inclusion in the collection requirements statement to enhance the analysis of digital evidence by further improving its contextual meaning and relevance.

CORRELATION AND ASSOCIATION

Digital evidence gathered during a forensic investigation, which is traditionally considered the primary records or indication of an event, is used to indicate the details about what happened during an incident; including, but not limited to, system, audit, and application logs, network traffic captures, or metadata.

For quite some time, the scope of a digital crime scene was somewhat limited to only the computer system(s) directly involved in the incident itself. However, today most organizations have environments that are made up of interconnected and distributed resources where events on one system are frequently related to events on other systems. This requires that the scope of an event be broadened outwards to include all systems that would be—in some form or another—involved in the incident.

With the expansion of the investigative scope, establishing a link between the primary evidence sources is needed so investigators can determine how, when, where, and by whom events occurred. To provide this additional layer of details, consideration needs to be given to other supporting data sources that can be used to establish the links between the content and context of digital evidence.

Under the chain-of-evidence model methodology, illustrated in Figure 7.1 below, each set of discrete actions performed by a subject[6] is placed into a group separate from each other based on the level of authority required to execute them. However, it is important that each group of actions in the different sources of digital evidence is linked to the adjacent action group in order to complete the entire chain of evidence link.

The ability to create a link between the various data sources is crucial for organizations to establish a complete chain of evidence and enhance their analytical capabilities by getting a better overall understanding of the incident. Using a chain-of-evidence model allows organizations to better plan for a complete trail of evidence across their entire environment. Following this model requires thinking in terms of gathering digital evidence in support of the entire chain of evidence instead of as individual data sources that may or may not be useful during the processing phase of the forensic investigations.

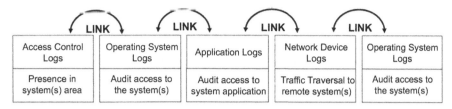

FIGURE 7.1

Chain-of-evidence model applied to the contextual awareness model.

CORROBORATION AND REDUNDANCY

Coupled together with how pervasive and distributed it has become in our personal lives, technology has also been so deeply embedded into business operations and functions where that when it comes to investigating an incident, there is no shortage of digital evidence to be gathered and processed. However when an incident does occur, organizations can be challenged with proving what happened because individual pieces of digital evidence on their own do not provide the context necessary to arrive at credible and factual conclusions.

With the aggregation of multiple data sources, there will most likely be some level of duplication in terms of the information content. This duplication of information should not be viewed negatively, but should instead be taken advantage to confirm the details of an incident during the forensic investigation.

The strength of digital evidence collected will ultimately improve when it can be vetted by across data sources. Generally, the goal of every forensic investigation is to use digital evidence as a means of providing credible answers to substantiate an event or incident. Achieving this requires that the same or similar digital evidence from multiple sources is gathered and processed as an entire chain of evidence because there will be most likely indicators of the same incident found elsewhere.

Over time, the continued gathering of data across multiple sources can provide a sufficient amount of digital evidence that minimizes the need for a complete forensic analysis of systems. By preserving digital evidence from multiple sources, it allows organizations to leverage a consistent toolset across the entire chain of evidence that can be used to support several investigative purposes such as incident response, digital forensics, or e-discovery.

STORAGE DURATION

Retention of different digital information types, regardless of whether it is preserved as digital evidence, has unique requirements for the length of time for which an organization must preserve it. In many instances, the length of time an organization must preserve digital information is stipulated by regulators and legal entities. Where this governance applies, organizations must ensure they formally document their preservation requirements in a data retention policy, as discussed further in chapter

"Evidence Management." Alternatively, if digital information is being preserved as digital evidence, organizations must ensure they safeguard it by implementing and following evidence management processes.

A common practice for many organizations, for example, is to retain in long-term storage digital information such as e-mail messages and security logs (ie, intrusion prevention systems, firewalls, etc.). Not only does retaining this digital information support regulator and legal requirements, but can also hold potential evidentiary value and might need to be recalled to support one of the business risk scenarios discussed in chapter "Define Business Risk Scenarios."

Organizations must carefully plan on which type of electronic storage medium will be used to support their long-term storage requirements. As an example, backups are commonly used for long-term storage; however, organizations should be diligent to ensure that the type of backup media selected is not susceptible to losing information each time they are used. To determine the most appropriate electronic storage medium, organizations should complete a CBA, as discussed in Appendix E: Cost-Benefit Analysis, to identify which solution best meets their needs for retention and recovery time objectives (RTO).

STORAGE INFRASTRUCTURE

The rapidly increasing size of electronic storage medium is most certainly the biggest challenge facing organizations today. As storage capacity increases so does the volume of potential digital evidence that needs to be gathered, processed, and preserved in support of the business risk scenarios discussed in chapter "Define Business Risk Scenarios."

Even though there have been significant advancements in how digital forensic tools and techniques have helped to reduce the time required to work with digital evidence, there still remains the underlying issue of the how organization can efficiently manage the data volumes that need to be gather and processed during a forensic investigation.

Foremost, there is a need to design a storage solution that can easily adapt to the continuously growing volumes of data that need to be accessed in both real time and near real time. Using storage solutions such as an EDW allows organizations to store both structured[7] and unstructured[8] data in a scalable manner that can easily and dynamically adapt to changing storage capacity requirements.

Second, as data volumes continue to increase organizations can start to experience inefficiencies in their potential to effectively perform data mining and analytics. Integrating into the EDW solution, the use of cataloging and indexing of metadata properties allows organizations to quickly identify data and reduce the length of time it take for data to be retrieved. Not only will organizations benefit from data being readily accessible as a result of cataloging and indexing, but the ease in which data processing can be performed will improve the overall evidence-based reporting, discussed in chapter "Maintain Evidence-Based Presentation," during a forensic investigation.

It is important to keep in mind when working with ESI that there is always the potential to inadvertently change the original data source. Therefore, when implementing any type of digital evidence storage solution, it is important that the principles, methodologies, and techniques of digital forensic are consistently adhered to. Organization must, at all times, ensure that their storage solutions adhere to the best practices for maintaining the integrity and authenticity of digital evidence and not risk the data being inadmissible in a court of law.

Appendix I: Data Warehouse Foundations, further discusses details on implementing a storage solution to support proactively gathering digital evidence.

DATA SECURITY REQUIREMENTS

Having such a large amount of data located in a common centralized storage solution can become a problem if adequate security controls are not enforced. Securing the data repository depends on the organization's diligence and attention to compliance regulations, awareness of potential threats, and the identification of both the risk and value of the ESI collected.

There is a significant amount of preliminary work that needs to be completed before data gathering and storage can take place. Complementary to the architectural design work that takes place, organization must incorporate current best practices and standards for implementing a data repository to ensure adequate security and reliability is maintained throughout the solution's lifetime. This requires that ongoing assessments of the centralized storage solution are completed to identify and understand the risks associated with each aspect of its eventual implementation, including:

- Analysis of requirements specific to:
  - the value to data being collected
  - the architectural design
- Interpreting security and compliance standards and guidelines
- Assessment of the effectiveness of security controls and designs

Analysis of security requirements begins with having an understanding of the business needs and desires for building the centralized storage solution. As described in the sections throughout this chapter, the capabilities and functionalities for the storage solution have been identified where now security controls, countermeasures, and data protection need to be established.

Generally, security requirements are complementary to the functional requirements whereby they address the need to ensure the protection of the system, its data, and its users. They are typically addressed separately and occur after the system's functional requirements have been documented. While security requirements can commonly be sourced from (international, federal, local) regulatory requirements, at a minimum organizations should adopt industry best practice standards as a measurement of due diligence to protecting the storage solution. Understanding that there are many different controls that contribute to the protection of the system, its data, and its users, the following are examples of how industry best practices can be applied to the seven security principles.

- *Confidentiality*: Applying data classification labels as a mechanism for enforcing mandatory access control.[9]
- *Integrity*: Generating cryptographic hash values, such as the message-digest algorithm family[10] (eg, MD5) or the Secure Hashing Algorithm family[11] (eg, SHA-2), for collected data stored in the centralized repository.
- *Availability*: Required backups are taken in support of disaster recovery capabilities.
- *Continuity*: Building cold, warm, or hot sites in support of business continuity capabilities.
- *Authentication*: Leveraging existing centralized directory services for subject identification.
- *Authorization*: Implementing role-based access controls[12] to objects.
- *Nonrepudiation*: Use of cryptographic certificates to associate the actions or changes by a specific subject, or to establish the integrity and origin of information.

Appendix J: Requirements Analysis, further discusses details how to perform a requirements assessment for gathering digital evidence.

SUMMARY

Developing a requirement statement for the collection of digital evidence requires organizations to conduct thorough planning and preparation. Not only does the storage solution need to be functionally assessed in terms of its architectural design, it is critical that further security assessments are completed to ensure the collected digital evidence is safeguarded from unauthorized access.

TAXONOMY

1 *Electronically stored information (ESI)*, for the purpose of the Federal Rules of Civil Procedure, is information created, manipulated, communicated, stored, and best utilized in digital form, requiring the use of computer hardware and software.
2 *Enterprise Data Warehouse (EDW)* is a central repository used to store amalgamated data from one or more disparate sources to support analytics and reporting.
3 *Objects* are passive elements that contain or receive information.
4 *Soft-delete* occurs when data is marked for deletion and is only prevented from being accessed.
5 *Hard-delete* occurs when data is deleted and can no longer be accessed through the file system.
6 *Subject* is an active element that operates on information or the system state.
7 *Structured* data is information that resides in a fixed field within a record or file (ie, databases, spreadsheets).
8 *Unstructured* data is information that does not resides in a traditional row–column arrangement (ie, e-mail, productivity documents).

9   *Mandatory access control* is a type of access control mechanism where a subjects ability to access resource objects is controlled by the system or an administrator.

10   *Message digest algorithm (MD)* is a family of one-way cryptographic hashing functions commonly used to creation a unique digital fingerprint with hash lengths that vary, depending on version, between 128-bit and 512-bit.

11   *Secure hashing algorithm (SHA)* is a family of one-way cryptographic hashing functions commonly used to create a unique digital fingerprint with hash lengths that vary, depending on version, between 160-bit and 512-bit.

12   *Role-based access control* is an approach where subjects have access to objects based on their associated roles.

Establish Legal Admissibility

## 8

This chapter discusses the fourth step for implementing a digital forensic readiness program as guaranteeing the authenticity of digital evidence for admissibility in a court of law. Though the implementing of controls to ensure digital evidence gathered is authentic, organizations can effectively demonstrate their due diligence when digital evidence is being admitted to a court of law.

INTRODUCTION

At this stage of implementing a digital forensic program, organizations will have a grasp on the totality of digital evidence available for proactive collection and have determined which of it, based on the business risk scenarios discussed in chapter "Define Business Risk Scenarios," can be gathered within the scope justified through the completion of a cost–benefit analysis.

With the organization's collection requirements defined, steps must now be taken to implement a series of controls to guarantee that the secure preservation of digital evidence is maintained when it is being gathered from relevant data sources. These steps are important for organizations to establish so they can ensure that data has been preserved as authentic records and cannot be disputed when admitted to a court of law as digital evidence.

LEGAL ADMISSIBILITY

Essentially, admissibility is the determination of whether information that is presented before the trier of fact[1] (ie, judge, jury) is worthy to be accepted in court of law as evidence. Generally, in order for digital evidence to be admissible in a court of law it must be proven to have relevance (ie, material, factual) and is not overshadowed by invalidating considerations (ie, unfairly prejudicial, hearsay[2]).

Within the legal system, there are a set of rules that is used as precedence for governing whether, when, how, and for what purpose digital evidence can be placed before a trier of fact. Traditionally, the legal system viewed digital evidence as being hearsay because its authenticity could not be proven, beyond a reasonable doubt, to be factual. However, exceptions do exist under the *Federal Rules of Evidence 803(6)* where digital evidence can be admitted into a legal proceeding only if it demonstrates "records of regularly conducted activity" as a business record; such as an act, event, condition, opinion, or diagnosis.

In order for digital evidence to qualify under this exception, organizations have to demonstrate that their business records are authentic, reliable, and trustworthy. As stated in the *Federal Rules of Evidence*, in order to attain these qualifying properties, organizations must be able to demonstrate that their business records:

- was created as a regular practice of that activity;
- were created at or near the time by—or from information transmitted by— someone with knowledge;
- have been preserved in the course of a regularly conducted activity of a business, organization, occupation, or calling;
- are being presented by the custodian, another qualified witness, by a certification that complies with either Rule 902(11) or Rule 902(12), or with a statute granting certification;
- do not show that the source of information or method or circumstances of its preparation indicate a lack of trustworthiness.

Furthermore, even if a business record qualifies under these exceptions, organizations must still determine if the business record falls within the context of being either:

- Technology-generated data that has been created and is being maintained as a result of programmatic processes or algorithms (eg, log files). These records fall within the rules of hearsay exception on the basis that the data is proven to be authentic as a result of properly functioning programmatic processes or algorithms.
- Technology-stored data that has been created and is being maintained as a result of user input and interactions (eg, word processor document). These records fall within the rules of hearsay exception on the basis that author of the data is reliable, trustworthy, and has not altered it.

Even if a business record meets the above criteria for being admissible as digital evidence, there is the potential that it will be challenged during legal proceedings. The basis for these contests is directed at the authenticity of the data and whether it has been altered or damaged either after it was created or as a result of interactions and exchanges with the data.

In an effort to reduce these oppositions the *Federal Rules of Evidence 1002* described the need for proving, beyond a reasonable doubt, that the trustworthiness of digital evidence must be demonstrated through the production of the authentic and original business record. Meeting this rule requires that organizations demonstrate their due diligence in preserving the authenticity of the original data source through the implementation of safeguards, precautions, and controls to guarantee that business records can be admitted as digital evidence during legal proceeding.

PRESERVATION CHALLENGES

Collecting business records is not as straight forward as it seems. As an example, where organizations operate in multiple jurisdictions and countries, they are bound in each location to multiple factors that determine how they can effectively preserve their business records.

First and foremost, organizations need to answer two preliminary questions before determining how they will guarantee the authenticity of their business records.

Can digital evidence be gathered without interfering with business operations and function?

The overall strategy for implementing digital forensic readiness, summarized as "the ability to maximize potential use of digital evidence while minimizing investigative costs," includes an objective to gather admissible digital evidence without interrupting business operations and functions.

Typically, forensic investigations are performed in reaction to an event and requires the assistance of several support resources to gather relevant digital evidence. In some instance, this reactive approach commonly results in roadblocks where business records are not readily available which requires support resources to be removed from the day-to-day business operations to assist. Where gathering business records has been identified as beneficial to digital forensic readiness, organizations need to assess the work effort required of resources to implement the proactive collection requirements while not impeding their day-to-day business operations.

Can digital evidence be gathered legally?

Aligned with the overall strategy for implementing digital forensic readiness noted above, another objective of gathering admissible digital evidence is to do it in a way that does not violate any laws or regulations. This determination should not be done without obtaining legal advice to ensure that the evidence collection requirements are met and upheld.

In some countries, there are relevant laws around data protection, privacy, and human rights that will dictate what business records can be collected and, if it can be collected, where or how it is stored. For organizations to ensure that they demonstrate a reasonable assurance, the collection of all business records must adhere to all applicable laws or regulations.

PRESERVATION STRATEGIES

Having answered these questions and knowing the constraints around what, how, and where business records can be gathered, organizations can now implement strategies to ensure they are compliant with applicable laws and regulations. As these strategies are being identified and developed, it is important to keep in mind that they should encompass a series of complimentary administrative, physical, and technical security controls.

ADMINISTRATIVE CONTROLS

Before any type of technical or physical security controls can be implemented, there must first and foremost be a foundational governance structure in place. This governance structure is established in the form of administrative controls that include the creation and approval of organizational policies, standards, and guidelines that support the preservation of digital evidence authenticity and integrity.

Policies

These documents are created with the intent of building a formal blueprint that describes the goals for preserving digital evidence. They are designed to provide generalized direction that allows organizations to consider any subsequent physical or technical security controls that are required to safeguard their digital evidence.

Guidelines

Building off of the policy documentation, guidelines can now be created as documents that provide recommendations for how to implement the generalized direction set previously. The context of these documents is intended to be subjective where organizations will use the recommendations as a way of gathering requirements for how to preserve the authenticity and integrity of their digital evidence.

Standards

Following the interpretation of the guidelines, standard documents are created to outline the minimum level of technical and physical security controls necessary. These documents should contain the exact configurations, architectures, and specifications for implementing technical and physical security controls in support of policies and guidelines.

Procedures

The previously noted administrative controls do not have direct oversight of interactions with collected digital evidence. Through the implementation of standard operating procedures, the exchanges and interfaces between administrators, operators, and investigators and digital evidence are documented.

For further information about how these administrative controls support the overall evidence management life cycle, including specific examples of governance documentation, refer to chapter "Evidence Management" of this book.

TECHNICAL CONTROLS

Stated previously in this chapter, even if a business record meets the criteria for being admissible during a legal proceeding, organizations will still be faced with the challenge of proving it has not been altered or damaged after it was created or as a result of interactions and exchanges with it.

As a means to mitigate the potential for the authenticity of business records being challenged in a court of law, organizations should implement several technical controls to guarantee that business records can be admitted as digital evidence. Understanding that every organization's business environment is different, at a minimum the following technical controls must be in place to ensure secure preservation of business records as digital evidence.

Storage Security

Organizations can select any different type of electronic storage medium to preserve their collected digital evidence, such as hard drives or backup tapes. Regardless of how the information is being stored, organizations must consider the data-at-rest[4] implications by ensuring the preserved digital evidence is not exposed if unauthorized access to the storage medium is gained. Through the use of cryptography, inactive data can be protected through one of the following implementations.

*   *Full-disk encryption* applies cryptographic algorithms to the physical storage medium, regardless of its content, to encrypt all information.
*   *Encrypted file system* applies cryptographic algorithms at the file system level to encrypt logical data sets.

The use of disk encryption does not replace the need for file encryption in all situations. In some instances, the two can be used in conjunctions with each other to provide a more layered defense to guaranteeing the authenticity and integrity of digital evidence.

Integrity Monitoring

All types of digital data, whether technology-generated or technology-stored, are prone to issues of trustworthiness where the content and context of the information cannot be easily validated and is often challenged for its authenticity. These issues of data integrity and authenticity are some of the contributors that render business records inadmissible as digital evidence in a court of law.

However, organizations can get the upper hand on the matter of data integrity and authenticity through the use of solutions such as file integrity monitoring. With these technologies, validation of both system and data integrity can be achieved by authenticating specific data properties of the current data state against the known-good state of the data. Examples of data properties that can be used in as part of this verification and validation include the following:

*   Subject[3] permissions and entitlements
*   Actual data content of files
*   Metadata attributes (ie, size, creation date/time)
*   Cryptographic values (ie, Message Digest Algorithm family[5] (MD5), Secure Hashing Algorithm (SHA) family[6])

Implementation of integrity monitoring is an essential security control to guarantee the authenticity and integrity of business records as digital evidence. In addition to the use of integrity monitoring as means of proving authenticity of data, these solutions have also been established as a requirement for several regulatory compliance objectives, including:

- Payment Card Industry Data Security Standard—Requirement 11.5
- Sarbanes–Oxley Act—Section 404
- Federal Information Security Management Act—National Institute of Standards and Technology (NIST) Special Publication (SP) 800-53 Rev3
- Health Insurance Portability and Accountability Act of 1996—NIST SP800-66

The online reference to the above regulatory objectives can be found in the *Resources* section at the end of this chapter.

Cryptographic Algorithms

Every interaction with and exchange of digital information introduces the potential of that data being modified; whether knowingly or unintentionally. Proving the authenticity of digital information to the original source and maintaining that level of integrity throughout a forensic investigation is critical for it to be admissible as digital evidence.

Cryptography supports many information security-centric services, such as authentication and nonrepudiation that are fundamental to the digital forensic science discipline and digital evidence management, as discussed in chapter "Evidence Management." Examples of common cryptographic algorithms that are used in digital forensics as part of evidence management are the following:

- The Message Digest Algorithm family (eg, MD5) is commonly used during a forensic investigation to generate a unique cryptographic identifier of files, data streams, and other digital evidence. However, in 2010, researchers were able to generate collisions where the same 128-bit hexadecimal value could be generated for two distinctively different pieces of digital information.
- The SHA family (eg, SHA-2) is also used during forensic investigations to generate a unique cryptographic identifier for digital evidence. From the collisions identified within specific versions of the Message Digest Algorithm family, specifically MD5, the SHA family of hash functions has become popular as a means of establishing the integrity and authenticity of digital evidence.
- Cyclic Redundancy Check[7] is commonly used during the forensic duplication of digital evidence to detect modifications to the underlying data. Using these calculations allows forensic investigators to use the duplicate data during analysis instead of risking potential contamination of the original evidence source.

When implemented correctly, cryptography provides organizations with an acceptable level of assurance that the integrity of collected business records can be proven when authenticated to the original data source.

Remote Logging

Technology-generated data stored on local systems, such as security or audit log files, is inevitably more vulnerable to being (1) manipulated to conceal activities or events or (2) planted to incriminate other individuals. These data integrity issues lessen the credibility of the information and render it inadmissible as evidence in a court of law.

As a best practice, remote logging capabilities should be leveraged to redirect the logging of technology-generated data off local systems and into a centralized remote logging infrastructure, such as a data warehouse as discussed in *Appendix E: Cost-Benefit Analysis*.

Enforcing this safeguard will reduce the likelihood of data tampering on local systems and maintain the integrity of technology-generated data as admissible digital evidence.

Secure Delivery

Where remote logging capabilities exist, organizations must consider the data-in-transit[8] implications for collected digital evidence. Regardless of whether information is traveling across a public or private network, there is a need to ensure the secure delivery of digital evidence to maintain its authenticity and integrity.

Network communications are, in general, insecure where information traveling across them can readily be accessed or modified by unauthorized subjects if appropriate controls are not in place. Knowing this, organizations should be concerned with the confidentiality and integrity of digital evidence as it is being collected into their remote logging solution(s). As a countermeasure, organizations should implement an encrypted communication channel using, as an example, Internet Protocol Security[9] to mitigate the risk of data-in-transit security concerns.

PHYSICAL CONTROLS

Generally, physical security controls are designed to control and protect an organization's physical assets (ie, building, systems, etc.) by reducing the risk of damage or loss. As organizations design their approach to ensure the secure preservation of digital evidence, they must take into account the costs of building, operating, and maintaining physical security controls that work in conjunction with their administrative and technical security controls.

While physical security controls may not always have the same direct interaction with digital evidence that technical controls have, they provide an additional layer of defense to safeguard the physical medium (ie, tapes, hard drives) where digital evidence is stored. Physical security controls indirectly contribute to preserving the authenticity and integrity of digital evidence as implemented in one of the following categories.

Deter

The goal of these physical security controls is to convince potential intruders and attackers that the likelihood of success is low because of strong defenses. Typically, the implementation of deterrent security controls are found in the combined use of physical barriers (ie, walls), surveillance (ie, closed caption television (CCTV)), and lighting (ie, spot lights).

Crime Prevention Through Environmental Design

Crime prevention through environmental design (CPTED) is an approach to planning and developing physical security controls that use natural or environmental surroundings to reduce the opportunities for crime. As part of a comprehensive approach to guaranteeing the authenticity and integrity of digital evidence, examples of CPTED controls that can be implemented include, but are not limited to:

- Natural surveillance such as implementing lighting designed to illuminate points of interest that do not generate glare or blind spots
- Natural access controls such as multilevel fencing to control access and enhance visibility
- Natural territorial reinforcements such as restricting activities to defined areas through the use of signage

Detect

Generally, detective controls are intended to discover and interrupt potential intruders and attackers before an incident or event occurs. Optimally, these controls should be implemented to reveal the presence of potential intruders and attackers while they are collecting information about how they can gain access to the physical medium where digital evidence is being stored.

While it also plays a part in the deterrence of potential intruders and attackers, the use of CCTV is one of the most common physical controls for discovering an incident or event. Additionally, physical alarm systems and sensors can be used in combination with other types of controls (ie, barriers, guards) to trigger a response when a breach has been detected.

Deny

Identical to the use of authentication and authorization mechanisms to control logical access to systems and data, the same type of restrictive security controls must be used to deny physical access to the organization's assets. The primary objective of these physical controls is to deny potential intruders and attackers the ability to cause damage to systems and information.

Within the context of preserving authenticity and integrity, examples of physical controls that can be used to deny access to collected digital evidence including, but are not limited:

- Constructing secure storage facilities, such as lockers and restricted areas, that have true floor-to-ceiling walls
- Entrances that are constructed of material resistant to tampering and have internally facing hinges
- Mechanisms to control and restrict access into secure lockers and restricted areas; such as lock and key, biometric scanner, or card/badge readers

Delay

Where the implementation of physical security controls is unable to deter or detect potential intruders and attackers, such as having obtained a key that provides access into the secure storage area, additional controls must ensure that their ability to easily gain access to digital evidence is delayed.

Typically, these types of controls are the last line of defense when all previous implementation (deter, detect, delay) have failed to deliver the level of protection that they were intended for. Examples of how these security controls provide the last line of defense in physical protecting digital evidence include the following:

- placing secure lockers inside restricted areas that located away from the exterior of the building and requiring multiple checkpoints in order to gain access
- requiring security guards to conduct searches and inspection of people, parcels, and vehicles as they leave buildings

Implementing physical safeguards provides organizations with a layer of security controls complimentary to their administrative and technical controls. Not only do these physical security controls help to guarantee the authenticity and integrity of collected digital evidence, but it also support data protection requirements as part of the overall evidence management life cycle.

SUMMARY

In order for business records to be admissible in legal proceedings, organizations must prove its authenticity by meeting specific criteria that direct rules for digital evidence. Through a layered implementation of safeguards, precautions, and controls that encompass the administrative, technical, and physical requirements for ensuring secure evidence preservation, organizations can guarantee that their business records can be admitted as digital evidence during legal proceedings.

RESOURCES

PCI-DSS: Requirements and Security Assessment Procedures v3.1. Requirement 11.5. https://www.pcisecuritystandards.org/documents/PCI_DSS_v3-1.pdf. PCI Security Standards Council, 2015.

SOX Act of 2002. Section 404. https://www.sec.gov/about/laws/soa2002.pdf. US Securities and Exchange Commissions, 2002.

FISMA SP800-53 R4. Requirement SI-7. http://csrc.nist.gov/drivers/documents/FISMA-final.pdf. NIST, 2013.

HIPAA SP800-66. Section 4.16. http://csrc.nist.gov/publications/nistpubs/800-66-Rev1/SP-800-66-Revision1.pdf. NIST, 2008.

TAXONOMY

1 *Trier of fact*, or finder of fact, is any person or group of persons in a legal proceeding who determines whether, from presented evidence whether something existed or some event occurred.

2 *Hearsay evidence* is secondhand or indirect evidence that is offered by a witness of which they do not have direct knowledge but, rather, their testimony is based on what others have said to them.

3 *Subject* is an active element that operates on information or the system state.

4 *Data-at-rest* refers to the protection of inactive data that is physically stored in any digital form (ie, database, enterprise data warehouse, tapes, hard drives, etc.).

5 *Message digest algorithm (MD)* is a family of one-way cryptographic hashing functions commonly used to creation a unique digital fingerprint with hash lengths that vary, depending on version, between 128-bit and 512-bit.

6 *Secure hashing algorithm (SHA)* is a family of one-way cryptographic hashing functions commonly used to create a unique digital fingerprint with hash lengths that vary, depending on version, between 160-bit and 512-bit.

7 *Cyclic redundancy check* is an error-detecting calculation that is commonly used in digital networks and storage devices to identify accidental changes to raw data.

8 *Data-in-transit* is the flow of information over any type of public or private network environment.

9 *Internet protocol security* is a protocol suite for securing network communications by establishing mutual authentication between nodes by encrypting each data packet of an entire communication session.

Establish Secure Storage and Handling

## 9

This chapter discussed the fifth step for implementing a digital forensic readiness program as the need to establish governance over the secure storage and handling of collected digital evidence. Following a defense-in-depth approach of layered administrative, technical, and physical controls, organizations must ensure that the proper handling of digital evidence will support the preservation of its authenticity and integrity.

INTRODUCTION

Taking into account the safeguards and controls implemented to ensure collected digital evidence is admissible in a court of law, organizations must now determine how they will uphold these requirements as their digital evidence is being handled by several individuals and technologies. Likewise, as digital evidence is being transferred from one storage facility to another, such as long-term or off-line storage, consideration must be given to ensure the data is securely preserved and readily available when needed.

Establishing a governance framework over the handling and storage of digital evidence can be achieved by following the traditional approach of implementing complimentary administrative, technical, and physical controls. Through the combination of these different controls in a layered fashion, organizations can ensure that their digital evidence will be handled correctly and stored securely.

SECURE STORAGE ATTRIBUTES

Storage solutions such as an Enterprise Data Warehouse (EDW), discussed further in *Appendix I: Data Warehouse Introduction*, provides a centralized repository for aggregating digital evidence from multiple data sources. While it can be complex to implement, when done correctly an EDW can generate significant benefit such as allowing digital evidence to be analyzed over a longer period of time for improved data mining and analytics.

However, as discussed previously in chapter "Establish Legal Admissibility," there are several administrative, technical, and physical controls that must be implemented to ensure that digital evidence being collected into any storage solution will be admissible in a court of law. Having identified the safeguards required to maintain admissibility, organizations must now determine how to properly implement these controls to ensure that their digital evidence is being handled correctly, throughout its entire lifecycle, and that its authenticity and integrity are maintained as it is transferred between different storage facilities.

LEAST PRIVILEGE ACCESS[1]

Even though the modern threat landscape has changed, the delivery channels and attack vectors used by potential intruders and attackers continue to rely on the absence or weakness in both system and application access controls. In the context of admissibility in a court of law, the deficiencies in strong access controls are a blueprint for disaster when it comes to preserving the authenticity and integrity of digital evidence in secure storage.

One of the fundamental cornerstones in the information security discipline is the concept of applying the principle of least privileged access. Generally, implementing least privilege implies that subjects[2] only have access to the objects[3] that are absolutely necessary as part of normal business operations and functions. However, as illustrated in Figure 9.1, when privileges are assigned they are typically granted beyond the scope of what is necessary permitting access that is otherwise not required.

Exercising rigid controls over subjects that have administrative access into storage solutions housing digital evidence is critical. Without enforcing the use of least privilege access to these secure storage facilities, organizations cannot demonstrate admissibility in a court of law because the potential for unauthorized subject access puts into questions the authenticity and integrity of their digital evidence.

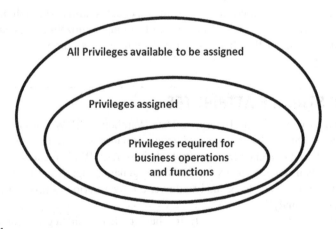

FIGURE 9.1

Privilege assignments.

END-TO-FND CRYPTOGRAPIIY

Outlined previously in chapter "Establish Legal Admissibility," cryptography supports several information security-centric services that are fundamental to the digital forensic discipline. Supporting several use cases for preserving digital evidence, examples of how cryptography can be applied were identified as data-at-rest[4] controls, used to guarantee that unauthorized access to the storage medium does not expose the digital evidence (eg, full disk encryption), or data-in-transit[5] control, used for securing the transmission of digital evidence across any type of network infrastructure (eg, Internet protocol security[6]).

Additionally, following along with the principles of least privilege access, digital evidence being stored should only be readable by those authorized. Through the use of cryptography, organizations can achieve a much stronger data-in-use[7] security control mechanism that will allows for the authenticity and integrity of the digital evidence to be maintained.

As digital evidence is being collected it should be encrypted, using a mechanism such as a secret key, to help enforce the principle of least privilege and restrict access to only those authorized subjects. As an example, while the application of an encrypted file system (EFS) contributes to the protection of data-at-rest, it also provides data-in-use controls where only those users in possession of the secret key can access and read the digital evidence.

INTEGRITY CHECKING

Outlined previously in chapter "Establish Legal Admissibility," integrity monitoring is an essential security control to guarantee the authenticity and integrity of digital evidence. With the known-good state of digital evidence captured, ongoing verification and validation must be implemented to ensure that no alteration to preserved digital evidence has been made.

When digital evidence is being preserved in a storage solution such as an EDW, integrity checks should be scheduled in alignment with the organization requirements for regulatory compliance and to effectively demonstrate legal admissibility. However, if digital evidence has been transferred into off-line storage, such as backup tapes, routinely performing integrity checks cannot be easily achieved. In this situation, organizations must take an alternate approach to preserving the authenticity and integrity of their digital evidence as follows:

1. Prior to digital evidence being transferred to off-line storage, an integrity check must be completed by comparing the known-good state (set #1) to the current state of the digital evidence (set #2) through a cryptographic hash values such as the message digest algorithm family[8] (eg, MD5) or the secure hashing algorithm family[9] (eg, SHA-2).
2. Once the initial integrity checking is completed, set #2 of hash values must be maintained for the duration of the transfer process for use in subsequent integrity checking after digital evidence has been stored on the off-line storage.

3. After all digital evidence have been transferred to off-line storage, a new set of hash values (set #3) is produced and compared against set #2 to guarantee the authenticity and integrity of digital evidence has been preserved.

PHYSICAL SECURITY

Outlined previously in chapter "Establish Legal Admissibility," physical security controls are designed to control and protect an organization's assets (ie, people, building, systems, etc.) by reducing the risk of harm, damage, or loss. While physical security controls may not always have the same direct interaction with digital evidence that technical controls have, they provide layers of defense that deter, detect, deny, and delay potential intruders and attackers from accessing digital evidence preserved in any type of storage solution.

Where digital evidence is preserved in a storage solution, physical security controls are focused on reducing the risk of unauthorized access to the infrastructure housing the digital evidence. However, if digital evidence has been transferred into off-line storage, such as backup tapes, the scope of physical security controls extends beyond protecting only the infrastructure.

Digital evidence housed in off-line storage is subject to the same requirement for demonstrating authenticity and integrity in order for it to be admissible in a court of law. For example, the Good Practices Guide for Computer-Based Electronic Evidence, developed by the Association of Chief of Police Officers (ACPO) in the United Kingdom, was created with four overarching principles that must be followed when handling evidence in order to maintain evidence authenticity:

- *Principle #1*: No action taken by law enforcement agencies or their agents should change data held on a computer or storage media which may subsequently be relied upon in court.
- *Principle #2*: In circumstances where a person finds it necessary to access original data held on a computer or on storage media, that person must be competent to do so and be able to give evidence explaining the relevance and the implications of their actions.
- *Principle #3*: An audit trail or other record of all processes applied to computer-based electronic evidence should be created and preserved. An independent third party should be able to examine those processes and achieve the same result.
- *Principle #4*: The person in charge of the investigation (the case officer) has overall responsibility for ensuring that the law and these principles are adhered to.

When digital evidence has been transferred to off-line storage such as backup tape, a chain of custody for this new storage medium must be established to guarantee its authenticity and integrity by tracking where it came from, where it went after seizure, and who handled it for what purpose. From this point forward, the chain of custody must accompany the off-line storage and be maintained throughout the lifetime of the evidence. A chain of custody template has been provided as a reference in the *Templates* section of this book.

Furthermore, tapes should be stored using physical security controls that are intended to deny or delay potential intruders and attackers access to digital evidence. Achieving these layers of defenses can be accomplished by implementing the following physical security controls:

- Off-line storage medium, such as backup tape, should be placed in an evidence bag that, at a minimum, supports the following characteristics:
  - Bags contain a secure pouch to store the media and an externally accessible pouch for accompanying documentation
  - Proper labeling is affixed to correctly and efficiently identify the contents
  - Tamper proof tape or locking mechanism is used to seal evidence inside
  - Chain of custody is placed in the externally accessible pouch

Physical access to digital evidence in off-line storage must also be controlled following the same security principles of least privilege access. Once digital evidence has been properly sealed in evidence bags, these bags should be stored in a secure locker, safe, or library for long-term retention. It is important that at all times the chain of custody is updated to demonstrate ownership and location of the digital evidence.

ADMINISTRATIVE GOVERNANCE FOUNDATIONS

Forensic viability can only be accomplished when digital evidence has been tracked and protected right from the time it was created and meets the requirements for legal admissibility throughout its entire lifecycle. Although technical and physical security controls have a more direct contribution to the secure handling and storage of digital evidence, they cannot be effective unless there is an organizational requirement to adhere to. Therefore, to guarantee that digital evidence is forensically viable, organizations must have an established governance framework in place to ensure the collection, preservation, and storage of digital evidence is done properly.

Ultimately, the objective of this governance framework is to establish direction on how the organization will preserve the authenticity and integrity of their digital evidence. Management, with involvement from key stakeholders such as legal, privacy, security, and human resources, must work together to define a series of documents that describe exactly how the organization will go about achieving these goals. Illustrated in Figure 9.2, and discussed further in chapter "Evidence Management," an information security management framework consists of a hierarchy of different types of documents that have direct influence and precedence over other documents.

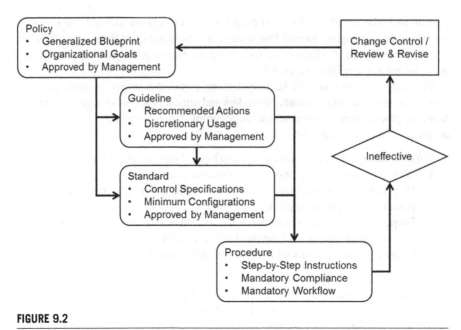

FIGURE 9.2

Information Security Management framework.

Within the context of guaranteeing forensic viability of digital evidence, governance documentation should be created to address the following areas:

PERSONNEL

- Provide continuous training and awareness regarding the governance framework to all stakeholder involved in the collection, preservation, and storage of digital evidence.
- As acknowledgment of their adherence with the governance framework, stakeholders should be required to sign the necessary document to indicate their understanding of and commitment to them. Management, legal, privacy, security, and human resources should all be involved to ensure that these signed documents can be legally enforced.
- Require enhanced background checks to be routinely conducted for personnel who have access to digital evidence.

EVIDENCE STORAGE

- Document all operational aspects of the digital evidence storage solutions and facilities, including, but not limited to, normal operations and maintenance, scheduled backups, and error handling.

- Provide clear guidance and direction regarding the installation and updates to hardware and software components.
- Ensure storage solutions are designed and architected to meet the requirement and specification of their intended business strategy and/or function.
- Enforce the principle of least privilege access and implement the use of multi-factor authentication mechanism including:
  - Something you have (eg, smart card)
  - Something you know (eg, password)
  - Something you are (eg, fingerprint)
- Apply a layered defense-in-depth approach to physical security using a combination of control that are designed to deter, detect, deny, and delay potential intruders and attackers.

EVIDENCE HANDLING

- Apply integrity monitoring and checks to ensure digital evidence has not been tampered or modified from its know-good and authenticated state;
- Prohibit the alteration or deletion of original source data;
- Restrict the storage of, transmission of, and access to digital evidence without the use of cryptographic encryption;
- Enforce the principle of least privilege access to only authorized personnel;
- Ensure that the long-term storage of digital evidence uses any form of storage medium that is write once read many (WORM);
- Seal digital evidence in appropriate containers (ie, evidence bag, safe) to preserve authenticity and integrity during long-term storage;
- Define the long-term retention and recovery strategies for digital evidence.

INCIDENT AND INVESTIGATION RESPONSE

- Require that each incident and investigation is tracked and reported separately.
- Ensure that digital evidence used is proven to be authentic to the original source.

ASSURANCE CONTROLS

- Require routinely audits and control assessments are conducted.

Essentially, the culture and structure of each organization influences how these governance documents are created. Regardless of where (internationally) business is conducted or the size of the organization, there are five simple principles that should be followed as generic guidance for achieving a successful governance framework:

- *Keep it simple*: All documentation should be as clear and concise as possible. The information contained within each document should be stated as briefly as possible without omitting any critical pieces of information. Where documentation is drawn out and wordy, it is typically more difficult to understand, less likely to be read, and harder to interpret for implementation.

- *Keep it understandable*: Documentation should be developed in a language that is commonly known throughout the organization. Leveraging a taxonomy, as discussed in *Appendix F: Building A Taxonomy*, organizations can avoid the complication of using unrecognized terms and slangs.
- *Keep it practicable*: Regardless of how precise and clear the documentation might be, if it cannot be practiced then it is useless. An example of an unrealistic documentation would be a statement indicating that incident response personnel is to be available 24 hours a day; even though there is no adequate mean of contacting them when they are not in the office. For this reason, documentation that is not practicable is not effective and will be quickly ignored.
- *Keep it cooperative*: Good governance documentation is developed through the collaborative effort of all relevant stakeholders, such as legal, privacy, security, and human resources. If key stakeholders have not been involved in the development of these documents, it is more likely that problems will arise during its implementation.
- *Keep it dynamic*: Useful governance document should be, by design, flexible enough to adapt with organizational changes and growth. It would be impractical to develop documentation that is focused on serving the current needs and desires of the organization without considering what could come in the future.

BACKUP AND RESTORATION STRATEGIES

Even though digital evidence has been put into off-line storage for long-term retention, there might come a time when it is needed in support of a business risk scenario, as discussed previously in chapter "Define Business Risk Scenarios." When this time comes, it is critical that in addition to the integrity of digital evidence being authenticated, the data itself must also be restored and made readily available so that there is no delay in the investigative process.

The recovery time objective (RTO)[10] that an organization accepts for restoring digital evidence from backups is what drives the type of backup strategy that will be implemented. RTO is commonly represented in units of time as minutes, hours, days, or longer depending on the needs for restoring digital evidence. When setting the RTO targets, it is important that organizations realize that lower values will result in more expensive backup solutions than the higher values. Recognizing that every organization has different RTO targets for restoring digital evidence, Table 9.1 provides an approximation of values and the backup solution required to meet the service levels.

Table 9.1 Data Restoration Targets

RTO Value	Backup Solution Required
<1 hour	Near real-time data replication
1–6 hours	Data replication
6–24 hours	Data restoration from online backup media
2–14 days	Data restoration from off-line backup media

NEAR REAL-TIME DATA REPLICATION

Meeting service levels with this type of backup solution requires that data is synchronously replicated across multiple identical and distributed instances of the storage solution. Because this type of backup strategy requires multiple instances of the storage solution to be highly available for near real-time data clustering, it is considered to be the most expensive, complex, and resource intensive.

DATA REPLICATION

Performed on a consistent schedule, this backup solution replicates data to two or more identical and distributed instances of the storage solution. Similar to the requirements of the near real-time strategy, this type of solution still requires the implementation of two or more identical and distributed instances of the storage solution. However, with more moderate RTO targets, this type of backup solution is considered to be just as expensive but slightly less complex and resource intensive.

DATA RESTORATION FROM ONLINE BACKUP MEDIA

With data replications set to occur on a schedule, this backup solution replicates data to highly available online media; such as network attached storage. Service levels for this type of strategy are reduced to allow for data to be restored into the production storage solution when required, which makes this type of backup solution less expensive, complex, and resource intensive.

DATA RESTORATION FROM OFF-LINE BACKUP MEDIA

Discussed previously in this chapter, data can be transferred to off-line media, such as backup tapes, for long-term storage. This type of backup strategy is the least expensive because it does not have the complexities of implementing additional storage infrastructures. However, the RTO targets for this solution are extremely relaxed because of the time required to restore from off-line media.

SUMMARY

Preserving the authenticity and integrity of digital evidence extends beyond the implementation of technical and physical security controls. Through the implementation of a governance framework that ensures forensic viability right from when data is created, organizations can ensure that legal admissibility of digital evidence is maintained during secure handling and storage.

TAXONOMY

1 *Least privileged access* is the practice of limiting subject access to objects at the minimal level required to allow normal operations and functions.

2 *Subject* is an active element that operates on information or the system state.

3 *Objects* are passive elements that contain or receive information.

4 *Data-at-rest* refers to the protection of inactive data that is physically stored in any digital form (ie, database, enterprise data warehouse, tapes, hard drives, etc.).

5 *Data-in-transit* is the flow of information over any type of public or private network environment.

6 *Internet protocol security* is a protocol suite for securing network communications by establishing mutual authentication between nodes by encrypting each data packet of an entire communication session.

7 *Data-in-use* applies to data that is actively stored in a nonpersistent state, such as memory, for consumption or presentation.

8 *Message digest algorithm (MD)* is a family of one-way cryptographic hashing functions commonly used to creation a unique digital fingerprint with hash lengths that vary, depending on version, between 128-bit and 512-bit.

9 *Secure hashing algorithm (SHA)* is a family of one-way cryptographic hashing functions commonly used to create a unique digital fingerprint with hash lengths that vary, depending on version, between 160-bit and 512-bit.

10 *Recovery time objective (RTO)* is the targeted duration of time and service level within which a system, network, or application must be restored in order to avoid unacceptable consequences.

Enable Targeted Monitoring

10

This chapter discusses the sixth step for implementing a digital forensic readiness program as enabling targeted monitoring in critical locations through the organization to improve early incident detection. In addition to gathering digital evidence in support of the major business risk scenarios, discussed further in chapter "Define Business Risk Scenarios," data sources can be used to monitor and detect the occurrence of events before it escalates into a more serious incident.

INTRODUCTION

Until this chapter, emphasis has been placed on the requirements for organizations to ensure that the digital evidence they gather, in support of the major business risk scenarios, is done in a manner that guarantees it will be admissible in a court of law. In addition to gathering digital evidence for later use in legal proceeding, the aggregation of data sources can also be used to enhance monitoring capabilities to detect potential threats in a more effective and timely manner.

This step is not about simply gathering data for the sake of gathering data. The purpose of this step is about making sure that additional data source being collected can be effectively used in the process of proactively detecting potential threats. However, determining what is a potential threat is subjective to each organization as they have their own risk tolerance levels which beg the question, "At what point should we be suspicious?"

WHAT IS (UN)ACCEPTABLE ACTIVITY?

Through the creation of governance documents, such as policies and standards, organizations define what is considered to be acceptable and unacceptable activity within the scope of their business environment. Generally, acceptable activity includes any communication that is within the defined boundaries as stated in the organization's governance documentation. As an example, using secure e-mail solutions for the transmission of customer information is within the boundaries of acceptable activity.

On the other hand, unacceptable activity includes any communication that is specifically prohibited outside of the defined boundaries as stated in the organization's governance documentation, such as policies violations, potentially harmful behavior, or breach of confidentiality. Essentially, unacceptable activity is any activity that is not within the confines of what the organization has defined as acceptable. As an example, uploading customer information to unapproved cloud storage is considered to be an unacceptable activity.

To facilitate the monitoring and alerting for any activity, organizations should explicitly define in their governance documentation what they deem to be acceptable activity so that it is clear and concise what actions are acceptable and what are not.

TRADITIONAL SECURITY MONITORING

Monitoring activity that is not within the boundaries of what has been defined as acceptable is a type of technical security control. It should be implemented to increase the possibility of positively identifying unacceptable activities, such as threats or attacks (true-positive[1]), while decreasing the probability of alerting against acceptable activity (false-positive[2]). Achieving this goal requires organizations to invest efforts to understand their business environment so that monitoring technologies can be customized to efficiently sort out the false-positives and improve visibility into the true-positive alerts.

Deploying security controls for the purpose of monitoring activity must be done as part of an organization's overall defense-in-depth strategy. Illustrated in Figure 10.1, defense-in-depth security controls implemented throughout the organization help to improve monitoring capabilities by providing different views into the information flow across assets. Most commonly, the following security controls are implemented to facilitate security monitoring:

- Network devices, such as routers/switches and firewalls, with access controls lists to regulate data flow between different security zones (ie, demilitarized zone, between regional offices).
- Host-based hardening and vulnerability scanning to reduce the potential attack surface by applying configuration changes and software updates.

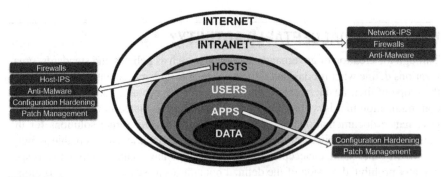

FIGURE 10.1

Traditional security controls layers.

- Subject[3] authentication and authorization to maintain the principles of least privileges for access to objects.[4]
- Signature-based technologies to detect and mitigate risk of threat actors[5] in both end point and network devices; such as anti-malware solutions or intrusion prevention systems (IPS).

First published in February 2010, and subsequently revised in February 2014, the Australian Signal Directorate (ASD) developed a list of security controls that, when used strategically, have been proven to be the most effective in mitigating cyber security incidents. This list was generated as a result of the ASD's experience in operational security, incident management, vulnerability assessments, and penetration testing.

It is important to understand that there is no single security control that can mitigate the risk of a cyber incident. However, the Australian government has proven that the effectiveness of implementing the following top four strategies has resulted in approximately ~85% of their cyber intrusions being mitigated:

- *Application white listing* of permitted/trusted applications to prevent the execution of malicious/unapproved applications
- *Patch applications* to mitigate the risk of application vulnerabilities being exploited
- *Patch operating system vulnerabilities* to mitigate the risk of operating system vulnerabilities being exploited
- *Restrict administrative privileges* to the principle of least privilege access for subject permitted access to only those objects required to perform their duties

While these top four strategies have been deemed as essential security controls and have been declared mandatory for Australian government agencies as of April 2013, organizations can selectively implement any of the top 30 security controls to address specific security needs.

MODERN SECURITY MONITORING

Organizations with effective information security programs have traditionally followed a defense-in-depth strategy that uses multiple layers of security controls. With this traditional approach, their defense-in-depth strategy has commonly focused on defining a physical perimeter as the boundary between the organization's internal network and the external Internet. However, as the modern threat landscape continues to change and cyber-crime evolves, the conventional approach to a defense-in-depth strategy is transforming.

More often today, organizations are building their business environments that stray away from the concepts that there needs to be a defined network perimeter and that all devices are—and will always be—connected to, trusted by, and managed by the organization. The distinction of what used to constitute for a defined network perimeter is being driven by the increasing demand for a more accessible and mobile workforce. In turn, this is further driving the need for organizations to allow their data to be accessed from locations and devices that are not guaranteed to be protected by traditional security monitoring strategies.

As modern technologies—such as mobile computing, desktop virtualization, or cloud infrastructures—continue to proliferate as tools for conducting business,

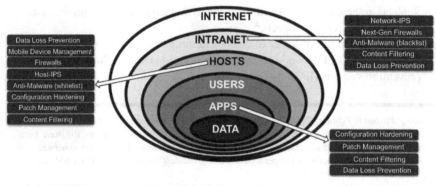

FIGURE 10.2

Next-Gen security controls layers.

organizations are increasingly faced with the need to expose their business records and applications beyond the borders of their traditional network perimeter controls. With this modern change in business practice, deploying security controls under the traditional methodologies will not be as effective in identifying unacceptable activity.

In order to ensure that security monitoring capabilities adapt to continuously evolving technology, threats, and business practices, organizations need to reengineer their security controls to concentrate more on the actual data. This is not to say that traditional security controls used for monitoring at the network and end point layers should be discarded; rather organizations should consider using a new layer of security controls to provide coverage for monitoring closer to the data. In addition to the security controls specified previously, Figure 10.2 illustrates examples of modern security controls that should be considered as part of data-centric security monitoring:

- Next-generation (Next-Gen) firewalls combine the traditional deep-packet inspection capabilities with applications awareness to better detect and deny malicious or unacceptable activity
- Data loss prevention (DLP) uses classifiers to detect and prevent potential data exfiltration through data-at-rest,[6] data-in-transit,[7] and data-in-use[8] scenarios
- Mobile device management allows remote administration and enterprise integration of mobile computing devices, such as smartphones and tablets
- Content filtering monitors activity and enforces compliance with defined acceptable use policies and standards
- White listing, which is the opposite of a known-bad signature-based black listing approach, controls application execution by permitting only trusted and known-good applications to operate

ANALYTICAL TECHNIQUES

Approaches to how security monitoring is performed depends on several factors such as the type of security control used or how the vendor designed the functionality of their technology. Regardless, the foundation of security monitoring is based on the concept that unacceptable activity is noticeably visible from acceptable activity and can be detected as a result of this difference. While there have been several security monitoring techniques suggested, the following are considered the three major categories used.

MISUSE DETECTION

Misuse detection is a technique that applies correlation between observed activity and known unacceptable or known-bad behavior. While this technique is effective in identifying threats or attacks, successfully performing misuse detection drives the need for organizations to define what they consider to be unacceptable or known-bad activity. Ultimately, it cannot be used to detect unacceptable behavior if it has not been defined, such as through the creation of a signature within an IPS. The typical model of the misuse detection technique consists of the following components:

1. Information is gathered from different data sources
2. Gathered information is translated and structured into a signature that can be interpreted by the applicable technologies
3. The signature is applied to analyze activity and characterize unacceptable or known-bad behavior
4. Activity detected as matching the signature is captured for reporting

Within the misuse detection technique, there are five implementation classes for how organizations can apply this approach to their security monitoring:

- *Simple pattern matching* uses text-based searching, such as GREP,[9] looking for an exact string of unacceptable or known-bad behavior within a single observed activity
- *Stateful pattern matching* applies the text-based searching capabilities looking for an exact string of unacceptable or known-bad behavior across multiple instances of observed activities
- *Protocol analysis* incorporates a layer of contextual intelligence where the composition of observed activity, such as the domain name system protocol, are examined to determine if there are variations in the way it is supposed to be structured
- *Heuristical analysis* involves varying levels of intelligence, learning, and logic about observed activity to determine is unacceptable or known-bad behavior is occurring

ANOMALY DETECTION

Anomaly detection is based on the assumption that an observed activity is unacceptable or known-bad behavior, if it is not within the predefined scope of acceptable behavior. This technique starts by establishing a baseline of what acceptable behavior is through the process of observing activity to learn and form an opinion. The typical model of the misuse detection technique consists of the following components:

1. A baseline of acceptable behavior is established from all observed activity.
2. The baseline is translated and structured into a model that can be interpreted by the applicable technologies.
3. Observed activity is compared against the baseline model to determine if a deviation from acceptable behavior exists.
4. Unacceptable or know-bad behavior is captured for reporting.

The main advantage of using this technique is because it applies the concept of white listing to detect unacceptable or known-bad behavior; versus the use of signatures in Misuse Detection. It is important that when establishing the baseline of acceptable activity, the organization is not currently under an attack or that abnormal activity is present. If this is the case, when the system is in the process of learning behavior it may misinterpret unacceptable behavior as acceptable resulting in increased false-positive or false-negative[10] detections.

SPECIFICATION-BASED DETECTION

Specification-based detection techniques do not follow the same methodologies as misuse or anomaly detection. Rather this technique uses behavior specifications, such as the principles of least privilege access,[11] to detect unacceptable or known-bad behavior that does not conform to the intended execution behavior. Essentially, instead of establishing a baseline of acceptable activity through a learning process stakeholders collectively define the threshold of acceptable behavior that are then used to capture reporting of unacceptable or known-bad behavior.

However, organizations need to consider the effort and complexity of establishing the specifications of a system's acceptable behavior. Although security monitoring technologies can help to automate the assessment of a system's behavior, organizations need to ensure that they conduct ongoing reviews to verify that the previously defined specifications for a system's acceptable behavior remain valid.

IMPLEMENTATION CONCERNS

Before organizations begin practicing any of the analytical techniques discussed previously, it is important that decisions are made regarding the deployment of the security monitoring solution. As a starting point, the implementation of the monitoring solution must be supported through existing governance documentation and justified through a formalized risk assessment, as discussed further in Appendix G: Risk Assessment. The following list outlines other areas of consideration that must be decided before a security monitoring solution can be implemented:

- Ensuring criticality-based deployment of monitoring capabilities to target high-value and high-risk employees, systems, networks, etc.
- Selecting the combination of analytical techniques to be used as part of the monitoring solution.

- Using a monitoring solution that meets the established Service Level Objectives[12] for responding.
- Conducting regular reviews of signatures and detection mechanisms to ensure accurate and timely identification of unacceptable or known-bad behavior.

SUMMARY

Before organizations implement any form of security monitoring, it is important that they understand the scope of what they need to monitor and how they will go about achieving it so they can implement targeted capabilities. Once established, using any combination of analytical techniques to monitor acceptable and unacceptable behavior will improve detection capabilities to identify events and/or incidents before they intensify.

TAXONOMY

1. *True-positive* occurs when results properly indicate the presence of a condition.
2. *False-positive* is an error in which results improperly indicate the presence of a condition when it should not be.
3. *Subject* is an active element that operates on information or the system state.
4. *Objects* are passive elements that contain or receive information.
5. *Threat actors* identify and/or characterize the malicious adversary with intent and observed behaviors that represent a threat.
6. *Data-at-rest* refers to the protection of inactive data that is physically stored in any digital form (ie, database, enterprise data warehouse, tapes, hard drives, etc.).
7. *Data-in-transit* is the flow of information over any type of public or private network environment.
8. *Data-in-use* applies to data that is actively stored in a nonpersistent state, such as memory, for consumption or presentation.
9. *GREP* is a utility for searching plain-text data sets for content that matching a specific pattern.
10. *False-negative* is an error in which results improperly indicate no presence of a condition when it should be.
11. *Least privileged access* is the practice of limiting subject access to objects at the minimal level required to allow normal operations and functions.
12. *Service level objectives* are specific quantitative characteristics used to measure service delivery in terms of availability, throughput, frequency, response time, or quality.

Map Investigative Workflows

## 11

This chapter discusses the seventh step for implementing a digital forensic readiness program as the need to establish the workflows for handling different types of investigations throughout the organization. Whether an incident has been detected through proactive security monitoring or by human watchfulness, every incident must be assessed to determine how it will be dealt with and who within the organizations needs to be involved.

INTRODUCTION

Forensic investigations can be triggered from many different types of events generated by a variety of security controls. Whether they originate as a result of human watchfulness, rule matching in an intrusion prevention system, or modification of data alerted on file integrity monitoring (FIM), organizations must demonstrate an acceptable level of due diligence by ensuring they review each event as they are generated.

While reviewing events, security analysts need to quickly assess the level of risk to the organization and make a decision of whether a full forensic investigation needs to be initiated. The criteria for deciding when an event becomes an investigation should not be simply left to the judgment of the security analyst, a series of policies and procedures must be established to clearly define when this escalation is performed. At the point an investigation is initiated, governance documentation should already be in place and include detailed information for how to proceed and whom to involve.

INCIDENT MANAGEMENT LIFECYCLE

A forensic investigation can be initiated from several types of events or incidents. Similar to how the digital forensic readiness model, as illustrated in Figure 11.1, provides a consistent and repeatable workflow for conducting a forensic investigation, the way in which organizations manage their incidents should also follow a consistent, repeatable, and structured workflow framework.

Incident management consists of several phases through which specific activities are performed to mitigate the impact of the incident by containing it and ultimately recovering from it. Illustrated in Figure 11.2, there are four major phases within the incident management lifecycle, each containing a subset of activities and

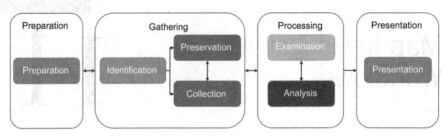

FIGURE 11.1

High-level digital forensic process model.

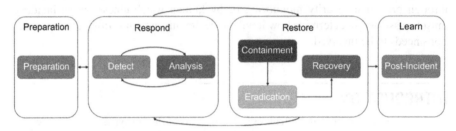

FIGURE 11.2

Incident management lifecycle.

steps that must be performed. Typically, the phases of an incident management lifecycle are completed in sequence and, similar to that of the digital forensic readiness model, may require that preceding phases are revisited as new events or findings are detected, making it very much a lifecycle.

INTEGRATING THE DIGITAL FORENSIC READINESS MODEL

When an incident has been declared, organizations must consider the implications their actions have on potential digital evidence, with respect to its admissibility in a court of law, as they work through the incident management lifecycle. Illustrated in Figure 11.3, the activities and steps performed during incident response have a direct and collateral effect on the organizations ability to support and conduct a forensic investigation.

Those members of the incident response team (IRT) responsible for performing forensic activities need to have knowledge of the principles, methodologies, procedures, tools, and techniques that apply throughout each phase of the incident management lifecycle. Not only does having this knowledge facilitate more efficient and effective response to incidents, it also ensures that the actions taken during incident handling and response will not interfere with the authenticity and integrity of digital evidence.

Included throughout the sections below, the integration points between each incident response phase and digital forensics have been specified.

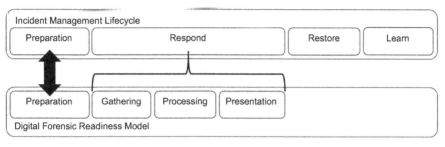

FIGURE 11.3

Incident response—forensic readiness integration.

INCIDENT HANDLING AND RESPONSE

There are four major phases included as part of the incident management lifecycle, including:

- Preparation (initiation)
- Respond (detection and analysis)
- Restore (containment, eradication, and recovery)
- Learn (postincident)

The activities and steps performed in some phases are common to all security incidents, such as when a detected incident has been validated and the IRT moves toward containment actions, while in some incidents there are activities and steps that may not be performed, such as when a detected incident has been invalidated and the IRT moves toward recovery actions. Making effective use of the incident management lifecycle requires that organizations minimize the number of impromptu decisions and subjective judgments being made during an incident. Not only will this facilitate in reducing stress related to potentially making an incorrect decision, but it also provides organizations with a comprehensive methodology that is demonstrably consistent and repeatable when challenged in a court of law.

PHASE #1: PREPARATION

The incident management lifecycle starts by completing activities that ultimately enables the organization to effectively respond and handle incidents. This is the most critical phase of the entire lifecycle because it establishes a foundation for how the subsequent phases will be executed within the capabilities throughout the organizations.

"Event" Versus "Incident"

One of the first actions that should be to taken is specified as part of a taxonomy, discussed further in Appendix F: Building a Taxonomy, what the organizations define as an "event" and "incident." Doing this as the first step provides a clear scope so that further decisions can be made as to roles and responsibilities, team structures, and escalation workflow criteria.

An "event" is any observable occurrence. Events can be physical or technical in nature such as a user accessing a restricted area or a firewall blocking a connection attempt. Additionally, an "adverse event" is a specific type of event that results in a negative consequence such as system failures, malware execution, or data exfiltration.

An "incident" is any violation or imminent threat of violating the organizations policies, standards, or guidelines. Examples of incidents can be:

- A distributed denial of service attack resulting in system failures
- The release of confidential or sensitive information to unauthorized parties

Policies, Plans, and Procedures

Organizing an effective incident handling and response capabilities requires organizations to establish formal incident management policies, plan, and procedures before an incident occurs.

This series of documentation must emphasize how interactions throughout the organization, as well as with external parties such as law enforcement, will be conducted.

Policies

At the highest level, policies are built as formalized blueprints used to describe the organization goals specific to incident management. These documents address general terms and are not intended to contain the level of detail that are found in the plans and procedures that are created afterward.

While the contents of these documents will be subjective to the organizations individual incident management needs, the following elements are commonly used across all policy implementations:

- Statement of management commitments to incident management
- Purpose and objective for creating the policy
- Scope of whom, how, and when the policy applies
- Inclusion of, or reference to, the organization's taxonomy which is used to define common terms and language, discussed further in Appendix F: Building a Taxonomy
- Prioritization or severity ranking of incidents
- Escalation and contact information
- Organizational structure including, but not limited to, roles and responsibilities, chain of command,[2] and information sharing rules

Plans

Building off of policies, plans are the documents that formally outline the focused and coordinated approach to incident management. It is important that each organization has a plan that is implemented to meet their unique requirements and provides the roadmap for how they will implement their incident response capabilities.

In addition to describing the resources and management support required, this document should also include the following components:

- Mission, strategies, and goals for incident management
- Approach and methodology used to support incident management
- Communication and information sharing plan
- Stakeholder (ie, management) approval of the document
- Service level objectives (SLO)[1] used to measure performance
- Roadmap for maturing incident management capabilities

Procedures

Standard operating procedures (SOPs) should be created and maintained based on the organizations implementation of governing policies, plans, and staffing models. Contained within these SOP documents should be comprehensive and detailed technical processes, checklists, and forms that will be used for handling and responding to an incident that align with digital forensics principles, methodologies, and techniques.

The goal for creating these SOP documents is to provide a consistently repeatable process, relevant to all incidents that can be accurately applied to all forensic activities. Suggested components for an SOP document, including the requirements for digital forensics, have been presented throughout the incident handling and response phases in the sections to follow.

Team Structure and Models

An IRT should always be readily available for anybody who identifies or suspects that an event within the organization has occurred. Beyond the availability of incident management documentation, the success of the IRT to analyze events and act appropriately depends on the involvement of key individuals through the organization. Generally, the IRT is responsible for:

- developing appropriate incident management documentation
- retaining resources necessary to perform incident management activities
- investigate the root cause of detected incidents
- manage digital evidence gathered and processed from the incident
- recommend countermeasures and security controls (administrative, technical, or physical)

The way in which an IRT is implemented depends largely on the organization's size. In business environments where operations are centralized to a smaller geographical region, it is quite effective to have a centralized IRT. However as business environments become more dispersed and operations are scattered across multiple geographical location, there could be a need to deploy regional IRTs. Where there are multiple IRTs distributed across a larger business environment, it is important that all teams are part of a single coordinated unit so that policies, plans, and procedures are consistently used for incident management throughout the organizations.

At the end of the day, the decision to use a centralized or distributed IRT comes down to the cost of deploying the model. Through a cost-benefit analysis, as discussed further in Appendix E: Cost-Benefit Analysis, organizations can determine which team model works best for them.

Roles and Responsibilities

It is important that there is participation of stakeholders throughout the organization to provide their expertise, judgment, and abilities throughout the incident management lifecycle. While the duties performed by each of these stakeholders may not have direct involvement in conducting incident response or handling related activities, their cooperation is essential to ensuring that the policies, plans, and procedures are consistently followed.

Depending on the size of the organization, not all business areas specified in the list might exist. Where this is the case, it is important to identify people who are experienced and knowledgeable in these subject matters so that when an incident occurs there will be no knowledge gap with how to proceed under certain circumstances.

- *Management* is ultimately accountable for establishing incident management documentation, budgets, and staffing. They are also held responsible for coordinating incident response and handling capabilities among stakeholders and dissemination of information.
- *Information security* resources provide supplementary support during different stages of the incident response and handling activities, such as validating security controls (ie, firewall rules).
- *Information technology (IT)* support and administration resources have the most intimate knowledge of the technology they manage on a daily basis. This expertise is important to have when ensuring that appropriate actions are taken for affected assets, such as the proper sequence for shutting down critical systems.
- *Forensic practitioners* who are knowledgeable in the scientific principles, methodologies, techniques of digital forensics. These individuals must be equipped with proper tools to ensure that incident response activities maintain the forensic viability and admissibility of digital evidence for eventual use in a court of law.
- *Legal* experts should review all incident management documentation to ensure the organization is compliant with applicable laws, regulations, guidance, and the right to privacy. Furthermore, their expertise should also be sought when it is believed that an incident will have some form of legal ramifications, such as prosecution of perpetrators or the creation of binding agreements for external information sharing.
- *Public and corporate affairs* will facilitate, depending on the nature and context of the incident, the communication and sharing of information with external parties (ie, media) and the public.
- *Human resource and employee relations* serve as mediators for disciplinary proceedings where an employee is suspect of being involved with the incident.
- *Business continuity planning* ensures that all incident management documentation is aligned and consistent with the organizations business continuity

practices. During an incident, their expertise can be used to help minimize operational disruptions and assist with communication. Additionally, these people should be made aware of the impact resulting from incidents so they can revise documentation accordingly, such as business impact and risk assessments.

Communication and Escalation

When an incident occurs, those individuals throughout the organization who have an invested interest in the process must be kept readily informed of what is happening. This requires that throughout each phase of the incident management lifecycle, the IRT must ensure they provide adequate and timely information about the incident.

Communication plans should account for the dissemination of information to a wide variety of audiences, across many different delivery channels (ie, in person, e-mail, paper), and be formatted based on the intended audience (ie, other IRTs, management, stakeholders). Not only should information be communicated on a periodic basis (ie, hourly updates, daily summary), but it should also be made available when requested on a "need to know" basis.

Recording and distributing information about an incident should be limited to specific IRT members, sometimes referred to as scribes, whose responsibility is focused solely on communication and escalations. These individuals work closely with other members of the IRT team(s) to document the activities, steps, and progresses through the incident management lifecycle and ensure that accurate and appropriate information is provided to those need it.

External Information Sharing

From time to time, organizations may need to communicate and share information with a variety of external parties such as law enforcement, media, industry experts, and so on. When required, key stakeholders—such as legal, executive management, and public/corporate affairs—should always be consulted prior to the dissemination of any information to external parties. Without having these teams involved to determine how and what level of detail information can be shared, there is a risk that sensitive or confidential information could be disclosed to unauthorized individuals.

Escalation Management

When required, the IRT may need to escalate specific activities about the incident to highlight issues so that appropriate individuals can respond and provide the required level of resolution. Most commonly, escalations are used during incident response to reprioritize, reassign, or monitor specific activities or actions so normal business operations, functions, and services can be restored as quickly as possible. Escalations can typically be grouped into one of the following categories.

Hierarchical Escalation

Hierarchical escalations are used to ensure that attention is given to the necessary actions for resolving an issue. During a hierarchical escalation, the focus is placed on following the documented chain of command until a resolution is achieved.

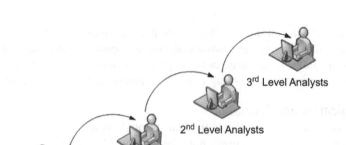

3rd Level Analysts

2nd Level Analysts

1st Level Analysts

Incident Notification

FIGURE 11.4

Hierarchical escalation.

Illustrated in Figure 11.4, an example of this can be seen during security monitoring where the first level analysts complete the initial event triage and if they are unable to resolve the issue it is escalated to the second level analysts, and so on until it is resolved.

Functional Escalation

Functional escalations are used to ensure that issue resolution is achieved within a given SLO.[1] During a functional escalation, the focus is placed on the priority for resolving the issue as a result of the combined importance and urgency.

Illustrated in Figure 11.5, a priority matrix demonstrates how priority can be determined to resolve issues within a given SLO.

Escalations should not be predominantly used as a means of deviating away from established incident management documentation. This typically happens when an organization incorrectly or vaguely defines when an escalation is to be used during the incident management lifecycle. If this occurs, the IRT will not know under what circumstance they should initiate an escalation, with whom they need to communicate, and how they are to perform the escalation. Examples of when an escalation can be triggered under both categories specified previously include the following:

- Evidence of a reportable crime exists
- Evidence indicates a fraud, theft, or other loss
- Estimate of possible damage exceeds the specified threshold
- Potential for embarrassment or reputational damage exists
- Immediate impact to customers, partners, or profitability is imminent
- Recovery plans have been invoked or are necessary
- Incident is reportable under legal or compliance requirements

The use of escalations should be limited to specific circumstances as defined in the incident management documentation. To ensure escalations are only performed

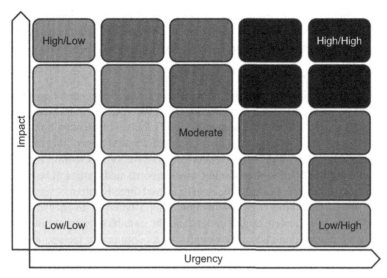

FIGURE 11.5

Functional escalation.

when required, the IRT should include a decision maker, such as the incident manager, who will decide whether an escalation is required.

PHASE #2: RESPOND

One of the most challenging aspects of the incident management lifecycle is accurately detecting and assessing potential incidents; primarily because incidents can originate from many different attack vectors[5] such as the loss or theft of equipment or lack of employee awareness.

While the established SOP documentation supports a consistent and repeatable process for responding to all incidents, the way in which organizations handles each incident varies.

Contained with the scope of this phase, activities and steps performed are focused primarily on the detection and analysis of incidents as they are received.

Detection

Incidents can be detected through many different sources other than the targeted security monitoring capabilities discussed previously in chapter Enable Targeted Monitoring. Regardless, the indicators of an incident can be grouped into one of the following categories:

- *Precursor* incidents are those events that imply that an incident may occur in the future.
- *Indicator* incidents are those events that signify that an incident has or is occurring now.

With both categories of events, organizations need to use supplemental information, as discussed further in chapter Determine Collection Requirements, to prevent the impeding incident from escalating and further impacting business operations.

Analysis

Generally, assessing incidents would be relatively simple if precursor and indicator events were guaranteed to always be accurate. However, even when events are confirmed to be accurate, it does not necessarily signify that an incident will or is about to occur. For this reason, it is important that those individual(s) responsible for completing the initial triage determine if the event is true-positive[3] or false-positive.[4] This validation is an important step in determining what activities and steps will be performed next, such as whether to contain the incident or moved directly into recovery activities.

Where initial validation corroborates that the existence of an incident, the IRT must work quickly to prioritize and understand the context to surrounding the incident. The following techniques are examples of recommended techniques that can effectively reduce the complexity of incident analysis:

- *Profiling* is the capability to characterize activity so that unknown or abnormal activity can be more easily identified. Examples of profiling techniques that can be used during incident analysis include file integrity monitoring (FIM) (chapter Establish Legal Admissibility) or misuse, anomaly, and specification-based detection (chapter Enable Targeted Monitoring).
- *Maintaining information knowledgebase*, such as a centralized incident and case management solutions, should be readily available for the IRT to reference quickly during an incident. The knowledgebase should contain a variety of information that can be used to assess an incident including the following:
  - *Observables* are the resulting outputs that might be or have been seen across an organization (eg, service degradation)
  - *Indicators* describe one or more observable patterns that, combined with other relevant and contextual information, represent artifacts and behaviors of interest (eg, file hashes)
  - *Incidents* are distinct instances of indicators that are affecting an organization accompanied by information discovered or decided upon during an investigation
  - *Adversary tactics, techniques, and procedures (TTP)* describe the attack patterns, tools, exploits, infrastructure, victim targeting, and other methods used by the adversary or attacker
  - *Exploit targets* describe a vulnerabilities, weaknesses, or configurations that might be exploited
  - *Courses of action* are specific countermeasures taken as corrective or preventative response actions to address an exploit target or mitigate the potential impact of an incident
  - *Campaigns* are instance of threat actors that are performing a set of TTPs or incidents potentially seen across an organization

- *Threat actors* identify and characterize the malicious adversary with intent and observed behaviors that represent a threat to an organization
- *Internet search engines* can help the IRT to find information about similar incidents or perpetrators. When performing Internet research, it is important to use systems that are not directly associated or connected with the organization so that anonymity can be maintained. Additionally through the use of "throwaway" systems, such as a virtual machine, organizations can avoid the potential of their searches being tracked or correlated by always using a system that operates within a preestablished and known operating state.

Prioritization

Following the analysis and assessment of an incident, the most critical decision to be made by the IRT is establishing the incident priority. As a rule of thumb, incidents that have been assessed should be handled by its priority and not on a first-come-first-serve basis; similar to how a hospital's emergency room might operate. Prioritizing incidents can be achieved by using the following factors.

Functional Impact

Incidents targeting an organization's IT assets will most typically have some impact on the organization's business operations. The IRT should consider not only the immediate negative impact to the business but also the likelihood of future impact if the incident is not contained. The criteria for prioritizing incidents that have a functional impact are illustrated in Table 11.1.

Table 11.1 Functional Impact Prioritization

Category	Criteria
None	No effect to business operations, functions, or services
Low	Minimal effect to business operations, functions, or services; no critical services have been impacted
Medium	Moderate effect to business operations, functions, or services; a subset of critical services have been impacted
High	Significant effect to business operations, functions, or services; all critical services have been impacted

Informational Impact

Incidents can affect the security properties of an organization's information, including confidentiality, integrity, availability, authentication, authorizations, and nonrepudiation. The IRT must consider the implications of sensitive or confidential information potentially being exfiltrated as a result of the incident. The criteria for prioritizing incidents that have an informational impact are illustrated in Table 11.2.

Table 11.2 Informational Impact Prioritization

Category	Criteria
None	No information was exfiltrated, lost, or otherwise compromised
Privacy breach	Sensitive information was exfiltrated, lost, or otherwise compromised (ie, personally identifiable information)
Proprietary breach	Internal information was exfiltrated, lost, or otherwise compromised (ie, architectural diagrams)
Integrity breach	Sensitive or proprietary information was exfiltrated, lost, or otherwise compromised (ie, financial records)

Recoverability Impact

Incidents can result in varying levels of impact to assets and operations. In some instances, it may be possible to quickly recover from an incident; however, in other incidents, additional resources might be required to facilitate the restoration of business assets and operations. The criteria for prioritizing incidents that have recoverability impact are illustrated in Table 11.3.

Table 11.3 Recoverability Impact Prioritization

Category	Criteria
Regular	Restoration time is predictable and can be achieved using existing resources
Supplemented	Restoration time is predictable but requires additional resources
Extended	Restoration time is unpredictable and requires assistance from existing, additional, and external resources
Not recoverable	Restoration time is unpredictable and not realistically possible

Once the criteria for prioritizing incidents have been established, the IRT needs to ensure that they notify and escalate, if required, to the appropriate stakeholders. Further details about requirements for notification and escalation have been specified in the following sections of this chapter.

PHASE #3: RESTORE

Once an incident has been responded to, appropriate actions must be taken to mitigate further impact and the organization can begin working to recover business operations, functions, and services.

While the established SOP documentation supports a consistent and repeatable process for restoring business operations, functions, and services, the ways in which organizations contain and eradicate each incident can vary.

Contained with the scope of this phase, activities and steps performed are focused primarily on the containment and eradication of incident and subsequent recovery of business operations, functions, and services.

Containment

Before an incident can intensify further, organizations need to determine the appropriate strategies for controlling the impact of the incident beyond the assets and resources it has currently affected. Every incident varies in context, and because of these variations there is no single containment strategy that can be used unanimously. Ultimately, deciding which containment strategy works best for controlling impact beyond the currently affected assets and resources requires organizations to understand the context under which the incident occurred. Examples of criteria that can be used to select an appropriate containment strategy include the following:

• Functional, informational, and recoverability prioritization
• Potential damage to or theft of assets and resources
• Effectiveness of the containment strategy
• Time required to implement the containment strategy

Although the IRT's primary goal is to select a containment strategy that will assist to eradicate and recover from the incident, careful consideration must be given to the need for preserving potential digital evidence in preparation for legal proceedings. Once the containment strategy has been selected, such as shutting down systems or isolating network segments, the IRT must ensure potential digital evidence is gathered and preserved in the order of the data's volatility rating.

Generally, the more volatile data within a system the more challenging it is to forensically gather it because it is only available for a specific amount of time. The ability to gather potential digital evidence prior to implementing a containment strategy comes with the inherent risk whereas the longer it takes to make the decision, the greater the risk of the incident intensifying and digital evidence being lost.

When deciding to preserve volatile data, it is important to keep in mind that the more volatile the data, the greater there is a need for knowledgeable individuals and specialized tools to ensure the data is gathered and preserved in a forensically sound manner. Illustrated in Table 11.4 is the order of volatility for digital evidence, ordered from most volatile to least volatile, as discussed further in chapter Understanding Digital Forensics.

Eradication and Recovery

After a containment strategy has been implemented, work can begin to remove the elements of the incident from where it exists throughout the organization. At this time, it is important that all affected assets and resources have been identified and remediated to ensure that when containment measures are removed, the incident does not come back or propagate further through the organization.

Recovery efforts that follow eradication involve restoring assets and resources to their normal and fully functional state, such as changing passwords, restoring data from backups, or installing patches. Recovery should be completed following the eradication of an incident's impact from a particular asset or resource, not in parallel. By completing these tasks as part of a phased approach, organizations can focus their priority on removing the threats from their environment as quickly as possible, then focusing on the work to keep the organization as secure as possible for the long term.

Table 11.4 Order of Volatility

Life Span	Storage Type	Data Type
As short as a single clock cycle	CPU storage	Registers
		Caches
	Video	RAM
Until host is shut down	System storage	RAM
	Kernel tables	Network connections
		Login sessions
		Running processes
		Open files
		Network configurations
		System date/time
Until overwritten or erased	Nonvolatile data	Paging/swap files
		Temporary/cache files
		Configuration/log files
		Hibernation files
		Dump files
		Registry
		Account information
		Data files
		Slack space
	Removable media	Floppy disks
		Tapes
		Optical disc (read/write only)
Until physically destroyed		Optical disc (write only)
	Outputs	Paper printouts

PHASE #4: LEARN

Every incident varies in context and can potentially include a new threat, attack vector, or threat actor that the IRT has not previously accounted for in their incident management program. However, the most commonly overlooked and disregarded phase of the incident management lifecycle involves learning from the incident.

By holding a "lessons learned" meeting with all stakeholders after an incident, the organization can identify additional controls to improve the organizations security posture and enhancing the IRT's capabilities for future incidents. This meeting is the organizations opportunity to formally close work being done on the incident and begin reviewing specific details about the incident including:

- What happened and at what time(s)?
- How well did stakeholders and the IRT deal with the incident?
- Were incident management processes and procedures followed'?
- Did incident management documentation contain adequate information?

- Did any activities, steps, or actions inhibit restoring business operations, functions, or services?
- How could notification, escalation, and information sharing be improved?

Following the completion of activities in this phase, the incident management lifecycle resets to the preparation phase. When this happens, the outputs from the postincident activities must be carried forward so the incident response process and accompanying documentation can be revised accordingly to reduce the likelihood of new incidents from occurring.

INVESTIGATION WORKFLOW

The logical flow from the time when the initial event occurs requires organizations to follow a consistent and repeatable incident handling and response process that encompasses several stages of information gathering (ie, preserving digital evidence, conducting interviewing), communication (ie, stakeholder reporting, escalations), and documentation (ie, SOPs, incident/case management knowledgebase).

The goal of following a logical investigative process, made up of clear and concise workflows, is to reduce the potential for impromptu and uninformed decisions to be made during incident handling and response. However, understanding that the context of every incident is different, the investigative workflow should still provide those involved with the ability to make the best and most educated decision for what actions are performed next.

Before an incident is escalated into an investigation, the IRT should have collected sufficient information to assess the impact of this decision on the organization, including the following:

- Can an investigation proceed at a cost that is proportional to the size of the incident?
- How can an investigation reduce the impact to business operations, functions, and services?

Understanding that each organization is subjective in how they will build their investigative workflow, the diagrams provided in the Templates section of this book can be used as a reference for starting to build a logical investigative workflow process.

SUMMARY

Forensic investigations are most commonly triggered as a result of some type of incident; whether an event was detected through security monitoring, a subpoena was received for legal proceeding, or whether the theft or loss of an asset occurred. Regardless, the logical investigative workflow used to handle and respond to all incidents must be well defined to reduce incorrect decision making but flexible enough to support the variety of incidents as they occur. In any case, organizations must ensure that their governance framework supports consistent and repeatable actions that can be used throughout their entire incident management capabilities.

TAXONOMY

1 *Service level objectives* are specific quantitative characteristics used to measure service delivery in terms of availability, throughput, frequency, response time, or quality.
2 *Chain of command* is the line of authority and responsibility along which order and commands are passed between different units.
3 *True-positive* occurs when results properly indicate the presence of a condition.
4 *False-positive* is an error in which results improperly indicate the presence of a condition when it should not be.
5 *Attack vectors* are paths or means by which an attacker or intruder gains access in order to deliver an exploit.

Establish Continuing Education

## 12

This chapter discusses the eighth step for implementing a digital forensic readiness program as the need to implement and ensure that stakeholders throughout the organizations are provided with continuous training and education to ensure they are knowledgeable in how they contribute to the success of the digital forensic readiness program. Based on the stakeholder's respective role within the digital forensic readiness program, organizations must ensure that all individuals are properly and adequately trained so that they have the knowledge necessary to perform their duties.

INTRODUCTION

Organizations cannot implement an effective digital forensics readiness program without ensuring that all stakeholders involved have an adequate knowledge of how they contribute to its overall success. Once stakeholders have established how they contribute to digital forensics readiness, the level of educational training and professional knowledge required will vary for each individual.

Without proper training and education, the people factor, not technology, becomes the weakest link of a digital forensic readiness program. Knowing this, it is essential that organizations implement a comprehensive and well-designed program to ensure that all those who have any involvement with digital forensic readiness are knowledgeable and experienced.

EDUCATION AND TRAINING

Much like other components of a digital forensic readiness program, a successful education and training program also starts with the implementation of organizational governance that reflects the need for (1) informing stakeholders of their responsibilities, (2) providing the appropriate level of training and education, and (3) establishing processes for monitoring, reviewing, and improving their level of knowledge.

Having different education and awareness programs in place for all stakeholders, depending on their involvement, is an effective way of distributing information about the benefits and value of digital forensic readiness throughout the organization. Illustrated in Figure 12.1 below, the following sections describe the difference between

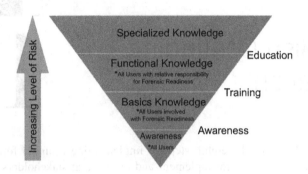

FIGURE 12.1

Continuing education hierarchy.

awareness, training, and education curriculums that organizations should consider as part of their overall continuing education for digital forensic readiness program.

Within each education and training curriculum illustrated above, organizations must ensure that the information is adapted according to the stakeholder's role (job function). As an example, a simplified concept for grouping the education and training information for applicable stakeholders has been placed into the following three categories:

- *All personnel* have a perspective that recognizes the importance of information security enough to positively contribute to the digital forensic readiness program.
- *Functional/specialized roles* emphasize the importance of performing their job duties to support the organizations digital forensic readiness program.
- *Management* needs to understand the functional, operational, and strategic value of the digital forensic readiness program so they can communicate and reinforce it throughout the organization.

AWARENESS

As the first stage of education and training, this general awareness is intended to change the behaviors of individuals and reinforce a culture of acceptable conduct. The objective here is not to provide users with in-depth or specialized knowledge, rather it is designed to provide stakeholders with the knowledge they need to recognize what the organization defines as unacceptable behavior and take the necessary steps from occurring.

With one of the business risk scenarios for implementing digital forensics readiness being to investigate employee misconduct against the organization's policies, this type of education and training will reduce the likelihood that an incident will occur requiring a formal forensic investigation.

The information provided at this level is generic enough that it can be provided to all stakeholders without being adapted according to their job function. Examples of topics and subject areas that should be included as part of general awareness education and training includes, but is not limited to:

- Policies, standards, guidelines
- Social engineering (ie, phishing)
- Privileged access
- Data loss prevention

Organizations should consider making it a mandatory requirement that all stakeholders complete the general awareness program as part of their employment condition. At a minimum, organizations should require existing stakeholders to complete the general awareness education and training annually. Alternatively, when new stakeholders are identified they should be expected to complete the general awareness program immediately.

BASIC KNOWLEDGE

As the next stage of education and training, the need for basic knowledge of digital forensic readiness provides stakeholders with the fundamental knowledge that is essential to ensuring they are competent. The distinction between basic knowledge and general awareness is that this level of education and training is designed to teach stakeholders the basic skills they will need to support a digital forensic readiness program.

The education and training provided at this level provides stakeholders with particular skill sets that continue to build off the foundations of the general awareness information. Creating in-house training courses can, for the most part, be designed to contain the same quality of information that could be obtained by enrolling in a formal college or university course.

The information provided at this level becomes more specific that it must be adapted to meet the knowledge required of each category of stakeholder. Examples of topics and subject areas that should be provided to each stakeholder group include, but are not limited to:

- Audit logging and retention
- Development life cycle security
- Incident handling and response
- Logical access controls

Completion of these basic knowledge courses can be positioned as either elective, where stakeholders can enroll themselves at their leisure to improve their professional development relating to digital forensic readiness, or mandatory, where stakeholders must complete the training in order to maintain their supporting role of digital forensics readiness.

FUNCTIONAL KNOWLEDGE

Taking education and training another level higher, there is a need for specific stakeholders to have a working and practical knowledge of the digital forensic discipline.

Essentially, these individuals must have the skills and competencies necessary to ensure that digital forensic principles, methodologies, and techniques are upheld in support of the organization's digital forensic readiness program.

Digital forensics requires individuals to have a significant amount of specialized training and skills to thoroughly understand and consistently follow the established scientific fundamentals. The information provided at this level of training is specific to the digital forensic discipline and requires stakeholders to have strong working and practical knowledge. Appendix B: Education and Professional Certifications provides a list of higher/postsecondary institutes that offer formal digital forensic education programs.

Professional Certification

Following completion of formalized education, there are several recognized industry associations that offer professional certifications in digital forensics. It is important to keep in mind that professional certifications are designed to test and evaluate an individual's knowledge and experience; they do not provide individuals with in-depth training on digital forensics and information technology (IT) as obtained through formalized education. Professional certifications, or professional designations, provide assurance that an individual is qualified to perform digital forensics.

Appendix B: Education and Professional Certifications provides a list of higher/postsecondary institutes that offer formal digital forensic education programs as well as recognized industry associations offering digital forensic professional certifications.

SPECIALIZED KNOWLEDGE

It was not too long ago that digital forensics was considered niche and now if you practice digital forensics you are recognized as somewhat of a generalist in the discipline. However, with the continuing advancements in technology and how it is being used to support business operations, simply being a digital forensic generalist is no longer practical for most individuals.

Having gained the necessary functional knowledge, the next level of education and training is to become a specialist or professional in a particular subject area of digital forensics profession. For this reason, it is common for individuals to expand their knowledge of digital forensics and how it can be integrated and applied to other disciplines throughout the organization. The following are examples of areas where digital forensic specialization can be achieved:

- *Cybercrime* which emphasizes applying investigative techniques and methodologies of digital forensics to subject areas including, but not limited to, the following:
  - *Electronic discovery (eDiscovery)* which relates to the discovery, preservation, processing, and production of electronically stored information (ESI) in support of legal or regulatory matters.

- *Network forensics and analysis* which relates to the monitoring and analysis of network traffic for the purposes of using it as digital evidence.
- *Memory forensics* which relates to the gathering and analysis of digital information as digital evidence contained within a system's Random Access Memory (RAM).
- *Cloud forensics* which, as a subset of network forensics, relates to the gathering and analysis of digital information as digital evidence from cloud computing systems.
- *Information assurance* which emphasizes applying investigative techniques and methodologies of digital forensics to subject areas including, but not limited to, the following:
    - *Incident handling and response* which relates to reducing business impact by managing the occurrence of computer security events; discussed further in chapter "Map Investigative Workflows."
    - *Threat modeling* builds appropriate countermeasures that effectively reduce business risk impact through the identification and understanding of individual security threats that have potential to affect business assets, operations, and functions; discussed further in Appendix H: Threat Modeling.
    - *Risk management* is an examination of what, within the organization, could cause harm to assets so that an accurate decision of how to manage the risk can be made; discussed further in Appendix G: Risk Assessment.
    - *Security monitoring* applies analytical techniques to identify unacceptable behavior patterns in the organization's systems and assets to detect potential threats in a more effective and timely manner; discussed further in chapter "Enable Targeted Monitoring."

DIGITAL FORENSIC ROLES

Illustrated in Figure 12.2, the *FORZA—digital forensic investigation framework* was developed as a mean of linking the multiple practitioner roles with the different procedures and processes they are responsible for throughout for the investigative workflow. Details on the roles described in the FORZA process model below have been described in Appendix A: Process Models.

Regardless of an individual's role in the investigative workflow, there are different activities and steps performed that require either general or specialized knowledge in order to maintain digital evidence admissibility and credibility. It is essential that all persons involved, at any phases of the investigative workflow, diligently follow the rules of evidence and thoroughly apply digital forensic principles, methodologies, and techniques to all aspects of their work.

The need for distinct roles, as described by FORZA process model, is subjective to the overall size of the organization and the arrangement of the digital forensic team. For example, organizations that are smaller or localized to a specific geographic location might only employ a few individuals that are responsible for all aspects of digital

	Why (Motivation)	What (data)	How (Function)	Where (Network)	Who (people)	When (Time)
Case leader (contextual investigation layer)	Investigation Objective	Event Nature	Requested Initial Investigation	Investigation Geography	Initial Participants	Investigation Timeline
System owner (if any) (contextual layer)	Business Objective	Business and Event Nature	Business and System Process Model	Business Geography	Organization and Participants Relationship	Business and Incident Timeline
Legal advisor (legal advisory layer)	Legal Objective	Legal Background and Preliminary Issues	Legal Procedures for Further Investigation	Legal Geography	Legal Entities and Participants	Legal Timeframe
Security/system architect/auditor (conceptual security layer)	System/Security Control Objective	System Information and Security Control Model	Security Mechanisms	Security Domain and Network Infrastructure	Users and Security Entity Model	Security Timing and Sequencing
Digital forensics specialists (technical preparation layer)	Forensic Investigation Strategy Objectives	Forensic Data Model	Forensic Strategy Design	Forensics Data Geography	Forensics Entity Model	Hypothetical Forensics Event Timeline
Forensics investigators/system administrator/operator (data acquisition layer)	Forensic Acquisition Objectives	On-site Forensics Data Observation	Forensics Acquisition / Seizure Procedures	Site Network Forensics Data Acquisition	Participants Interviewing and Hearing	Forensics Acquisition Timeline
Forensics investigators/forensics analysts (data analysis layer)	Forensic Examination Objectives	Event Data Reconstruction	Forensics Analysis Procedures	Network Address Extraction and Analysis	Entity and Evidence Relationship Analysis	Event Timeline Reconstruction
Legal prosecutor (legal presentation layer)	Legal Presentation Objectives	Legal Presentation Attributes	Legal Presentation Procedures	Legal Jurisdiction Location	Entities in Litigation Procedures	Timeline of the Entire Event for Presentation

FIGURE 12.2

FORZA—digital forensics investigation framework, 2006.

forensics. Alternatively, organizations that are larger, distributed in geographic location, or have clearly defined structures might employ multiple individuals who are each responsible for a particular aspect of digital forensics.

In any case, what remains consistent is the need for individuals who have strong IT knowledge as well as formalized training of digital forensic principles, methodologies, and techniques. These are essential and fundamental to ensuring that the integrity, relevancy, and admissibility of digital evidence are maintained. While not comprehensive, the following roles are commonly employed in support of digital forensics:

- *Forensic technicians* gather, process, and handle evidence at the crime scene. These individuals need to be trained in proper handling techniques, such as the order of volatility discussed in chapter "Understanding Digital Forensics," to ensure the authenticity and integrity of evidence is preserved for potential admissibility in a court of law.
- *Forensic analysts or examiners*, use forensic tools and investigative techniques to identify and, where needed, recover specific electronic information. Leveraging their technical skills, these individuals most often are the ones who are performing the work to process and analyze ESI as part of an investigation.
- *Forensic investigators* work with internal (ie, IT support teams) and external (ie, law enforcement agencies) entities to retrieve evidence relevant to the investigation. In some environments, these individuals might also perform the duties of both/either the forensic technician and the forensic analyst. It is important to note that in some jurisdiction, use of the term "investigator" requires individuals to hold a private investigator license that involves meeting a minimum requirement for both education and experience.
- *Forensics managers* oversee all actions and activities involving digital forensics. Within the scope of their organization's digital forensic discipline, these individuals can be accountable for ensuring their organization's digital forensic program continues to operate through activities such as leading a team, coordinating investigations and reporting, and ensuring the daily operations. Even though these individuals do not perform hands-on activities, it is expected that they are educated and knowledgeable of how digital forensic principles, methodologies, and techniques must be applied and followed.

While not typically a role within the digital forensic discipline, the terms specialist and professional are typically used to describe individuals who have been extensively trained, gained significant amounts of experience, and are recognized for their skills.

BALANCING BUSINESS VERSUS TECHNICAL LEARNING

Those individuals who are directly involved with practicing digital forensics cannot solely rely on their technical education and training to support them through an investigation. While formal education is great and should be obtained where needed, there is a business side to digital forensics that must be accounted for and recognized as equally important as the technical skill sets. The following subject areas should be considered important to develop and continuously improve upon to be recognized as a digital forensic professional.

- *Analytical skills* are about extracting meaning and finding the hidden patterns and unexpected correlations among the masses of data. It is not about knowing everything; it is about identifying what is relevant and getting closer to the meaningful pieces of information. To do this requires that a level of objectivity is maintained throughout the investigation by setting aside personal and professional influences or biases to focus in on the facts.
- *Communication and technical writing skills* involve translating the technical techniques, methodologies, and findings into a natural language that can be effectively communicated across business, civil, or criminal court settings. This can be an overwhelming task for a technical individual who, depending on their level of experience, has had limited involvement in the business aspects of digital forensics. Further discussion on how to formulate evidence-based reports for communicating information about an investigation can be found in chapter "Maintain Evidence-based Reporting."
- *Time management and task prioritization* are typically acquired through practical experience in dealing with investigations. Depending on the size and complexity of an investigation, there are certain processes and/or techniques that will produce results quickly or may take more time to execute. Deciding on the appropriate amount of time that will be required to complete the tasks is important to ensure that the investigation is not impact as a result of evidence being released or destroyed.
- *Interpersonal skills* are focused on building strategic relationships with key stakeholders to gain their confidence and cooperation. Regardless of whether the stakeholders are individuals with technical background, attorneys, or management, in the context of conducting an investigation there is a common goal to which everybody is striving to complete.
- *Critical thinking* can be developed through any number of workshops, sessions, or simulations using real-life case studies from a variety of security incidents. By analyzing real-life security incidents, skills can be obtained that are not focused on how to perform a task (ie, seizing evidence) but rather on how to identify relationships (ie, cause and effect).

SUMMARY

Over the course of an investigation, there can be a wide range of individuals involved at any given time. Through the implementation of different levels of education and training programs, organizations can prepare stakeholders for the various roles they may play before, during, or after an investigation.

Maintain Evidence-Based Reporting

13

This chapter discusses the ninth step for implementing a digital forensic readiness program as the need to provide answers to questions that arise during the investigation and demonstrate, through evidence-based reporting, why those answers are credible. Ultimately, the purpose of completing this step is to develop and implement a governance framework (ie, policies, procedures) that will be used to describe how evidence-based reporting should be constructed during an investigation.

INTRODUCTION

Conducting an investigation is more than simply supporting the business risk scenarios discussed in chapter "Define Business Risk Scenarios." From conducting an investigation, organizations must also be able to provide answers to questions—who, where, what, when, why and how—and demonstrate how their digital evidence supports the credibility of these answers.

   Achieving these goals requires that forensic viability of digital evidence, including the authenticity and integrity of the data, is maintained by following the steps outlined throughout this book; such as the need for governance over the collection, handling, and storage of digital evidence. Furthermore, by applying an evidence-based methodology for managing an investigation, organizations will be in a better position to establish credibility in the answers to questions as they arise.

IMPORTANCE OF FACTUAL REPORTS

Having processed all digital evidence, a formal report must be created to communicate the findings of the investigation. However, one of the biggest downfalls of any investigation is the deficiencies in the final report. Ultimately, if decision-makers cannot understand and interpret the information detailed within the report, the entire investigation could result in failure.

   As with any investigation, organizations should always conduct themselves on the basis that the matter will escalate into some form of legal proceeding. Therefore, creating a formal report should not only be done to share information within the context of the organization, but also created with the intention to present evidence as testimony in a court of law.

Required under Rule 26 of the US Federal Rules of Civil Procedure, any person(s) who will be presenting evidence as testimony has a duty to disclose a written report.

These reports must disclose all "facts or data" considered by the person(s) during the investigation, the basis how they established these "facts or data," and the information that was used in order to arrive at these "facts or data."

It is important to understand that Rule 26 defines the intent to exclude theories or opinions and the need for creating a credible investigative report that limits the disclosure of "facts or data" to only information that is "material of a factual nature."

TYPES OF REPORTS

Completed during the presentation stage of the digital forensic readiness model, discussed further in chapter "Investigative Process Models," investigative reports are essential in communicating facts about the evidence analyzed to various different stakeholders, such as presenting evidence as legal testimony.

As the first step to creating a report, it is important that the author(s) identify the target audience and the purpose for creating the report. Authors need to ensure that the content of the report is structured to be clear, concise, easy to follow, and understandable to their target audience. For example, when a report is being provided to management, the author(s) should consider accompanying any technical content with references or educational materials to clarify or further elaborate this information so that the reader does not become withdrawn from the report.

With the audience established the next step is to decide which type of report is required. Typically, investigative reports can be grouped into one of the following categories:

- *Verbal formal* reports are typically quite structured and are commonly used to present information to management or in front of a jury without producing any form of document. An important consideration when using this presentation style is the amount of time available to communicate the facts. If the pace is quick, there is a chance that the audience will not clearly understand the information; alternatively if the pace of delivering the report is too long, the author may not have enough time to share important pieces of information contained within the report. Author(s) must ensure that they organize the presentation of information in a way that clearly and concisely focuses on the facts of the investigation.
- *Verbal informal* reports are typically less structured and are commonly used to present information to management or in an attorney's office without producing any form of document. With respect to using this style for management communication, it is commonly done as an "elevator speech"[1] where the facts of the investigation need to be shared quickly. Alternatively, this presentation style can also be used when communicating with attorneys where there is a need to reduce the amount of written information that can later be discovered as part

of a legal proceeding. Author(s) must ensure that they are prepared to deliver this style of report by focusing on key, relevant, and meaningful facts of the investigation to avoid confusion or misinterpretation.

- *Written formal* reports are typically quite structured and result in the creation of a document that will be used to present information to management or as part of legal proceedings. Regardless of whom the audience is, this style of report is considered legally discoverable and can be used in a court of law. These reports require author(s) to pay a great deal of attention to detail and ensure that the report is focused specifically on communicating credible and factual information only. When writing these reports, it is recommended that the author(s) use a natural language, as discussed below, and not use words or grammar that is difficult for readers to understand. The arrangement of these reports is discussed in the section "Arranging Written Reports."
- *Written informal* reports are considered at high risk because the information being documented might not yet be proven as factual to the investigation. If this style of report must be produced, it is important for organizations to understand that these documents are discoverable in a court of law. Instead of making preliminary statements about information, may not be factual, author(s) should include the same level of information provided through a verbal informal report discussed above.

CREATING UNDERSTANDABLE REPORTS

Writing a report should flow just as naturally and logically as we think or speak. Each related fact and piece of information should be grouped together into a single paragraph and build upon each other from beginning to end.

The use of jargon or slang terminology should be avoided at all times. Where technical terms need to be used, they must be defined in a natural language as part of taxonomy, discussed further in Appendix F: Building a Taxonomy. Additionally, when using acronyms or abbreviations, they should be written in full expression on the first use and defined as part of the taxonomy.

Information being communicated most typically occurred before the report was written which means the author(s) should primarily write in the past tense; but can decide to change tense to use either present or future where appropriate.

ARRANGING WRITTEN REPORTS

Regardless of whether the investigation will proceed into a court of law, all investigative reports should be structured to communicate relevant and factual information. At a minimum, author(s) should ensure that the following goals are consistently applied to every type of report that is being presented:

- Report contains an accurate description of all event and incident details
- Content is clear, concise, and understandable to relevant decision-makers

- Content is deemed admissible and credible in a court of law
- Content not portray opinions or information that is open to misinterpretation
- Report contains sufficient information to establish factual relevance of conclusions
- Report is completed and presented in a timely manner

With verbal reports, whether formal or informal, the intention is to speak about the facts of the investigation. Alternatively, when using a written report the author(s) should ensure that they follow a consistent approach in the layout and presentation of the facts. In addition to ensuring the above-noted goals are achieved, a standardized template should be used that establishes a repeatable standard for how facts and information will be presented.

Understanding that the inclusion of information in a written formal report is subjective to the organization's needs, the minimum components required of a standardized report template should include the following:

- *Executive summary*: The subsections included within the executive summary are intended to provide readers with a high-level summary of the investigation. Most commonly, this section might be all that management reads to get an understanding of the investigation. For this reason, it is important that the information contained in these subsections is written in a natural and business language that does not include unnecessary technical details.
  - *Background*: Describes the event(s) or incident(s) that brought about the need for the investigation, the objectives of performing the investigation, as well as who authorized the investigation to be conducted.
  - *Summary of findings*: Summarizes the significant findings as a result of the investigation.
  - *Conclusions*: Establishes credible answers to questions that came about from the investigation.
- *Investigative details*: The subsections included within the investigative details are intended to provide readers with detailed information about the investigations. While the information contained within places emphasis on the digital evidence, it must be focused on detailing the credibility of facts as identified during the investigation.
  - *Chain of evidence*: Describes the continuity of all digital evidence relating to where it was identified, the techniques used to seize it, and methods used to transport it.
  - *Gathering of evidence*: Specifies the methodologies, tools, and equipment used to collect and preserve digital evidence.
  - *Processing of evidence*: Specifies the methodologies, tools, and equipment used to examine digital evidence.
  - *Analysis of evidence*: Details the meaningful, relevant, and factual findings from analyzing digital evidence.
- *Addendums*: The subsections included within the investigative details are intended to provide readers with in-depth supplementary information that

supports the findings outlined in the previous section. Examples of supplementary information that can be included are the following:

* tables listing the full pathnames of significant digital evidence
* the total number of digital evidence reviewed during the investigation
* all keywords, phrases, and search terms used and results of these searches

A template for creating written formal reports has been provided as a reference in the Templates section of this book.

INCULPATORY[2] AND EXCULPATORY[3] EVIDENCE

While the objective of performing an investigation is to determine root cause or identify a culprit, all conclusions derived from the analysis of evidence must be factual and credible. However, as conclusions are being drawn, it may become clear that there is the existence of inculpatory (indication of guilt) and exculpatory (indication of innocence) evidence that need to be considered further before any factual and credible conclusions can be established.

The totality of all digital evidence, whether inculpatory or exculpatory, is an important consideration when establishing credible facts. The suppression of exculpatory evidence, which indicates innocence, is a violation of the US Supreme Court Rules and can result in implausible facts. Organizations must ensure that they have clearly defined in their governance documentation, such as standard operation procedures, how to handle exculpatory evidence when it is encountered.

Brady v. Maryland 373 U.S. 83 (1963) is a milestone in court rulings that has set precedence for establishing the requirement to disclose all exculpatory evidence.

The State of Maryland prosecuted Brady for murder to which he claimed a companion has committed the actual crime. The prosecution willfully withheld from the defendants a written statement by the companion where a confession was made to committing the murder.

Under the Brady Rule, named after this matter, the Supreme Court ruled that suppression of evidence that is favorable to defendant is a violation of due process and established that evidence of information that proves innocence must be disclosed.

SUMMARY

When communicating the findings of an investigation, it is important that reports are created to focus specifically on the credible facts that have been established during the investigation. Regardless of whether findings from digital evidence demonstrate guilt or innocence, as long as reports are an accurate representation of the event(s), they are still considered relevant and credible.

TAXONOMY

1 *Elevator speech* is a short, clear, and brief message used to share information, quickly and simply.

2 *Inculpatory evidence* demonstrates a subject's[4] involvement in an event that establishes guilt.

3 *Exculpatory evidence* exonerates a subject's involvement in an event that establishes innocence.

4 *Subject* is an active element that operates on information or the system state.

Ensure Legal Review

14

This chapter discusses the 10th and final step for implementing a digital forensic readiness program as the need to ensure legal resources review the investigation and provide advice on whether additional actions are needed. From this legal advice, the organization can establish the strength of the current digital evidence and can suggest if additional actions, such as collection and processing of additional evidence, must be taken.

INTRODUCTION

At any time during the forensic investigation workflow, as discussed in chapter "Investigative Process Models," it may be necessary to obtain legal advice regarding the current state of the case. This advice will provide the investigation team with a level of assurance that either (1) there is credible digital evidence to support legal proceedings, or (2) that collected digital evidence does not support factual conclusions about the event(s) or incident(s).

Where the legal team determines that the strength of existing digital evidence is adequate, the investigation has been identified as meeting the criteria for progressing into formal legal proceedings. However, where the legal team determines that strength of existing digital evidence is deficient, the investigative team must work with the legal advisors to identify what additional actions and activities are required to progress into formal legal proceedings.

TECHNOLOGY COUNSELING

When required, legal team will be called upon to provide educated and accurate advisement on the current state of an investigation. When this happens, not only do they need to know about laws involving evidence admissibility, but they also need to be knowledgeable in applicable information technology (IT), cyber or Internet, and computing laws. This requires that legal advisors are adequately trained and experienced so that they are readily equipped to provide appropriate counsel in response to digital evidence being presented as part of an investigation report, as discussed in chapter "Maintain Evidence-Based Reporting."

As an example, an IT attorney is an individual who is educated and knowledgeable in legal matters as they relate to technology. In addition to having a law degree, these attorneys should be trained and knowledgeable in several areas of technology to provide organization support in terms of:

- drafting, negotiating, interpreting, and maintaining (where needed) technology-related documentation (ie, agreements, contracts, reports)
- ensuring digital evidence is gathered, stored, and handled in compliance with applicable privacy policies, regulations, and laws
- providing high-quality, specialized, and practical advice for how to proceed with investigative matters

LAWS AND REGULATIONS

In many geographic regions, there are laws and regulations that dictate how technology can be used, such as information privacy, anti-spamming, and data exporting. Designed to connect technology with risk, these laws and regulations can be generally grouped into one of the following categories.

IT LAW

Whether you know it or not, when you conduct any form of business transaction on the Internet there are IT laws affecting you. These IT laws provide a framework intended to govern the collection, storage, and dissemination of their electronic (digital) information. Not only do these laws ensure regulatory compliance, they are also designed to reduce the risk of potential disputes by having agreements in place to anticipate and address these concerns.

When disputes arise, IT attorneys can be much more effective at explaining technical concepts to a judge or jury and will likely have industry contacts to consult with. Examples of IT laws include the following:

- Payment Card Industry Data Security Standard (PCI-DSS)
- Sarbanes–Oxley Act (SOX)
- Federal Information Security Management Act—National Institute of Standards and Technology (NIST) Special Publication (SP) 800-53 Rev3
- Health Insurance Portability and Accountability Act of 1996—NIST SP 800-66

The online reference to the above can be found in the "Resources" section at the end of this chapter.

In 2014, the US Securities and Exchange Commission (SEC) laid charges against the chief executive officer (CEO) and chief financial officer (CFO) of a Florida-based computer equipment company for misrepresenting external auditors and shareholders the state of its internal controls over financial reporting.

As required through SOX, a management report describing the internal controls over financial reporting is required and must be included in the annual report. This management report must be signed by both the CEO and CFO as a means of confirming they have disclosed all significant deficiencies and certify the information in the management report is accurate.

Through an administrative proceeding, it was discovered that the CEO and CFO withheld information about deficiencies, the circumvention of inventory controls, and improper handling of accounts receivable and inventory recognition.

Corporate executives have an obligation to take the Sarbanes–Oxley disclosure and certification requirements very seriously.

Scott W. Friestad, Associate Director in the SEC's Enforcement Division

CYBER OR INTERNET LAW

International jurisdictions have implemented laws and regulations that are designed to help settle disputes and guide the development of laws relating to the use of the Internet. Cyber law or Internet law is constantly being developed by courts around the world to align legal disputes involving the Internet into preexisting legal frameworks.

The Internet is one of the most complex legal landscapes because of how it continues to advance and becomes more readily available to users around the world. As a result, there are increasing opportunities for cybercriminals to use the Internet as either a fruit of crime[1] or tool of crime.[2] Examples of cyber or Internet laws include the following:

- United States (US) Electronic Communications Privacy Act of 1986
- European Union (EU) ePrivacy Act of 2002
- Philippines (PH) Cybercrime Prevention Act of 2012

The online reference to the above can be found in the "Resources" section at the end of this chapter.

In 2006, law enforcement conducted a series of raids throughout central Sweden where they seized several servers and computer equipment involved in operating the file-sharing site known as The Pirate Bay (TPB).

In 2009, four individuals involved with operating TPB were put on trial for allowing its users to download copyrighted materials through their services and software offering. The defense argued that the activities of these four individuals are legal under Swedish copyright laws because TPB does not host copyrighted content; it simply acts as a search engine to direct its users to locations where they can download music and films.

As part of the ruling, it was ordered that TPB's site be shut down.

COMPUTER LAW

In the early days of computer crimes, discussed further in chapter "Understanding Digital Forensics," charges were laid under traditional legal proceeding which did not necessarily apply to the presence of computer-based evidence. As concerns of systems and data protection intensified, computer laws were developed to relate issues involving the design and use of computing technologies with multiple legal areas.

With international jurisdictions creating legislation to address computer crime, cooperation improved between law enforcement agencies to mitigate the continued risk to system and data protection. Examples of computer laws include the following:

- United Kingdom (UK) Computer Misuse Act of 1990
- Australian (AU) Cybercrime Act of 2001
- United States (US) Patriot Act of 2001

The online reference to the above can be found in the "Resources" section at the end of this chapter.

Between 1999 and 2000, at least 40 large US companies—such as Online Information Bureau, eBay, and Speakeasy—experienced similar attacks where perpetrators hacked into their networks and then attempted to extort money. From a digital forensic investigation, it was determined that Internet traffic for all of these attacks originated from a single Internet protocol address in Russia. Through further investigation, the Federal Bureau of Investigation (FBI) identified Alexey Ivanov as the perpetrator of these activities.

In 2000, the FBI constructed a false company called Invita Security to which they used as a front for inviting Ivanov to interview for a job. Accompanied by his companion Vasiliy Gorshkov, the pair was interviewed by Invita where it was explained that they were looking for hackers that could break into the network of potential customers in an effort to persuade those companies to hire Invita.

Ivanov and Gorshkov were charged with several crimes, including computer fraud, conspiracy, hacking, and extortion. A move was made to dismiss the indictment, claiming that the court lacked jurisdiction arguing that because they were physically in Russia when the offenses were committed, they cannot be charged with violations under the US law. The US court denied the motion on the basis that the intended and actual effects of their actions occurred within the United States and that because the statutes under which charges were laid already extend extraterritorially; the US Patriot Act increased the scope of the Computer Fraud and Abuse Act to expressly cover systems outside of the United States.

Both Ivanov and Gorshkov pled guilty to the charges and were sentenced to a US prison.

OBTAINING LEGAL ADVICE

With legal resources trained and educated in appropriate technology laws, organizations will be better equipped to determine if the findings of an investigation are credible enough to be upheld in a court of law or if additional actions are required. Throughout the investigation, legal advice could be required to facilitate decision-making related to the following issues.

CONSTRAINTS

Laws and regulations exist that impose controls over the proper and effective use of digital evidence during an investigation. Generally, the three areas where legal advice can be provided include the following:

- Security controls resulting from laws and/or regulations that set a precedent to restrict the necessary identification and disclosure of information protected as privileged or confidential.

- Practices governing the identification and disclosure of information within a reasonable time frame when formal legal proceedings have been filed.
- Rules of evidence on the admissibility of information for legal proceedings

DISPUTES

Depending on the nature of business performed, organizations can face commercial disputes over contractual commitment and obligations. When these disputes involve external entities such as business partners, competitors, shareholders, suppliers, or customers, consultation with the legal team is required to advise and guide the organization towards resolution.

EMPLOYEES

The purpose of conducting a forensic investigation is not to find fault or blame in the actions of an employee. However, where an investigation reveals credible facts about the involvement of an employee, based on the nature of the employee's actions a decision must be made on the most appropriate course of action to deal with the employee. Through consultation with the legal team, organizations can ensure that when it comes time to taking action and dealing with the employee, they do not go beyond the boundaries of their authority or violate any legal rights that could result in unwanted liabilities.

LIABILITIES

At any point during the investigation an action, circumstance, or event might be identified which could reasonably be expected to result in some form of legal action against the organization, such as a breach of customer information. When this occurs, the investigation team should involve legal resources to determine how to properly manage the situation and the best course of action to take; such as engaging public and corporate affairs to formally manage information sharing or contacting law enforcement due to the involvement of criminal actions.

PROSECUTION

As digital evidence is being analyzed, investigators work to correlate and corroborate different sources of digital evidence that might lead to credible findings where prosecution or punishment, both internal and external, are possible. In these circumstances, involving the legal team could improve the likelihood for the organization to get restitution for any losses they experienced or to ensure that claims (ie, insurance) are proper substantiated.

COMMUNICATION

One possible outcome of a successful cyber attack could be the unintentional or malicious exfiltration of sensitive or confidential information (ie, personally identifiable information[3]). In conjunction with other teams within the organizations (ie, privacy, public, and corporate affairs), legal can assist in assessing the severity of the information disclosure, the impact it has to partners, customers, and/or investors, and establish if (when required) the notification of the data exposure must be distributed.

Involving Law Enforcement

Depending on the severity and impact to the organization, a decision could be made to contact appropriate law enforcement agencies to further assist with the investigation. While a decision to involve law enforcement could help to identify whether organized crime is involved, or to engage law enforcement personnel in other jurisdictions, it is important that organizations understand that they could be required to surrender control of the investigation.

SUMMARY

At any point during an investigation, it may be necessary to obtain legal advice regarding the current state of the case. Making these decisions requires that attorneys who will be involved throughout in a forensic investigation are trained and educated in applicable laws and regulations. Having obtained this training and education will ensure that accurate and timely legal counsel is provided to determine if sufficient credible facts exist or if additional evidence is required to make an informed decision about the investigative findings.

RESOURCES

Computer Misuse Act of 1990. http://www.legislation.gov.uk/ukpga/1990/18/pdfs/ukpga_19900018_en.pdf. Parliament of the United Kingdom.

Cybercrime Act of 2001. https://www.comlaw.gov.au/Details/C2004A00937. Australian Government.

Cybercrime Prevention Act of 2012 (Republic Act No. 10175). http://www.gov.ph/2012/09/12/republic-act-no-10175. Congress of the Philippines.

Electronic Communications Privacy Act of 1986. http://www.loc.gov/law/opportunities/PDFs/ElectronicCommunicationsPrivacyAct-PL199-508.pdf. US Congress.

ePrivacy Act of 2002. http://eur-lex.europa.eu/LexUriServ/LexUriServ.do?uri=OJ:L:2009:337:0011:0036:en:PDF. European Parliament.

PCI-DSS: Requirements and Security Assessment Procedures v3.1. https://www.pcisecuritystandards.org/documents/PCI_DSS_v3-1.pdf. PCI Security Standards Council, 2015.

SOX Act of 2002. https://www.sec.gov/about/laws/soa2002.pdf. US Securities and Exchange Commissions, 2002.

FISMA SP800-53 R4. http://csrc.nist.gov/drivers/documents/FISMA-final.pdf. NIST, 2013.

HIPAA SP800-66. http://csrc.nist.gov/publications/nistpubs/800-66-Rev1/SP-800-66-Revision1.pdf. NIST, 2008.

Patriot Act of 2001. http://www.gpo.gov/fdsys/pkg/PLAW-107publ56/pdf/PLAW-107publ56.pdf. US Congress.

TAXONOMY

1 *Fruit of crime* applies to material objects that are acquired during a crime.
2 *Tool of crime* applies to material objects used to perpetrate criminal activities.
3 *Personally identifiable information* is any data that can be used to identify and distinguish one person from another.

Accomplishing Forensic Readiness

15

Digital forensic readiness is an organization's capability to proactively maximize their use of digital evidence while minimizing investigative costs. The 10 steps toward achieving digital forensic readiness, as proposed throughout this book, involve approaching the subject area from the business content that details the need for administrative, technical, and physical components.

INTRODUCTION

For the most part, digital forensic investigations are still being performed in reaction to an incident where organizations must work quickly to gather and process digital evidence. Ultimately, the availability of relevant and meaningful digital evidence is a critical requirement to effectively manage business risk.

When conducting investigations in a reactive mode, there is increased risk that the evidence necessary to support the investigation may or may not exist; resulting in difficulties in establishing credible facts about what occurred. Where organizations have identified opportunities to proactively gather digital evidence in anticipation of an incident, they will be better equipped to validate the impact, support litigation matters, and demonstrate regulatory compliance.

Digital forensic readiness is the ability of an organization to proactively maximize their prospective use of electronically stored information.[1] By following a systematic and proactive approach to gathering and preserving potential digital evidence, the added value of a digital forensic readiness program will be realized through reduced investigative cost and gains in operational efficiencies.

MAINTAIN A BUSINESS-CENTRIC FOCUS

One of the most significant barriers to implementing digital forensic readiness is that organizations do not effectively communicate their business risks to those who work with their IT systems. Essentially, making progress towards a successful implementation means following an approach established from a risk-based methodology.

As discussed in chapter "Understanding Digital Forensics," cybercrime continues to evolve as technology increasingly becomes more deeply entrenched in our business and personal lives. In response to this natural evolution, the traditional "wall-and-fortress" approach continues to focus on the technology aspect where each specific threat is addressed as it emerges. A successful digital forensic readiness implementation requires organizations to ensure that their approach is adequately balanced to (1) understand the business reasons (who should be involved under what circumstances) for executing this program to properly and (2) sufficiently support its technical elements (how do go about performing forensics).

DO NOT REINVENT THE WHEEL

Even if not formally acknowledged, many organizations already perform some information security activities, such as proactively gathering and preserving digital information, relative to a digital forensic readiness program. The systematic and proactive approach achieved from digital forensics readiness is complimentary to many business operations and functions within an organization, such as:

- enhancing the overall effectiveness of managing business risk
- demonstrating the organization's due diligence in meeting legal and/or regulatory requirements
- determining the need for preserving digital evidence in support of business functions, such as incident response and business continuity
- improving identification and detection of security events to mitigate potential impact

Integrating the elements of digital forensics readiness should not have to be a process that is started from the ground up. Included throughout this book is a collection of industry best practices, references, methodologies, and techniques that can be used to achieve digital forensics readiness. The investment in time, effort, and resources to accomplish digital forensics readiness must be focused on what is required for its successful implementation, and not on re-creating materials that are readily available for use.

UNDERSTAND THE COSTS AND BENEFITS

Implementing a digital forensic readiness program requires organization to follow the systematic methodology as outlined throughout this book. Decisions to skip, substitute, or not invest the required amount of time, effort, and resources into the digital forensic readiness methodology will most certainly result in a failed, incomplete, or misaligned digital forensic readiness program.

For these reasons, it is extremely important that organizations take their time to fully understand how digital forensic readiness creates value in mitigating their business risks and what bearing it will have on their budgetary needs. As found throughout this book, the assessment of costs versus benefits is not to be limited to just one aspect of digital forensic readiness and should be a recurring process to ensure that the goals of the program are achieved at a reasonable cost.

SUMMARY

Similar to how organizations understand the importance and need for having proper disaster recovery and business continuity plans in place, it is equally important that there is an understanding of the need to have proper digital forensic readiness planning. The continuing trend to take a reactive approach to dealing with incidents is both disruptive and riskier to business operations in terms of digital evidence being altered, lost, or incorrectly handled.

Digital forensic readiness is an organization's capability to proactively maximize their use of digital evidence while minimizing investigative costs. Organizations that understand the importance of establishing proactive controls to maintain the forensic viability and admissibility of digital evidence have a better chance of ultimately surviving and prospering in the continuously evolving threat landscape.

As stated previously, the intention of this book is to provide readers with a business perspective of the digital forensic discipline. This book was written from a nontechnical, business perspective and is intended as an implementation guide for preparing your organization to enhance its digital forensic readiness by becoming more proactive with investigations and moving away from the traditional reactive approach to incident. The methodology discussed throughout this book is also an effective way for organizations to demonstrate their due diligence and good corporate governance over their assets and business operation.

TAXONOMY

1 *Electronically stored information*, for the purpose of the Federal Rules of Civil Procedure, is information created, manipulated, communicated, stored, and best utilized in digital form, requiring the use of computer hardware and software.

Appendices

INTRODUCTION

Digital forensic readiness requires organizations to strategically integrate its business functions and processes with its administrative, technical, and physical information security controls to maximize the use of digital evidence while minimizing investigative costs. By doing so, organizations are in a much better position to proactively detect and deter security events before they escalate into a more serious incident or reactive investigation.

While not directly related to how the digital forensic discipline is practiced, the supplemental business functions and processes discussed in this section of the book are essential to successfully implementing a digital forensic readiness. Using these business functions and processes as part of a digital forensic readiness program allows organizations to make much more appropriate and informed decisions about their business risks specific to the digital forensic investigations.

In this section, the business function and processes discussed throughout the book have been included as supplemental content to digital forensic readiness. While these materials can be used as part of the digital forensic readiness program, they have been included as stand-alone materials and can be referenced as independent functions and processes that can also be used in other contexts.

Appendix A: Investigative Process Models

INTRODUCTION

Ever since forensic science became an established component of digital forensics, there have been a number of suggested and proposed process models. As early as 1984, law enforcement agencies began developing processes and procedures around computer forensic investigations. This led to the determination that as a result of bypassing, switching, or not following correct processes, the investigation could result in incomplete or missed evidence.

To examine the specified process models, the components of each model have been standardized to describe the activities performed as part of the investigative workflow. The term "process model" is used to represent all activities included in the proposed investigative workflow. The term "phase" is used to represent the high-level components within the process model and the term "task" is used to represent the specific activity within the higher-level components.

There has been several digital forensic process models developed over the years to address either a specific need, such as law enforcement, or with a generalized scope with the intention that the process model could be adopted universally. While there might be some process models absent from the table below, Table A.1 contains a chronological list of process models including a unique identifier, the author(s), the publication year, and the number of phases included in the model.

PROCESS MODELS

It is important to note that inclusion of the process models in Table A.1 does not suggest that these are better or recommended over other models that were not included. The following sections further dissect all process models, identified in Table A.1, in greater detail to extract the phases and better understand how the process model is structured.

[M01] COMPUTER FORENSIC INVESTIGATIVE PROCESS (1995)

Consisting of four phases, this model was proposed as a means of assuring evidence handling during a computer forensic investigation followed scientifically reliable and legally acceptable methodologies (Figure A.1).

- *Acquisition* requires that digital evidence is collected using acceptable methodologies only after receiving proper approval from authorities
- *Identification* interprets digital evidence and converts it into a readable human format
- *Evaluation* determines the digital evidence's relevancy to the investigation
- *Admission* documents relevant digital evidence for legal proceedings

Table A.1 Digital Forensic Process Models

ID	Name	Author(s)	Year	Phases
M01	Computer Forensic Investigative Process	M. Pollitt	1995	4
M02	Computer Forensic Process Model	US Department of Justice	2001	4
M03	Digital Forensic Research Workshop Investigative Model (Generic Investigation Process)	Palmer	2001	6
M04	Scientific Crime Scene Investigation Model	Lee et al.	2001	4
M05	Abstract Model of the Digital Forensic Procedures	Reith et al.	2002	9
M06	Integrated Digital Investigation Process	Carrier and Spafford	2003	5
M07	End to End Digital Investigation	Stephenson	2003	9
M08	Enhanced Integrated Digital Investigation Process	Baryamureeba and Tushabe	2004	5
M09	Extended Model of Cybercrime Investigation	Ciardhuain	2004	13
M10	A Hierarchical, Objective-Based Framework for the Digital Investigations Process	Beebe and Clark	2004	6
M11	Event Based Digital Forensic Investigation Framework	Carrier and Spafford	2004	5
M12	Four Step Forensic Process	Kent et al.	2006	4
M13	Framework for a Digital Forensic Investigation	Kohn et al.	2006	3
M14	Computer Forensic Field Triage Process Model	K. Roger et al.	2006	12
M15	FORZA—Digital Forensics Investigation Framework	Ieong	2006	6
M16	Common Process Model for Incident and Computer Forensics	Freiling and Schwittay	2007	3
M17	Dual Data Analysis Process	Bem and Huebner	2007	4
M18	Digital Forensic Model Based on Malaysian Investigation Process	Perumal S.	2009	7
M19	Generic Framework for Network Forensics	Pilli et al.	2010	9
M20	Generic Computer Forensic Investigation Model	Yusoff	2011	5
M21	Systematic Digital Forensic Investigation Model	Agarwal et al.	2011	11

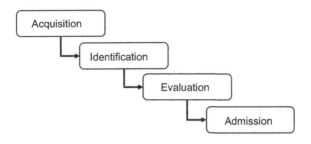

FIGURE A.1

Computer forensic investigative process 1995.

[M02] COMPUTER FORENSIC PROCESS MODEL (2001)

Consisting of four phases, this model was proposed in the *Electronic Crime Scene Investigation: A guide to first responders* publication and focused on the basic components of a digital forensic investigation (Figure A.2).

- *Collection* involves searching for digital evidence sources and ensuring its integrity is maintained while gathering
- *Examination* evaluates digital evidence to reveal data and reduce volumes
- *Analysis* examines the context and content of digital evidence to determine relevancy
- *Reporting* includes presenting digital evidence through investigation documentation

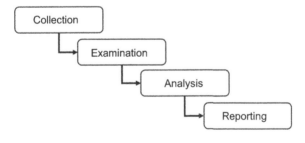

FIGURE A.2

Computer forensic process model 2001.

[M03] DIGITAL FORENSIC RESEARCH WORKSHOP (DFRWS) INVESTIGATIVE MODEL (2001)

Consisting of six phases, this model was proposed as a general purpose process for digital forensic investigations (Figure A.3).

- *Identification* involves detection of an incident or event
- *Preservation* establishes proper evidence gathering and chain of custody
- *Collection* gathers relevant data using approved techniques
- *Examination* evaluates digital evidence to reveal data and reduce volumes

- *Analysis* examines the context and content of digital evidence to determine relevancy
- *Presentation* includes preparing reporting documentation

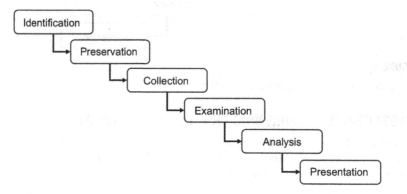

FIGURE A.3

Digital forensic research workshop investigative model 2001.

[M04] SCIENTIFIC CRIME SCENE INVESTIGATION MODEL (2001)

Consisting of four phases, this model was proposed to strictly address scientific crime scene investigations, and not the entire investigative process (Figure A.4).

- *Recognition* identifies items or patterns seen as potential evidence
- *Identification* classifies evidence and compares it to known standards
- *Individualization* determines evidence uniqueness in relation to the investigation
- *Reconstruction* provides investigative details based on collective findings

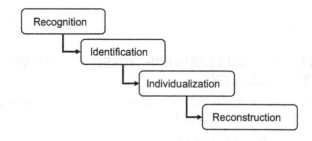

FIGURE A.4

Scientific crime scene investigation model 2001.

[M05] ABSTRACT MODEL OF THE DIGITAL FORENSIC PROCEDURES (2002)

Consisting of nine phases, this model enhances the DFRWS model by including three additional phases; *preparation*, *approach strategy*, and *returning evidence* (Figure A.5).

- *Identification* involves detection of an incident or event
- *Preparation* includes activities to ensure equipment and personnel are prepared
- *Approach strategy* focuses on maintaining evidence integrity during acquisition
- *Preservation* establishes proper evidence gathering and chain of custody
- *Collection* gathers relevant data using approved techniques
- *Examination* evaluates digital evidence to reveal data and reduce volumes
- *Analysis* examines the context and content of digital evidence to determine relevancy
- *Presentation* includes preparing reporting documentation
- *Returning evidence* includes, where feasible, returning evidence to its original owner

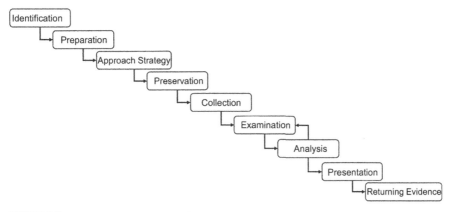

FIGURE A.5

Abstract model of the digital forensic procedures 2002.

[M06] INTEGRATED DIGITAL INVESTIGATION PROCESS (2003)

Consisting of five phases, this model was proposed with the intention of merging the various investigative processes into a single, integrated model. This model introduced the idea of a digital crime scene created as a result of technology where digital evidence exists (Figure A.6).

- *Readiness* includes activities to ensure equipment and personnel are prepared
- *Deployment* enables the detection and validation of an event or incidents
- *Physical crime scene* involves the collection and analysis of physical evidence
- *Digital crime scene* involves the collection and analysis of digital evidence
- *Review* assesses the entire investigative process to identify opportunities for improvement

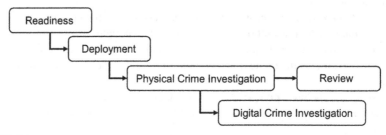

FIGURE A.6

Integrated digital investigation process 2003.

[M07] END TO END DIGITAL INVESTIGATION (2003)

Consisting of six phases, this model was proposed a general purpose process for digital forensic investigations (Figure A.7).

- *Collecting evidence* involves acquiring and preserving digital evidence
- *Analysis of individual events* examines digital evidence to assess relevancy
- *Preliminary correlation* assesses events to determine when events occurred and what technology is involved
- *Event normalizing* deduplicates and standardizes events into a unified structure
- *Event deconfliction* consolidates multiple common events into a single event
- *Second level correlation* assesses the normalized events to further refine when events occurred and what technology is involved
- *Timeline analysis* builds the chronological sequence of events
- *Chain of evidence construction* establishes the correlation based on sequential events
- *Corroboration* validates evidence and events against other evidence and events

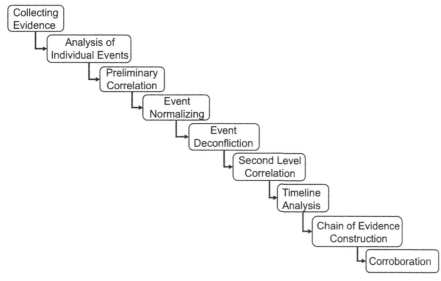

FIGURE A.7

End to end digital investigation 2003.

[M08] EXTENDED MODEL OF CYBERCRIME INVESTIGATION (2004)

Consisting of 13 phases, this model was proposed as a generalized approach to the investigative process to assist the development of new tools and techniques (Figure A.8).

- *Awareness* allows the relationship with investigation events to be identified
- *Authorization* involves obtaining approval to proceed with the investigation
- *Planning* scopes out how and where evidence will be collected
- *Notification* informs stakeholders of the investigation
- *Search for and identify evidence* locates and identifies evidence sources
- *Collection of evidence* involves acquiring and preserving evidence
- *Transport of evidence* includes moving evidence into a secure location
- *Storage of evidence* includes placing evidence in a protective custody
- *Examination of evidence* evaluates evidence to reveal data and reduce volumes
- *Hypothesis* constructs a theory based on the events that occurred
- *Presentation of hypothesis* allows for a decision on the appropriate course of action
- *Proof/defense of hypothesis* involves demonstrating the validity of the theory
- *Dissemination of information* distributes information to stakeholders.

FIGURE A.8

Extended model of cybercrime investigation 2004.

[M09] ENHANCED INTEGRATED DIGITAL INVESTIGATION PROCESS (2004)

Consisting of five phases, this model is based on the integrated digital investigation process. This model introduces the *traceback* phase which allows investigators to backtrack to the actual technology used in the crime (Figure A.9).

- *Readiness* includes activities to ensure equipment and personnel are prepared
- *Deployment* enables the detection and validation of an event or incidents
- *Traceback* tracks back to the source crime scene including technology and location
- *Dynamite* involves conducting investigations at the primary crime scene with intentions of identifying the potential offender(s)
- *Review* assesses the entire investigative process to identify opportunities for improvement

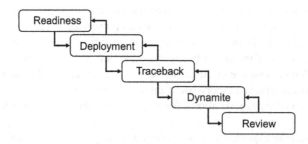

FIGURE A.9

Enhanced integrated digital investigation process 2004.

[M10] A HIERARCHICAL, OBJECTIVE-BASED FRAMEWORK FOR THE DIGITAL INVESTIGATIONS PROCESS (2004)

Consisting of six phases, this model was proposed as a means of addressing all phases and activities described in preceding process models (Figure A.10).

- *Preparation* includes activities to ensure equipment and personnel are prepared
- *Incident response* detects and acknowledges an event or incident
- *Data collection* gathers digital evidence in support of the response and investigation
- *Data analysis* validates the detected event or incident using collected digital evidence
- *Presentation* of findings communicates findings to stakeholders
- *Incident closure* includes acting upon decisions and assessing the investigative process

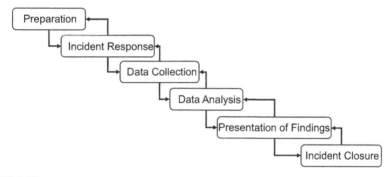

FIGURE A.10

A hierarchical, objective-based framework for the digital investigations process 2004.

[M11] EVENT-BASED DIGITAL FORENSIC INVESTIGATION FRAMEWORK (2004)

Consisting of five phases, this model proposes following the processes for investigating physical crime scenes while considering the digital crime scene investigation as a subset (Figure A.11).

- *Readiness* includes activities to ensure equipment and personnel are prepared
- Deployment involves the detection of an incident and notification of investigators
- *Physical crime scene investigation phases* is a series of steps and activities to search for identify and collect physical evidence to reconstruct physical events
- *Digital crime scene investigation phases* is a subset of the physical crime scene investigation that involves a series of steps and activities to examine digital evidence
- *Presentation* includes preparing reporting documentation

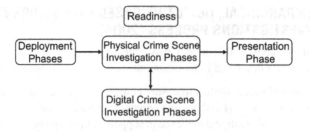

FIGURE A.11

Event-based digital forensic investigation framework 2004.

[M12] FOUR-STEP FORENSIC PROCESS (2006)

Consisting of four phases, this model proposes that forensic investigations can be conducted by even nontechnical persons through increased flexibility of steps and activities performed (Figure A.12).

- *Collection* involves searching for digital evidence sources and ensuring its integrity is maintained while gathering
- *Examination* evaluates digital evidence to reveal data and reduce volumes
- *Analysis* examines the context and content of digital evidence to determine relevancy
- *Reporting* includes presenting digital evidence through investigation documentation

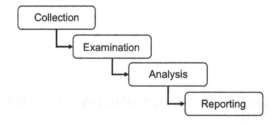

FIGURE A.12

Four-step forensic process 2006.

[M13] FRAMEWORK FOR A DIGITAL FORENSIC INVESTIGATION (2006)

Consisting of three phases, this model proposes merging existing process models into a broader and more adaptable model (Figure A.13).

- *Preparation* includes activities to ensure equipment and personnel are prepared
- *Investigation* involves all steps and activities performed to preserve, analyze, and store evidence
- *Presentation* includes preparing reporting documentation

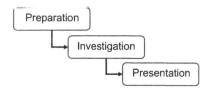

FIGURE A.13

Framework for a digital forensic investigation 2006.

[M14] COMPUTER FORENSIC FIELD TRIAGE PROCESS MODEL (2006)

Consisting of six primary phases and six subtasks, this model proposes performing investigative tasks on-site, in a short time frame, without seizing technology or acquiring forensic images (Figure A.14).

- *Planning* includes activities to ensure equipment and personnel are prepared
- *Triage* identifies evidence and determines its relevance to the investigation
- *User usage profile* focuses on analyzing user activity and behavior
- *Chronology timeline* establishes a date/time sequence of digital evidence events
- *Internet* examines artifacts from Internet-related service activities
- *Case-specific* places focus on digital evidence relating directly to the investigation

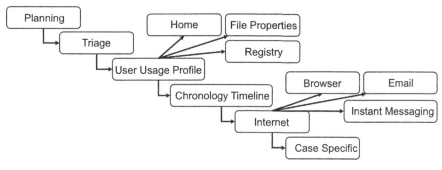

FIGURE A.14

Computer forensic field triage process model 2006.

[M15] FORZA—DIGITAL FORENSICS INVESTIGATION FRAMEWORK (2006)

Consisting of six layers, this model proposes linking the eight practitioner roles and their associated procedures together throughout the investigative process (Figure A.15).

- *Contextual investigation layer* understands the background details of the event
- *Contextual layer* recognizes the involvement of business elements to the event
- *Legal advisory layer* determines the legal aspects of the event

	Why (Motivation)	What (data)	How (Function)	Where (Network)	Who (People)	When (Time)
Case leader (contextual investigation layer)	Investigation Objective	Event Nature	Requested Initial Investigation	Investigation Geography	Initial Participants	Investigation Timeline
System owner (if any) (contextual layer)	Business Objective	Business and Event Nature	Business and System Process Model	Business Geography	Organization and Participants Relationship	Business and Incident Timeline
Legal advisor (legal advisory layer)	Legal Objective	Legal Background and Preliminary Issues	Legal Procedures for Further Investigation	Legal Geography	Legal Entities and Participants	Legal Timeframe
Security/system architect/ auditor (conceptual security layer)	System/Security Control Objective	System Information and Security Control Model	Security Mechanisms	Security Domain and Network Infrastructure	Users and Security Entity Model	Security Timing and Sequencing
Digital forensics specialists (technical preparation layer)	Forensic Investigation Strategy Objectives	Forensic Data Model	Forensic Strategy Design	Forensics Data Geography	Forensics Entity Model	Hypothetical Forensics Event Timeline
Forensics investigators/system administrator/operator (data acquisition layer)	Forensic Acquisition Objectives	On-site Forensics Data Observation	Forensics Acquisition / Seizure Procedures	Site Network Forensics Data Acquisition	Participants Interviewing and Hearing	Forensics Acquisition Timeline
Forensics investigators/ forensics analysts (data analysis layer)	Forensic Examination Objectives	Event Data Reconstruction	Forensics Analysis Procedures	Network Address Extraction and Analysis	Entity and Evidence Relationship Analysis	Event Timeline Reconstruction
Legal prosecutor (legal presentation layer)	Legal Presentation Objectives	Legal Presentation Attributes	Legal Presentation Procedures	Legal Jurisdiction Location	Entities in Litigation Procedures	Timeline of the Entire Event for Presentation

FIGURE A.15

FORZA—digital forensics investigation framework 2006.

- *Conceptual security layer* explores the design of systems and relevant security controls
- *Technical presentation layer* determines the strategies and steps required of the digital forensics investigation
- *Data acquisition layer* involves executing the identified digital forensic strategies and steps to collect evidence
- *Data analysis layer* involves executing the identified digital forensic strategies and steps to examine evidence
- *Legal presentation layer* involves discussing legal component as a result of the digital forensic investigation

[M16] COMMON PROCESS MODEL FOR INCIDENT AND COMPUTER FORENSICS (2007)

Consisting of three phases, this model proposes the combination of incident response and digital forensics into an overall process for investigations (Figure A.16).

- *Preanalysis* contains all steps and activities that are initially completed
- *Analysis* includes all steps and activities performed during evidence examination
- *Postanalysis* documents all steps and activities completed throughout the investigation

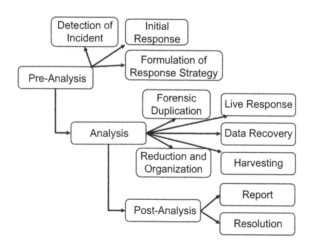

FIGURE A.16

Common process model for incident and computer forensics 2007.

[M17] DUAL DATA ANALYSIS PROCESS (2007)

Consisting of four phases, this model proposes following parallel investigative streams; first stream with a less experienced "computer technician" and the second stream with a "professional investigator" (Figure A.17).

- *Access* locates and identifies evidence sources
- *Acquire* involves collecting evidence and ensuring its integrity is maintained
- *Analysis* examining the context and content of digital evidence to determine relevancy
- *Report* includes presenting digital evidence through investigation documentation

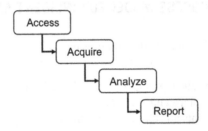

FIGURE A.17

Dual data analysis process 2007.

[M18] DIGITAL FORENSIC MODEL BASED ON MALAYSIAN INVESTIGATION PROCESS (2009)

Consisting of seven phases, this model is based on the Malaysian investigation process focusing on data acquisition and fundamental phases in conducting analysis (Figure A.18).

- *Planning* involves obtaining authorization and associated documentation to conduct an investigation
- *Identification* identifies evidence to be seized while considering data volatility
- *Reconnaissance* involves the gathering and storage of digital evidence
- *Analysis* examines the context and content of digital evidence to determine relevancy
- *Result* includes preparing reporting documentation
- *Proof and defense* proves hypothesis with supporting evidence
- *Archive storage* maintains evidence for future reference

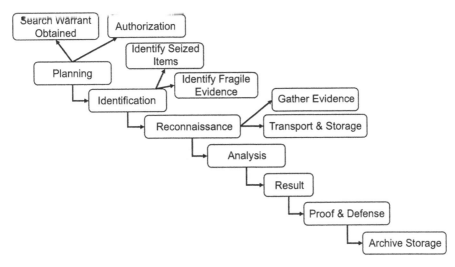

FIGURE A.18

Digital forensic model based on Malaysian investigation process 2009.

[M19] GENERIC FRAMEWORK FOR NETWORK FORENSICS (2010)

Consisting of nine phases, this model was proposed to specifically formalize a methodology for network-based digital investigations (Figure A.19).

- *Preparation and authorization* includes activities to ensure equipment and personnel are prepared
- *Detection of incident/crime* indicates that an incident or event has occurred
- *Incident response* consists of acknowledging and responding to an event or incident
- *Collection of network traces* acquires data from sensors that collect network traffic data
- *Preservation and protection* involves the gathering and storage of digital evidence
- *Examination* evaluates digital evidence to reveal data and reduce volumes
- *Analysis* examines the context and content of digital evidence to determine relevancy
- *Investigation and attribution* reconstructs the event or incident using collected evidence
- *Presentation* includes preparing reporting documentation

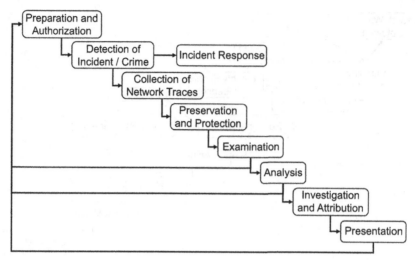

FIGURE A.19

Generic framework for network forensics 2010.

[M20] GENERIC COMPUTER FORENSIC INVESTIGATION MODEL (2011)

Consisting of five phases, this model was proposed as a means of generalizing the investigative process (Figure A.20).

- *Preprocess* includes obtaining approval to proceed and activities to ensure equipment and personnel are prepared
- *Acquisition and preservation* involves the gathering and storage of digital evidence
- *Analysis* examines the context and content of digital evidence to determine relevancy
- *Presentation* includes preparing reporting documentation
- *Postprocess* includes returning evidence, where feasible, and identifying opportunities for improvement

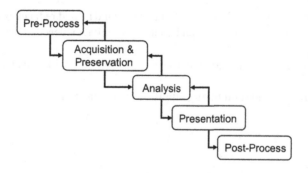

FIGURE A.20

Generic computer forensic investigation model 2011.

[M21] SYSTEMATIC DIGITAL FORENSIC INVESTIGATION MODEL (2011)

Consisting of 11 phases, this model was proposed with the goal of aiding in establishing appropriate policies and procedures in a systematic manner (Figure A.21).

- *Preparation* involves becoming familiar with the investigations and activities to ensure equipment and personnel are prepared
- *Securing the scene* secures the crime scene from unauthorized access and mitigates evidence tampering
- *Survey and recognition* involves assessing the crime scene for potential evidence sources and establishes an appropriate search plan
- *Documenting the scene* ensures crime scene documentation is recorded including photographs, sketches, etc.
- *Communication shielding* terminates all data exchange capabilities from technology
- *Evidence collection* focuses on gathering of relevant data using approved techniques
- *Preservation* establishes proper evidence gathering and chain of custody
- *Examination* evaluates evidence to reveal data and reduce volumes
- *Analysis* examines the context and content of digital evidence to determine relevancy
- *Presentation* includes preparing reporting documentation
- *Result* identifies opportunities for improvement

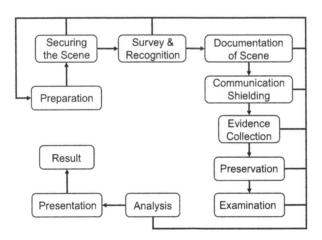

FIGURE A.21

Systematic digital forensic investigation model 2011.

COMPARATIVE ANALYSIS

Understanding the phases and tasks compromised within each process model, it is evident that each author had different influences into the development of their respective workflows. Most notable is the use of nonparallel characteristics—such as the interchangeable use of procedures, processes, phases, functions, tasks, and steps—to describe their proposed investigative workflow.

Even though all identified process models have their own unique characteristics, each author developed it with the intention of upholding the application of forensic science to the investigative process. Having standardized on terminology being used to objectively compare these process models, we can easily recognize the phases of each model and extract them for further comparison.

Note: [M15] FORZA—Digital forensics investigation framework 2006 was not included in this comparison below because of the significant differences in the process model's characteristics; where it uses layers and roles instead of phases for describing the investigative workflow.

As illustrated in Figure A.22, we can easily see which phases are more often applied across multiple process models and how frequently they occur. Of special note, highlighted in the graphic below are seven phases that have the highest frequency of reoccurrence: *preparation, identification, collection, preservation, examination, analysis, and presentation*. Without getting caught up on the subtle differences in naming convention, it is quite apparent that there is an opportunity to consolidate all phases identified throughout each process model into these common phases.

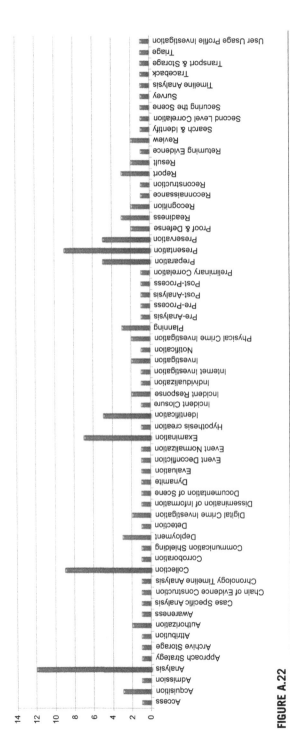

FIGURE A.22

Process model phase frequency.

SUMMARY

Since the formalization of digital forensic science, several process models have been developed and proposed to meet a specific investigative need. Regardless of the difference in structure of each process model, the underlying fundamental workflow and concepts of mandatory investigative activities remain consistent as represented within the higher-level phases.

Appendix B: Education and Professional Certifications

INTRODUCTION

Digital forensics requires that individuals have strong information technology knowledge as well as formalized training of digital forensic principles, methodologies, techniques, and tools. These are essential and fundamental to maintaining the integrity, authenticity, credibility, and admissibility of digital evidence.

DIGITAL FORENSIC CERTIFICATIONS

Following completion of formalized education, there are several recognized industry associations that offer professional certifications in digital forensics. It is important to keep in mind that these professional certifications do not provide the in-depth level of education and training on digital forensics and information technology that formalized education provides. Professional certifications, or professional designations, provide "assurance" that an individual has gained the necessary knowledge to properly perform digital forensics.

While there might be some certifications absent, the following is a list of digital forensic professional certifications grouped/ordered by association and then ordered by the certification name. It is important to note that inclusion of these digital forensic professional certifications does not suggest that these are better or recommended over other digital forensic professional certifications that were not included.

INDUSTRY NEUTRAL CERTIFICATIONS

7SAFE
Certified MAC Forensics Specialist
Certified Forensic Investigation Practitioner
Certified Forensic Investigation Specialist
American Society for Industrial Security (ASIS) International
Professional Certified Investigator (PCI)
International Council of Electronic Commerce Consultants (EC-Council)
Computer Hacking Forensic Investigator (CHFI)
High Tech Crime Network (HTCN)
Certified Computer Crime Investigator (CCCI) Basic
Certified Computer Crime Investigator (CCCI) Advanced
Certified Computer Forensic Technician (CCFT) Basic Certified
Computer Forensic Technician (CCFT) Advanced

Information Assurance Certification Review Board (IACRB)
Certified Computer Forensics Examiner (CCFE)
International Association of Computer Investigative Specialists (IACIS)
Certified Forensic Computer Examiner (CFCE)
Certified Advanced Windows Forensic Examiner (CAWFE)
International Information Systems Forensic Association (IISFA)
Certified Information Forensics Investigator (CIFI)
International Information Systems Security Certification Consortium (ISC)^2
Certified Cyber Forensics Professional
International Society of Forensic Computer Examiners (ISFCE)
Certified Computer Examiner (CCE)
SysAdmin, Audit, Networking, and Security (SANS)
Global Information Assurance Certification (GIAC)—Certified Forensic Analyst (GCFA)
Global Information Assurance Certification (GIAC)—Certified Forensic Examiner (GCFE)

VENDOR-SPECIFIC CERTIFICATIONS

AccessData
AccessData Certified Examiner (ACE)
AccessData Mobile Phone Examiner (AME)
BlackBag Technologies
Certified BlackLight Examiner (CBE)
Macintosh and iOS Certified Forensic Examiner (MiCFE)
Guidance Software
Encase Certified Examiner (EnCE)

DIGITAL FORENSIC EDUCATION

The number of higher education or postsecondary institutions offering formalized education programs focusing specifically on digital forensic continues to grow. While each education programs might be slightly different in the curriculum offered, they all cover the fundamental principles, methodologies, and techniques of digital forensics as required for individuals who are directly involved in the investigative workflow.

While there might be some higher/postsecondary institutions absent, the following is a list of digital forensic education programs grouped/ordered by geographical location and then ordered by the educational institute's name. It is important to note that inclusion of these digital forensic education programs does not suggest that these are better or recommended over other digital forensic education programs that were not included.

AUSTRALIA

- Charles Sturt University
    Graduate Certificate Information Systems Security (Digital Forensics)
    Master Information Systems Security (Digital Forensics)
- Edith Cowan University
    Master of Digital Forensics
- Macquarie University
    Postgraduate Diploma in Computer Forensics (PGDipCFR)
    Postgraduate Certificate in Computer Forensics (PCertCFR)
- Melbourne University
    Graduate Certificate in Digital Forensics
    Master of e-Forensics and Enterprise Security
- Murdoch University
    Cyber Forensics and Information Security (BSc)
- University of South Australia (UniSA)
    Graduate Certificate in Science (Forensic Computing)
    Master of Science (Information Assurance)
- Swinburne University of Technology, Melbourne
    Graduate Certificate in eForensics

CANADA

- Algonquin College
    Computer Systems Technology—Security, Advanced Diploma (CST8606
    Introduction to Digital Forensics)
- BCIT Centre for Forensics and Security Technology Studies
    Bachelor of Technology (BTech)—Computer Crime Studies Option
    Forensic Investigation Advanced Specialty Certificate (ASC)—Computer
    Crime Studies Option
- Canadian Police College Technological Crime Learning Institute
    Advanced Internet Child Exploitation (AICE)
    Canadian Internet Child Exploitation (CICEC)
    Cell Phone Seizure and Analysis (CSAC)
    Computer Forensic Examiner (CMPFOR)
    Digital Technologies for Investigators (DTIC)
    Internet Evidence Analysis (IEAC)
    Live Analysis Workshop (LAW)
    Network Investigative Techniques (NITC)
    Using the Internet as an Intelligence Tool (INTINT)
    Advanced Computer Forensic Workshop (ACFW)
    Registry Analysis Workshop (RAW)
    Wireless Networks Workshop (WNETW)

- Ecole Polytechnique, University of Montreal's Engineering School
    Certificat en cyberenquête
- Fleming College
    Computer Security and Investigations program

ENGLAND

- University of Bedfordshire
    (MSc) Computer Security and Forensics
- Birmingham City University
    BSc (Hons) Forensic Computing
- University of Bradford
    MSc Forensic Computing
- Canterbury Christ Church University
    BSc (Hons) Forensic Computing
    MSc Cybercrime Forensics
- Coventry University
    Forensic Computing MSc
- Cranfield University (based at the Defense Academy of the UK)
    Forensic Computing MSc/PgDip/PgCert
- De Montfort University
    Forensic Computing BSc (Hons)
    Forensic Computing MSc/PG Dip/PG Cert
- University of Derby
    BSc (Hons) Computer Forensic Investigation
    MSc Computer Forensic Investigation
- University of Gloucestershire
    Forensic Computing Honors Degree (3 or 4 year sandwich)
- University of Greenwich
    BSc (Hons) Computer Security and Forensics
    Computer Forensics and Systems Security, MSc
- Kingston University
    Cyber Security and Computer Forensics BSc (Hons)
- University of Central Lancashire
    Forensic Computing BSc (Hons)
- Leeds Metropolitan University
    BSc (Hons) Computer Forensics
    BSc (Hons) Computer Forensics & Security
    MSc Digital Forensics & Security
- Liverpool John Moores University
    Computer Forensics BSc (Hons), BSc
- University of East London
    Information Security and Computer Forensics (ISCF)
    Block Mode MSc

- London Metropolitan University
  Computer Forensics and IT Security (BSc Hons—Single)
  Computer Networking and Computer Forensics (BSc Hons—single)
  Computer Forensics and IT Security (MSc)
- University of London—Royal Holloway
  Computer Forensics and IT Security (BSc Hons—Single)
- Manchester Metropolitan University
  BSc (Hons) Computer Forensics and Security
- Middlesex University
  BSc Honors Forensic Computing
- Northumbria University
  Digital and Computer Forensics BSc (Hons)
- The Open University
  M889 Computer Forensics and Investigations
- University of Portsmouth
  BSc (Hons) Forensic Computing
  MSc Forensic Information Technology
- Sheffield Hallam University
  BSc (Honors) Computer Security with Forensics
- Staffordshire University
  Digital Forensics BSc (Hons)
  Digital Forensics and Cybercrime Analysis MSc, Postgraduate Certificate
  (PgC), Postgraduate Diploma (PgD)
- University of Sunderland
  BSc (Hons) Computer Forensics
- Teesside University
  BSc (Hons) Computer and Digital Forensics
- University of the West of England
  BSc (Hons) Forensic Computing
- University of Westminster
  MSc Computer Forensics

GERMANY

- University of Erlangen, University of Munich, University of Applied Sciences
  Albstadt-Sigmaringen (joint program)
  Digitale Forensik (Master)/Masters in Digital Forensics

INDIA

- Gujarat Forensic Sciences University
  MS—Digital Forensics and Information Assurance
- University of Madras
  Cyber Forensics and Information Security MSc

- Institute of Forensic Science, Mumbai
    Post Graduate Diploma in Digital and Cyber Forensic and
    Related Law
- The National Law Institute University, Bhopal
    Master of Science in Cyber Law and Information
    Security (MSCLIS)

IRELAND

- Blanchardstown Institute of Technology
    Bachelor of Science in Computing in Information Security and Digital
    Forensics
    Bachelor of Science (Honors) in Computing in Information Security and
    Digital Forensics
    Master of Science in Computing (Information Security & Digital Forensics
    Stream)
- University College Dublin
    Forensic Computing and Cybercrime Investigation
    (FCCI) Programme
    MSc Digital Investigation and Forensic Computing
- Dublin City University
    MSc in Security and Forensic Computing
- Letterkenny Institute of Technology
    Bachelor of Science in Computing with Computer Security and Digital
    Forensics
    Bachelor of Science (Hons) in Computer Security and Digital Forensics
- Waterford Institute of Technology
    BSc (Hons) in Computer Forensics

ITALY

- University of Bologna
    Forensic Computer Science
- University of Milan
    Computer Forensics
- University of Piemonte Orientale
    Corso di Informatica Forense

MEXICO

- Instituto Politecnico Nacional
    Maestría en Ingeniería en Seguridad y Tecnologías de la Información
    (Master of Security and Information Technology)

NETHERLANDS

- Universiteit van Amsterdam (UvA)
    Computer Forensics (part of Master's in Artificial Intelligence
    and Master's in Forensic Science)
- Hogeschool Leiden
    Forensisch ICT

NEW ZEALAND

- AUT University
    Master of Forensic Information Technology

NORWAY

- Norwegian Police University College
    Digital forensics further education

SCOTLAND

- Abertay University (Dundee)
    BSc (Hons) Digital Forensics
- Edinburgh Napier University
    Computer Security & Forensics BEng/BEng (Hons)
- University of Glasgow
    Computer Forensics & E-Discovery
- Glasgow Caledonian University
    Digital Security, Forensics and Ethical Hacking
    BEng/BEng (Hons)

SOUTH AFRICA

- University of Cape Town (UCT)
    Postgraduate Diploma in Management in Information Systems
    (CG022)—INF4016W: Computer Forensics

SWEDEN

- Högskolan Dalarna
    Digitalbrott och eSäkerhet, 180 högskolepoäng
- Högskolan i Halmstad
    IT-forensik och informationssäkerhet, 120/180 hp

UNITED ARAB EMIRATES

- Zayed University
  Graduate Certificate in High Technology Crime Investigation
  Master of Science (MS) in Information Technology (Specialization in Cyber Security)

UNITED KINGDOM

- Bournemouth University
  Forensic Investigations BSc
  Forensic Computing and Security BSc

UNITED STATES OF AMERICA

- American InterContinental University
  Bachelor of Information Technology (BIT): Specialization in Digital Investigations
- American Public University System
  Undergraduate Certificate—Digital Forensics
  Graduate Certificate—Digital Forensics
- Anne Arundel Community College
  Cybercrime Degree Program, Cybercrime Certificate
- Bloomsburg University of Pennsylvania
  Digital Forensics (BS)
- Boston University
  Digital Forensics Graduate Certificate
- Bristol Community College
  Associate Degree in Science in Computer Information Systems (Computer Forensics)
- Bunker Hill Community College
  Digital and Computer Forensics and Investigations Option—Computer Information Technology Program—(Associate in Science Degrees)
- Butler County Community College
  Computer Information Systems—Computer Forensics and Security, AAS
- California State University, Fullerton
  Certificate in Computer Forensics I
- Carnegie Mellon University
  Master of Science in Information Security Technology and Management (MSISTM)—Cyber Forensics and Incident Response
- Catawba Valley Community College
  Cyber Crime Technology
- Central Piedmont Community College
  Digital Evidence Training

- Century College
    Computer Forensics—Associate in Applied Science Degree, Computer
    Forensics—Certificate
- Champlain College
    Bachelor of Science, Computer & Digital Forensics
    Bachelor of Science, Computer Forensics & Digital Investigations
    Degree (online)
    Computer Forensics & Digital Investigations Certificate (online)
    Master of Science in Digital Forensic Management
    Master of Science in Digital Forensic Science
- Chestnut Hill College
    Certificate in Computer Forensics and Electronic Discovery
- College of Lake County
    Computer Information Technology (CIT) program with various computer
    forensics courses
- College of Western Idaho
    Information Technology: Information Security and Forensics
- Colorado State University–Pueblo
    Bachelor of Science (BS) degree in Computer Information Systems
    (CIS)—CIS 462/562, Computer Forensics and Investigations
- Community College of Philadelphia
    Computer Forensics Courses
- Dakota State University
    MSIS Information Assurance (Forensics Classes)
- Defiance College
    Digital Forensic Science (Bachelor of Science degree)
- DelMar College
    Associate of Applied Science (AAS) degree—Information Systems
    Specialization—Digital Media Forensics Associate Emphasis (pdf)
- DeSales University
    Master of Arts in Criminal Justice Online with a concentration in
    Computer Forensics
- DeVry University
    Bachelor of Science, Computer Information Systems with a Specialized
    Track in Computer Forensics
- Dixie State University
    BS in Criminal Justice—Digital Forensics Emphasis (pdf file)
- Drexel University
    Minor in Computer Crime
    BS in Computing and Security Technology—Concentration: Computing
    Security—CT 212 Computer Forensics (Elective)
- Edmonds Community College
    Digital Forensics Certificate
    Information Security and Digital Forensics Associate of Technical Arts
    Degree (pdf)

- Florida State College
    Computer Forensics Technician (6947)
- Fountainhead College of Technology
    Network Security and Forensics
- George Mason University
    MS in Computer Forensics
- Herkimer County Community College
    Cybersecurity AS
- Highline Community College
    Data Recovery/Forensic Specialist (Certificate & AAS options)
- Illinois Institute of Technology
    Computer and Network Forensics, IT 538
- Indian Hills Community College
    Digital Forensics Associate of Applied Science Degree (AAS)
- International Academy of Design & Technology
    Bachelor of Science in Computer Forensics (BS)
- Iowa State University
    CprE 536: Computer and Network Forensics
- James Madison University
    Master's Degree in Computer Science concentration in Digital Forensics
- Johns Hopkins University
    MSc Security Informatics (650.457 Computer Forensics, 650.657 Advanced
    Topics in Computer Forensics)
- John Jay College of Criminal Justice
    Master of Science in Digital Forensics and Cybersecurity, Certificate in
    Applied Digital Forensic Science
- Kaplan University—Hagerstown Campus
    Bachelor of Science in Criminal Justice
    Master of Science in Criminal Justice
    Associate of Applied Science in Criminal Justice
    Computer Forensics Post Baccalaureate Certificate
- Kennesaw State University
    ISA 4350. Computer Forensics. 3-0-3.
- Lamar Institute of Technology
    ITDF 1300 Introduction to Digital Forensics 3:3:0
- Las Positas College
    Computer Networking Technology—Introduction to Computer Forensics
    and Computer Forensics II
- Lawrence Technological University
    Graduate Certificate in Information Assurance Management (MIS5213 High
    Tech Cyber Crime)
- Marshall University
    Computer and Information Technology Major—Computer Forensics Area of
    Emphasis

Graduate Certificate in Digital Forensics
Master of Science Degree Program—Emphasis on Digital Forensics
- Metropolitan State University
  Computer Forensics (BAS)
  Computer Forensics Minor
  Computer Forensics Certificate
- Middlesex Community College
  Certificate and Associate Degree Programs in Computer Forensics
- Missouri Southern State University
  Bachelor Science in CIS—Computer Forensics
- Northcentral University
  Business PhD Computer and Information Security Specialization
- Pittsburgh Technical Institute
  Network Security and Computer Forensics Concentration
- Purdue University Cyber Forensics Lab
  CIT 420/556 Computer Forensics
  CIT557 Advanced Research Topics in Computer Forensics
- Regis University
  Information Assurance Certificate (options available in Computer Forensics and Network Forensics)
- Rich Mountain Community College
  Computer Forensics Certificate
- Richland College
  Digital Forensics AAS Degree
  Digital Forensic Analyst Advanced Technical Certificate
  Digital Forensics Certificate Programs in Information Security/Information Assurance
- Rochester Institute of Technology (RIT)
  BS in Information Security and Forensics (ISF)
- St. Ambrose University
  BA in Computer Investigations and Criminal Justice
- St. Petersburg College
  Digital Forensics and Computer Investigations (AS Degree and Certificate)
- Sam Houston State University
  Digital Forensics (various classes)
- Solano Community College
  Certificate and Associate Science Degree in Criminal Justice: Computer Forensics
- Stanly Community College
  Cyber Crime Technology
- Stark State College
  Cyber Security and Computer Forensics Technology
- Stevenson University
  Master's Degree in Cyber Forensics

- The George Washington University
  Master of Science in the field of High Technology Crime Investigation (HTCI)
- Tompkins Cortland Community College
  Computer Forensics AAS Degree
- University of Alabama at Birmingham (UAB)
  Master of Science in Computer Forensics and Security Management (MSCFSM)
- University of Advancing Technology
  BS in Technology Forensics
- University of Central Florida
  Certificate Program
  Master of Science in Digital Forensics (MSDF)
- University of Nebraska Omaha (UNO)
  CSCI-4380 (Computer and Network Forensics)
- University of New Haven
  Digital Forensics focus area (various degrees)
- University of New Orleans
  Information Assurance Program
- University of Northwestern Ohio
  Computer Forensics Associate Degree (pdf)
- University of Rhode Island (USA)
  Digital Forensics Minor
  Digital Forensics Professional Certificate (online)
  Digital Forensics Graduate Certificate (online)
  Computer Science Master's degree with concentration in Digital Forensics
  PhD with a concentration in Digital Forensics
- University of Southern California
  Information Technology Program—Digital Forensics Specialization
  Computer and Digital Forensics Minor
- University of Texas at Arlington
  CRCJ 3320 Cybercrime (pdf)
- University of Texas at San Antonio
  MS IT and Infrastructure Assurance—6363 Computer Forensics class
- University of Washington in Seattle
  Certificate in Digital Forensics
- Utica College
  Online Cybersecurity and Information Assurance Bachelor's program (Cybercrime Investigations and Forensics Concentration Courses)
- Walsh College
  Digital Forensics Certificate
- Waynesburg University
  Bachelor of Science in Computer Security (Computer Forensics)
- West Virginia University
  Certificate in Computer Forensics

- Westchester Community College
    - Computer Security and Forensics Certificate
    - Computer Security and Forensics AAS
- Westwood College
    - Major in Computer Forensics
    - Major in Computer Forensics Online
- Wilmington University
    - Computer and Network Security Bachelor of Science (credits in Electronic Discovery and Computer Forensics)

WALES

- Cardiff University
    - Computer Science with Security and Forensics (BSc)
    - Computer Science with Security and Forensics with a year in industry (BSc)
- University of Glamorgan
    - BSc (Hons) Computer Forensics
    - MSc Computer Forensics
- Newport University
    - Forensic Computing—BSc (Hons)
    - Cybercrime Forensics MSc

Appendix C: Tool and Equipment Validation Program

INTRODUCTION

All digital forensic tools and equipment work differently, and may behave differently, when used on different evidence sources. Before using any tools or equipment to gather or process evidence, investigators have to be familiar with how those tools operate by practicing on a variety of evidence sources.

This testing must demonstrate that these tools and equipment follow the proven principles, methodologies, and techniques used throughout digital forensic science. This process of testing introduces a level of assurance that the tools and equipment being used by investigators are forensically sound, will not result in the evidence being inadmissible or discredited.

STANDARDS AND BASELINES

For data to be admissible as evidence in legal proceedings, testing and experimentation must be completed that generates repeatable[1] and reproducible[2] results; meaning that results must consistently produce the same results.

In 1993, the US Supreme Court decided in *Daubert v. Merrell Dow Pharmaceuticals, 509 U.S. 579* that Rule 702 of the Federal Rules of Evidence (1975) did not incorporate a "general acceptance" test as the basis for assessing whether scientific expert testimony is based on reasoning or methodology that is scientifically valid and can properly be applied to facts.

The Court stated that evidence based on innovative or unusual scientific knowledge may be admitted only after it has been established that the evidence is reliable and scientifically valid. Under this ruling, the *Daubert Standard* was established with the following criteria applied for determining the reliability of scientific techniques:

1. Has the theory or technique in question undergone empirical testing?
2. Has the theory or technique been subjected to peer review and publication?
3. Does the theory or technique have any known or potential error rate?
4. Do standards exist, and are they maintained, for the control of the theory or technique's operation?
5. Has the theory or technique received general acceptance in the relevant scientific community?

These criteria require that scientific theory or techniques must be subjected to hypotheses and experimentation—based on gathering, observing, and demonstrating repeatable and reproducible results—to prove or falsify the theory or techniques.

As a result of the Daubert Standard, all digital forensic tools and equipment must be validated and verified to meet specific evidentiary and scientific criteria in order for evidence to be admissible in legal proceedings. In the context of applying the

Daubert Standard to software testing, there is a clear distinction between the activities and steps performed as part of both validation[3] and verification.[4]

BUILDING A PROGRAM

The ability to design, implement, and maintain a defensible validation and verification program is an essential characteristic that a digital forensic professional should have. With this type of program in place, the digital forensic team will be able to provide a level of assurance of what the capabilities of their tools and equipment are as well as to identify what, if any, limitations exist so that compensating actions can be applied; such as acquiring other tools and equipment or creating additional procedures.

The methodology for performing tools and equipment testing consists of several distinct activities and steps that must be completed in a linear workflow. To formalize this workflow, a process model must be implemented to govern the completion of each activity and step in the sequence they must be executed. Illustrated in Figure C.1, the phases proposed in chapter "Investigative Process Models" for both the *high-level digital forensic process model* and *digital forensic readiness process model* are consistently applied to the activities and steps performed in tool and equipment testing. Consisting of four phases, the digital forensic tool testing process model focuses on the basic categories of tools and equipment testing.

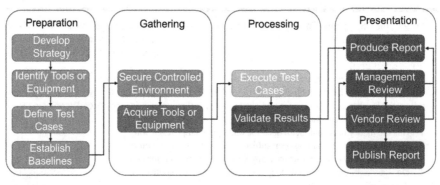

FIGURE C.1

Digital forensic tool testing process model.

PREPARATION

Similar to how a project charter establishes scope, schedule, and cost, the testing plan of digital forensic tool or equipment must follow an identical structure. The starting point of this strategy is to define and capture the objective and expectation of the testing specific to how the tool or equipment is expected to behave. Following the objective setting, further details of the testing plan must be documented using a formalized structure to include, at a minimum, the following sections:

- *Introduction*: A summary of the objectives and goals of the testing
- *Background*: Description of why the testing is being performed
- *Purpose/scope*: Specifications of technical and business functionality the testing is expected to generate
- *Approach*: Procedures, activities, and steps that will be followed throughout the testing
- *Deliverables*: Definition of test cases and the success criteria for testing documented functionality
- *Assumptions*: Identification of circumstances and outcomes that are taken for granted in the absence of concrete information
- *Constraints*: Administrative, technical, or physical activities or steps that directly or indirectly restrict the testing
- *Dependencies*: Administrative, technical, or physical activities or steps that must be completed prior to testing
- *Project team*: Visualization of the testing team structure and governing bodies

GATHERING

This phase of the testing program is either the longest and most time-consuming or the easiest and fastest. The determination for this depends on how well the plan's objectives, scope, and schedule were documented during the preparation phase that took place previously. In this phase, the tactical approaches outlined in the plan's strategy are completed to acquire the tool or equipment that will be subject to the testing. Prior to making any purchases, it is essential that both parties enter into contractual agreement with each other; such as a nondisclosure agreement (NDA) and statement of work (SOW).

- An NDA is a formal document that creates a mutual relationship between parties to protect nonpublic, confidential, or proprietary information and specifies the materials, knowledge, or information that will be shared but must remain restricted from disclosure to other entities.
- An SOW is a formal document that contains details often viewed as legally equivalent to a contract to capture and address details of the testing.

Both documents contain terms and conditions that are considered legally binding between the parties involved. These documents must be reviewed and approved by appropriate legal representatives before each party commits to them by signing. In the absence of providing wording for how the content within these documents should be structured, at a minimum the following sections should be included:

- *Introduction*: A statement referring to NDA as the governing agreement for terms and provisions incorporated in the SOW
- *Description/purpose*: Summarizes the objectives and goals of the testing and provides information pertaining to the tool or equipment being tested; including, but not limited to, technology name, version, release date, and creator

- *Location of work*: Describes where people will perform the work and the location of tools or equipment
- *Deliverables schedule*: A listing of the items that will be produced, the start and finish time, and the individuals responsible for providing results
- *Success criteria*: Baselines that will be used for measuring the success criteria against each test case including the criteria for measuring success or failure, scenario for how the test will be executed, tools or equipment subject to the test, and the business value for conducting the test case
- *Assumptions*: Identification of circumstances and outcomes that are taken for granted in the absence of concrete information
- *Key personnel*: Provides contact information for the individuals, from all parties, who will be involved in the testing
- *Payment schedule*: A breakdown of the fees, if any, that will be paid—up front, in phases, or upon completion—to cover expenses for individuals and tools or equipment involved in the testing
- *Miscellaneous*: Items that are not part of the terms or provisions but must be listed because they are relevant to the testing and should not overlooked

Following the creation of these formal documents, the tools or equipment that is subject to testing can be procured. In parallel, the team can secure and build the controlled environment where the test cases, as defined in the SOW, will be executed. This controlled environment must be built following previously defined baselines as well as the SOW deliverables. Once the controlled environment is created, and before it is used for the testing, the environment itself must be tested and validated to ensure that it matches the specifications of the baselines and test cases. By documenting the validity of the controlled environment, it can easily be reused in future testing because a level of assurance has been established.

PROCESSING

Software testing is one of many activities used as part of the systems development life cycle (SDLC) to determine if the output results meet the input requirements. This phase is where the documented test cases are executed and success criteria are measured to verify and validate the functionality and capabilities of the tool or equipment. Before starting the activities and steps involved in executing test cases, it is important to understand the differences between verification and validation.

Verification

In general terms, a verification process answers the question "did you build the right thing" by objectively assessing if the tool or equipment was built according to the requirement and specifications. Verification focuses on determining if the accompanied documentation consistently, accurately, and thoroughly describes the design and functionality of the tool or equipment being tested. Techniques used during the verification tools or equipment can be split into two distinct categories:

- *Dynamic analysis* involves executing test cases against the tool or equipment using a controlled data set to assess the tool's or equipment's documented functionality. This category applies a combination of black box[5] and white box[6] testing methodologies to support:
  - functional assessments of documented features to identify and determine actual capabilities
  - structural review of individual components to further assess specific functionalities
  - random evaluation to detect faults or unexpected output from documented features
- *Static analysis* involves performing a series of test cases using the tool or equipment following manual or automated techniques to assess the nonfunctional components. This category applies a series of programmatic testing methodologies to support:
  - consistency of internal coding properties such as syntax, typing, parameters matching between procedures, and translation of specifications
  - measurement of internal coding properties such as structure, logic, and probability for error

Validation

In general terms, a validation process confirms through objective examination and provisioning if "you built it right" to prove that requirements and specifications have been implemented correctly and completely. Validation activities rely on the application of an all-inclusive testing methodology that happens both during and after the SDLC. Techniques used during the validation of tools or equipment can be performed by:

- intentionally initiating faults into different components (eg, hardware, software, memory) to observe the response
- determining what the probability of reoccurrence is for a weakness identified in different components (eg, hardware, software, memory), and subsequently selecting countermeasures as a means of reducing or mitigating exposures

Completing test cases can be a lengthy and time-consuming process. Completing test cases should be thorough because it is fundamental in proving that the tool or equipment maintains and protects the admissibility and credibility of digital evidence; ultimately protecting the credibility of forensic professionals. While there are indirect factors such as caseload or other work responsibilities that impact the amount of time spent on testing, the following direct influences cannot be overlooked and must be maintained during testing.

- Regulating testing processes within secure and controlled lab environments
- Following proven, repeatable, reproducible, and consistent scientific methodologies

- Limiting the duplication of test results from others without subsequent validation
- Preventing use of generalized processes or technologies that suggest arbitrary use

As the test cases are being executed, it is important to keep a record of all actions taken and the outputted results. Using a formalized document to track test case execution provides a level of assurance that the tests have been completed as specified in the strategy plan and SOW. A formalized test case report template has been provided in the *Templates* section of this book, which includes a matrix for recording and tracking execution of each test case.

PRESENTATION

Once testing has concluded a summary of all activities, test results, conclusions, etc. must be prepared using a formalized test case report; as seen in the template provided in the *Templates* section of this book. While the initial draft of the final report might be performed by a single person, it should be reviewed for accuracy and authenticity by peers and management before being finalized. This review process will ensure that, as illustrated in the test case report template, the scope and results of the testing meet the specific business objectives so that when it comes time to obtain approvals to finalize, the testing process will not be challenged.

Having obtained final authorizations and approvals on the test case report, it can now be published and distributed to stakeholders who will be influenced as a result of the testing outcomes. Using the testing results, these stakeholders can now develop standard operating procedures (SOP) to use the tool or equipment for gathering and processing digital evidence.

SUMMARY

Maintaining the integrity of digital evidence throughout its lifetime is an essential requirement of every digital forensics investigation. Organizations must consistently demonstrate their due diligence by providing a level of assurance that the principles, methodologies, and techniques used during a digital forensic investigation are forensically sound.

TAXONOMY

1 *Repeatability* refers to obtaining the same results when using the same method on identical test items in the same laboratory by the same operator using the same equipment within short intervals of time.
2 *Reproducibility* refers to obtaining the same results being obtained when using the same method on identical test items in different laboratories with different operators utilizing different equipment.

3 *Validation* is the process of evaluating software to determine whether the products of a given development phase satisfy the condition imposed at the start of that phase.

4 *Verification* is the process of evaluating software during or at the end of the development process to determine whether it satisfies specified requirements.

5 *Black box* is a methodology that examines the functionality of an application, system, or object without knowledge of internal structures or workings.

6 *White box* is a methodology that examines the nonfunctional, internal structures or workings of an application, system, or object.

Appcndix D: Service Catalog

INTRODUCTION

Information security controls can be either administrative, technical, and physical in implementation. For every security control that exists within the organization, it must deliver value in support of business functions throughout the organization. Unfortunately, with the inner workings of information security typically not made common knowledge, the business value being delivered and the role it plays in achieving successful business outcomes is not usually recognized. This leaves the overall information security program vulnerable to not be seen as strategically relevant to the organization's business functions. To be successful in demonstrating value, information security needs to be strategically aligned to business functions and positioned as an empowering contributor to the organizations success.

As part of the overall service management life cycle, a service portfolio is the entire set of services[1] managed and offered by the provider. The service catalog, also referred to as an information technology (IT) service catalog, is a subset of the service portfolio that acts as a centralized register and entry point for details about the organization's available services. Through the creation of a service catalog, the value of information security can be demonstrated more effectively by aligning the delivered outcomes to business functions in a format that is easily understood.

BUSINESS BENEFITS

At a minimum, a service catalog provides organizations with a centralized way to see, find, invoke, and execute services regardless of where the service exists within the organizational. Organizations utilize a service catalog to eliminate the need for developing or supporting localized implementations that may be otherwise redundant.

Implementing a service catalog demonstrates a positive return on investment (ROI)[2] back to the organization in the form of direct financial savings or through maximizing effectiveness and efficiencies. From the strategic alignment of information security to business functions, organization can realize the ROI through the following positive effects of a service catalog:

- Provides a platform to better understanding and communicate business requirements
- Positions the overall information security program to be run like a business
- Reduces operational costs by identifying essential services and either eliminating or consolidating both redundant or unnecessary services
- Enhances operational efficiencies through the strategic structuring of resources and funding
- Helps market the awareness and visibility of the information security program to build stronger business relationships

Inevitably, if a service catalog does not already exist, somebody within the organization will understand the benefits of having it in place and what it provides in terms of visibility to the information security program. Once identified, creating a service catalog should not be viewed as a straight forward task. By taking a laid back approach to creating a service catalog, the organization may not realize the true ROI and will most likely be wasting resources, time, effort, and money. Guidance and oversight should be in place right from the start of creating the service catalog to make sure the organization properly utilizes its assets throughout the entire process.

DESIGN CONSIDERATIONS

The creation of services that deliver business value will differ from one organization to the next. Before starting the work of defining services, every organization should consider including the four consistent elements to support the service in delivering value:

- People—Human resources and organizations structure(s)
- Processes—Service management documentation
- Products—Technology and infrastructure
- Partners—Dependencies on external entities

Service catalogs include descriptive elements so that users within the organization can easily find and request the desired service. There are no predefined requirements indicating what specific elements must be included in a service catalog; leaving the decision to include or exclude elements entirely up to the subjectivity of the organization. The most common descriptive elements that organizations should use in any service catalog implementation include the following.

SERVICE NAME

The service name should clearly illustrate, in both business and IT terminology, how the service is commonly referred to throughout the organization. Structuring the name in such a way eliminates any confusion that may exist about the service.

SERVICE DESCRIPTION

The description should be written at a very high level, with no more than two to three lines, in a nontechnical, business language that is simple and easy to understand.

SERVICE FAMILY/GROUP/CATEGORY

Illustrated in Figure D.1, the hierarchical use of families, groups, and categories allows for individual services to be classified and aligned into the organization's common areas of functionality. The purpose of classifying individual services into the larger areas is to simplify resource management and cost analysis.

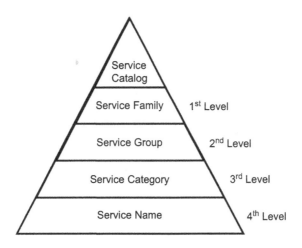

FIGURE D.1

Operational service catalog hierarchy.

Service Family
In the first level of the service catalog hierarchy, the purpose of a service family is to translate services into core business driven functions; such as *IT services* or *business services*.

Service Group
In the second level of the service catalog hierarchy, the purpose of a service group is to expand the individual business functions contained within the service family, such as *security services* or *compliance*.

Service Category
In the third level of the service catalog hierarchy, the purpose of a service category is to specify the individual service functions, such as *security operations* or *investigations*.

SERVICE OWNER
The owner is the person within the organization who provides funding for the service; commonly assigned to the executive management person where the service is offered.

KEY CONTACT(S)
The key contact(s) of the service are those within the organization who functions as the focal point for all communications between IT departments and the business communities. These individuals are responsible for understanding and supporting the level of service being delivered in line with established service level objectives.[3]

SERVICE COSTS

Documenting all services as quantifiable provides organizations with a better understand where funding is allocated across the total cost for operating the service. Having identified all of the contributors to the total service cost, organizations can then implement a chargeback model for performing cost allocations based on the services activities costs.

Cost Elements

The fixed (eg, software licensing, capital) and variable (eg, remuneration, outside data processing) costs associated with operating the service.

Cost Driver

The specific fixed (eg, software licenses) or variable (eg, billable work hours) unit(s) of service activity that results in a change in cost to the requestor.

Cost Per Unit

The measurement used to identify the cost of delivering one unit of service activity.

$$(\text{Total fixed costs} + \text{Total variable costs})/\text{Total units produced}$$

Cost Allocation

The distribution of service costs through the organization to areas that consume the service activities.

A service catalog template has been provided as a reference in the *Templates* section of this book.

SUMMARY

Every administrative, technical, and physical security control contributes to an organization's overall service offering. With Information Security service offerings mostly being considered as overhead to an organization, it is important that associated resources and technologies are identified so that cost elements can be allocated appropriately.

TAXONOMY

1 *Service* is a means of delivering value outcomes to customers without requiring the customer to directly own the specific costs and risks.
2 *Return on investment* is the benefit to the investor resulting from an investment of some resource.
3 *Service level objectives* are specific quantitative characteristics used to measure service delivery in terms of availability, throughput, frequency, response time, or quality.

Appendix E: Cost–Benefit Analysis

INTRODUCTION

Completing a cost–benefit analysis is a critical step for successful project management execution. It details the potential risks and gains of a proposed solution through a comparative assessment of the program's benefits against the costs associated with implementing it. If the results of this assessment identify that the benefits of the program outweigh the costs incurred to operate it, then the organization will be able to demonstrably agree to follow through with the implementation.

While completing a cost–benefit analysis requires those involved to maintain a quantitative perspective on the outcome, the activities involved in this process can be viewed as somewhat of an art form than a science. Although performing a cost–benefit analysis can be a challenging task to complete, organizations that are willing to invest resources, effort, and time into brainstorming, researching, and analyzing data can generate an assessment that is thorough, accurate, and relevant.

WHAT IS COST–BENEFIT ANALYSIS?

Cost–benefit analysis involves the estimation and evaluation of the benefits associated with alternative courses of action. This assessment involves identifying and comparing the net present value (NPV)[1] of benefits against the projected benefits and selecting the best solution according to specified criteria. The goal of the cost–benefit analysis is for organizations to make an educated decision on whether implementing a solution is worth investing their resources, time, and effort.

All activities and steps performed in the cost–benefit analysis can be grouped into four major phases, as illustrated in Figure E.1, including:

- *Problem statement* documents an in-depth analysis of the current situation
- *Quantitative assessment* assigns monetary value to all known cost and projected benefits
- *Comparative analysis* assesses if projected benefits outweigh known costs and identifies what alternate solutions exist
- *Stakeholder validation* determines the reliability of the decision generated from the analysis

PROBLEM STATEMENT

The first phase of the cost–benefit analysis workflow is extremely important in any decision-making process. Documenting the problem statement is the only way an organization can identify alternate and appropriate solutions. This task involves

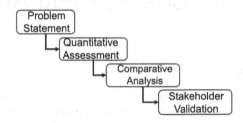

FIGURE E.1

Cost–benefit analysis workflow.

analyzing and having a good understanding of the issues, risks, and baseline scenarios for why the cost–benefit analysis is required.

Contained within the problem statement, organizations should include specifications of the objectives they are setting for this analysis and the plan they will follow to achieving these objectives. It is important that when defining these specifications, the outputs are precise and concrete as possible so the desired future state stands alone and successful achievements can be measured. By setting these specifications too broad, focus on the original problem statement will be lost and the cost–benefit analysis will lead to inappropriate assumptions and incorrect results.

This phase of the workflow involves generating all possible alternative solutions and, if required, narrowing down the list by removing options that are not feasible; including solutions that do not align with basic budgetary, legal, or organizational restrictions. As a means of narrowing down the list of alternatives, organizations should answer the following questions:

- How will performing this analysis meet our objectives?
- Will this analysis involve new capital expenditures?
- Will there be a need to replace existing tangible assets?
- Will there be a need to enhance existing tangible assets?
- What are the constraints of this analysis?
- What stakeholders will be affected by this analysis?
- How will stakeholders be affected by this analysis?

Ideally, organizations should limit the list of alternatives that they will assess further to a minimum of two and a maximum of five. By reducing the list of alternatives before performing quantitative analysis allows organizations to better manage resources, time, and costs.

QUANTITATIVE ASSESSMENT

With the problem statement documented and alternatives identified, the second phase of the cost–benefit analysis workflow is to quantify all relevant costs and benefits. Completing a detailed and accurate quantitative assessment of costs and benefits, for each alternative, should not be taken lightly. This phase requires that organizations invest its resources, time, and effort into identifying and thoroughly understanding all relevant effects of the solution, both positive and negative, and assign a monetary value to it.

IDENTIFYING COSTS

Dismissing, overlooking, or assuming any cost or benefit relating to an alternative can significantly impact the organization's ability to accurately determine which alternative should be recommended as the final solution. To mitigate this, organizations must ensure they are comparing "apples-to-apples" by categorizing costs as either tangible[2] or intangible[3] and categorizing benefits based on commonalities.

Tangible Costs

Using the service catalog as the source, a thorough and itemized list of quantifiable costs must be made. Where actual costs cannot be taken from the service catalog, as discussed in Appendix D: Service Catalog, factual research should be completed to determine estimates. Types of tangible costs included, but are not limited to, the following:

- Capital expenditures, or physical assets, such as property or equipment
- Software expenses such as licensing
- Shipping, handling, and transportation fees
- Remuneration overhead such as employee salary or training expenses
- Premises payments such as utilities, insurance, and taxes
- Outside data processing such as professional services and contingent workforce

Most likely, there could be a span of several years before an alternative has been fully implemented where ongoing costs will need to be carried forward and incurred until completion.

Intangible Costs

Associated costs can also include those that are not quantifiable. Even though these costs do not have any directly quantifiable value and cannot be bought or sold, based on factual evidence organizations are able to arrive at a hypothetical monetary value for these items. Types of intangible costs included, but are not limited to:

- change in customer dissatisfaction
- drop in employee morale
- decline in quality of product/service

PROJECTING BENEFITS

Benefits are positive effects that are realized from implementing a solution in response to issues or risks. They are achieved through any means of enhancement to the way an organization performs a business function.

Benefits can also be presented as being either tangible or intangible. Identifying benefits is done in the same way that cost contributors are documented in the previous step; although projecting them relies more on the educated estimates than direct facts. Generally, benefits can be grouped into one of the following categories:

* Cost savings or avoidance
* Error reduction
* Operational efficiencies
* Increased flexibility
* Improved planning and control

Tangible Benefits

Similar to costs, tangible benefits are the components of business functions or information technology that can be measured directly through known valuation. Referring back to the service catalog as the definitive source for measuring tangible value, these types of benefits can be realized as one of the following potentials:

* Increased operational efficiencies
* Decreased operational funding
* Reduced workforce overhead
* Reduced rate of budgetary increase
* Lower software costs and maintenance
* Lower physical equipment costs and maintenance
* Lower outside data processing fees
* Lower internal development costs

Intangible Benefits

Also similar to costs, intangible benefits do not have any directly quantifiable value and organizations will have to assign a hypothetical monetary value to these types of benefits. As indicated previously, making assumptions on the monetary values can be challenging to determine the value of intangible benefits as one of the following potentials:

* Improved asset utilization
* Improved resource control
* Improved business planning
* Improved organizational flexibility
* Quicker access to information
* Higher quality of information
* Enhanced organizational training, awareness, and learning
* Increased goodwill within workforce
* Increased job satisfaction
* Enhanced decision-making capabilities
* Quicker decision-making process
* Reduce error rates
* Improved organizational image
* Improved customer satisfaction
* Increased customer loyalty

Guessing as a means of estimating the quantitative value of intangible benefits has the potential to significantly impact the organization's ability to accurately determine which alternative should be recommended as the final solution. Instead, organizations can approach the valuation of intangible benefits in any of the following manners:

- Organizations may decide that it would be acceptable to leave intangible benefits entirely out of the cost–benefit analysis. This decision can be related to the degree of difficulty in assigning monetary values or that intangible benefits do not demonstrate significant improvements to business functions.
- Leave intangible benefits out of the cost–benefit analysis but their potential effects to business functions in an appendix. This way, they do not have direct influence to the assessment but can be presented as an additional consideration for selecting an alternative solution.
- Identify a stand-in measurement that can be used to include the intangible benefit valuation in the cost–benefit analysis. In this case, a stand-in measurement could be taken as the value of a similar benefit or cost that is more easily assigned a monetary value. Caution must be given when selecting a stand-in measurement to ensure that it provides an accurate and equivalent approximation of the actual benefit or cost.
- By conducting a survey of key stakeholders, the valuation of the intangible benefits can be determined. This survey is designed to ask stakeholders to assign a monetary value to the intangible benefit which can then be used for inclusion in the cost–benefit analysis.
- Use of a shadow price[4] to function as the unit of measurement to generate estimates on the monetary value of the intangible benefit. No rules or procedures exist for determining a shadow price; requiring that organizations employ an experienced matter expert to generate the valuation. The use of this option should only be explored when none of the preceding approaches will provide an accurate and equivalent approximation of the intangible benefit.

COMPARATIVE ASSESSMENT

With all identified costs and benefits assigned a common unit of measurement, each alternative solution documented in the problem statement can now be accurately assessed.

Discounting Future Value

Before starting the comparative assessment, organization should take special consideration where there are either costs or benefits that span across several years. In these cases, it is important that organizations take note that the immediate and present value (PV) of an alternative will diminish over its lifespan.

The process of discounting can be applied to reduce the monetary value of future costs and benefits back to a common time dimension that will be used for the assessment. Discounting allows organizations to realize the immediate value of an alternative, over the future value, and provides a way of reflecting the opportunity costs. In preparation, the organization should document the following series of parameters to be used in the baseline for discounting:

- The total evaluation period[5] for the alternative
- Which year is to be used as the base discount year[6]
- What discount rate will be used for the evaluation period
- Which price year[7] is appropriate to use for cost estimates
- Which price year is appropriate to use for the level of inflation[8]
- If analysis of relative prices is needed for specific cost items

Discounting is performed on the finance principle of time value of money (TVM)[9] assumed that value or monies or cash flow depends on the period in which they are received. In other terms, this principle suggests that monies received in the future are worth less than monies received today because monies received today can be invested and begin to accrue interest immediately. This allows organizations to determine the economic worth of the alternatives under assessment.

Present Value (PV) Assessment

The PV of costs or benefits is the representation of costs and benefits received in the future, discounted back into today's current value. The PV of each cost and benefit should be calculated for each alternative being considered as a solution. The resulting PV can then be used for selecting criteria to identify which alternative is most valuable to the organization. The PV of costs and benefits is calculated as:

$$\text{Present value (PV)} = V_t/(1+d)^t$$

where V is the cost or benefit represented in the evaluation period t, and d is represented as the discount rate. At a minimum, the PV should be calculated and used as the primary decision criteria for identifying which alternative provides the best return on investment.[10]

Tables E.1 and E.2 show examples of estimated costs and benefits for two alternatives identified through defining the problem statement. For the purposes of this example, an assumption is made that the discount rate has been set at 3%. The final

Table E.1 Cost–Benefit Analysis for Alternative #1

	V_0 ($)	V_1 ($)	V_2 ($)	V_3 ($)
Costs				
Capital	10,000	2000	1000	1000
Expenses	9000	1000	1000	1000
Workdays	2000	1000	1000	0
Benefits				
Process automation	0	6000	4000	3000
Increased productivity	0	12,000	9000	9000

NPV calculations for these two alternatives, presented in Tables E.3 and E.4, clearly demonstrate that the benefits of both alternative outweigh the present value of costs; with the second alternative being larger.

The values illustrated in Tables E.1 and E.2 are high-level representations of individual costs and benefits. An NPV template has been provided as a reference in the *Templates* section of this book.

Having arrived at the final NPV calculations for each alternative, organizations can elect to use additional criteria for determining which alternative is the best solution. These additional criteria should be used as a supplemental assessment and not as a replacement of the NPV.

Table E.2 Cost–Benefit Analysis for Alternative #2

	V_0 ($)	V_1 ($)	V_2 ($)	V_3 ($)
Costs				
Capital	8000	1000	1000	1000
Expenses	9000	2000	2000	1000
Workdays	2000	1000	0	0
Benefits				
Increased productivity	0	8000	5000	3000
Reduced workforce	0	6000	9000	9000

Table E.3 Present Values (PV) for Alternative #1

Costs	
PV =	$((10{,}000+9000+2000)/(1+0.03)^0+((2000+1000$ $+1000)/(1+0.03)^1+((1000+1000+1000)/(1+0.03)^2$ $+((1000+1000+0)/(1+0.03)^3)$ $\quad = 29{,}542$
Benefits	
PV =	$((6000+12{,}000)/(1+0.03)^1+((4000+9000)/(1+0.03)^2$ $+((3000+9000)/(1+0.03)^3)$ $\quad = 40{,}711$

Table E.4 Present Values (PV) for Alternative #2

Costs	
PV =	$((8000+9000+2000)/(1+0.03)^0+((1000+2000$ $+1000)/(1+0.03)^1+((1000+2000+0)/(1+0.03)^2$ $+((1000+1000+0)/(1+0.03)^3)$ $\quad = 27{,}542$
Benefits	
PV =	$((8000+6000)/(1+0.03)^1+((5000+9000)/(1+0.03)^2$ $+((3000+9000)/(1+0.03)^3)$ $\quad = 37{,}770$

Benefit–Cost Ratio

Organizations can use these criteria to select the alternative that provides the maximum ratio of benefits in comparison to costs and is calculated as the PV of identified benefits divided by the PV of known costs. This calculation is presented as follows:

$$\text{Benefit/Cost Ratio (BCR)} = B/C$$

where B is represented as the total value of identified benefits and C is represented as the total value of known costs.

The benefit–cost ratio (BCR) calculation for the alternatives noted in Tables E.1 and E.2 are presented below in Table E.5.

Table E.5 Benefit–Cost Ratios (BCR)

Alternative #1	BCR = 40,711/29,542	= 1.378072
Alternative #2	BCR = 37,770/27,542	= 1.37136

Net Present Value of Net Benefits

Organizations can use these criteria to select the alternative that provides the largest NPV of net benefits and is calculated as the present value of identified benefits minus the present value of known costs that have been discounted back to the present. This calculation is presented as follows:

$$\text{NPV of Net Benefits} = (Bt - Ct)(1 + r)^t$$

where B is represented as the value of identified benefits, C is represented as the value of known costs, r is the discount rate, and t is the number of evaluation periods that the benefits and costs occur in.

The calculation for the alternatives noted in Tables E.1 and E.2 are presented in Tables E.6 and E.7.

Table E.6 NPV of Net Benefits for Alternative #1

NPV =	$((0-21,000)/(1+0.03)^0) + ((18,000-4000)/(1+0.03)^1) + ((13,000-3000)/(1+0.03)^2) + ((12,000-2000)/(1+0.03)^3)$	= 11,170

NPV, net present value.

Table E.7 NPV of Net Benefits for Alternative #2

NPV =	$((0-19,000)/(1+0.03)^0) + ((14,000-4000)/(1+0.03)^1) + ((14,000-2000)/(1+0.03)^2) + ((12,000-2000)/(1+0.03)^3)$	= 10,229

NPV, net present value.

Internal Rate of Return[11]

Organizations can use these criteria to evaluate the rate of growth a project is expected to generate. Determining the rate of growth is most commonly performed through trial and error until a discount rate resulting in a zero value NPV is found.

To help in the identification of this rate, financial calculators should be used.

Payback Period[12]

Organizations can use these criteria to select the alternative that recovers its costs in the shortest amount of time. The major concern with using this calculation is that it does not take into consideration the time value of money (TVM); potentially leading to inconsistent results when cash flows occur in later time periods. However, the advantage of this calculation is that organizations can arrive at a value quickly because it requires no knowledge of the PV of costs or benefits.

The calculation for the alternatives noted in Tables E.1 and E.2 are presented in Tables E.8 and E.9.

An NPV is a recommended part of cost–benefit analysis that supports business decision-making. The overall ranking of all alternatives to ultimately identify a preferred solution demands that the NPV, and supplemental criteria (ie, BCR, Internal rate of return, etc.), is completed as thoroughly as possible. However, while the NPV ranking provides organizations visibility to which alternative will provide the best value, each alternative must be subjected to validation of the robustness under different scenarios.

Table E.8 Payback Period for Alternative #1

	Cash Flows (In and Out)	Cumulative Cash Flow
Year 0 (base)	21,000	
Year 1	14,000	14,000
Year 2	10,000	24,000
Year 3	10,000	34,000

Table E.9 Payback Period for Alternative #2

	Cash Flows (In and Out)	Cumulative Cash Flow
Year 0 (base)	19,000	
Year 1	10,000	10,000
Year 2	12,000	22,000
Year 3	10,000	32,000

Sensitivity Analysis

Obtaining a unique figure is not always the simplest of tasks when there are so many positive and negative influences on the final NPV calculation. Having finally arrived at an NPV for each alternative, these results must be subjected to further analysis with the purpose of determining how sensitive the NPV is to changes in key variables, such as resource overhead.

The sensitivity analysis performed here allows decision-makers within the organization to test the robustness of the results to collect additional information about how the solution will perform under different scenarios. Keep in mind that the analysis performed here does not reduce the project risk, instead better illustrates the actual feasibility of a successful solution implementation to the organization's decision-makers.

Creating a series of scenarios, most of which will be subjective to every organization, should focus on worst cases where assumptions and estimates are scrutinized. While there are many ways of performing sensitivity analysis, the most commonly used method is to validate the degree of error and reliability of costs, benefits, and other parameters (ie, discount rate) recorded in the final NPV and supplemental criteria.

By creating additional NPV and criteria documents that illustrate both high and low values, the degree to which these documents differ identifies how susceptible alternatives will be to changing values or parameters. By modifying a single value or parameter, the ranking of preferred alternatives could change leading to a different solution being identified as the most valuable.

Organizations must be cautious when performing sensitivity analysis where there are a large number of values and parameters included in the NPV and supplemental criteria. Where a value or parameter will be subjected to this sensitivity analysis, a degree of error must be completed using both high and low comparisons; resulting in $(X)^2$ for the number of outputted documents.

Gap Analysis

Graphic aids, such as a gap analysis, are excellent tools for helping stakeholders to clearly understand the differences between continuing to operate with the current risks and issues in comparison with implementing the highest ranked alternative. Working from the baseline and future scenarios created while documenting the problem statement, the costs and benefits of each identified solution(s) can be used to visually demonstrate the value of implementing an alternative as illustrated in Figure E.2.

To ensure that the gap analysis accurately captures the differences between current and future state scenarios, the baseline has to be properly defined and relevant. Having a baseline scenario does not mean that nothing will happen to the current situation over time. The reality is that business moves on as usual and in the current situation, the risks and issues identified in the problem statement could still be subjected to legal, regulatory, or corporate policies; regardless of the future state scenario.

On this account, the impact of changes in the current situation must be properly reflected in the baseline scenario. Organizations have to make a distinction between

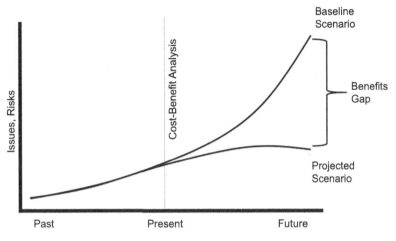

FIGURE E.2

Baseline-future scenario gap analysis.

what they consider as "do nothing" and "do minimum" when it comes to the level of interactions that will happen in the current situation that do not take into account the future state scenario.

Investing in an alternative that demonstrates the highest ranked value can be misleading; not because cost, benefits, or parameters have been inaccurately recorded, but because the NPV could be hiding the fact that even without implementing an alternative the current situation might not remain constant. Using an optimized baseline scenario that accounts for changes in the current situation, a more accurate comparison to the future state scenario can be performed.

STAKEHOLDER VALIDATION

There are usually several different stakeholders that will be affected when the selected alternative is implemented. Each group of stakeholders should be identified and an assessment of whether they will gain (ie, operational efficiencies) or lose (ie, private costs) as a result of the implemented solution is done. Communication to stakeholders on their involvement should contain detailed information so that it is clearly understood who will be the beneficiaries, who will be the losers, and by what amount. Whether positive and negative, different types of impact that should be communicated to stakeholders as part of the overall communication plan include:

- Determining the ability to remain profitable when a reduction in workforce from enhanced operational efficiencies influences economic opportunities
- Identifying change, whether an increase or decrease, in operational (eg, processes), regulatory (eg, taxes), and individual (eg, consumer) costs as a result of changes in the way core business functions are performed

In addition to impact assessment, the final recommendations from the cost–benefit analysis should be formally documented and presented in the form of a business case. This business case should contain sufficient details about the cost–benefit analysis so that stakeholders have enough details to support their decision-making on whether the organization should proceed with implementing the final recommendation. A formalized business case template has been provided in the *Templates* section of this book.

SUMMARY

By completing a cost–benefit analysis, organization can gain a better understanding of the benefits and potential risks of implementing a solution. While performing this analysis can be challenging at times, it is important that resources, effort, and time are invested to generate results that are thorough, accurate, and relevant.

TAXONOMY

1 *Net present value (NPV)* is the sum of the present values of incoming and outgoing cash flows, also described as costs and benefits, over a period of time.
2 *Tangible* costs are quantifiable costs related to an identifiable source or asset (eg, software licensing).
3 *Intangible* costs are unquantifiable costs related to an identifiable source (eg, employee productivity).
4 *Shadow price* is the gain from an increase, or loss from a decrease, of relaxing the constraint, or, equivocally, the change in the total cost of strengthening the constraint.
5 *Evaluation period* is the time period in which effectiveness of cash flows is measured against subjective or objective standards.
6 *Base discount year* is the time period used to first start measuring the effectiveness of cash flows.
7 *Price year* is any subsequent time period following the base year used to continue measuring the effectiveness of cash flows.
8 *Level of inflation* is the sustained increase in the level of costs measured as an annual percentage.
9 *Time value of money (TVM)* is the principle that the value of money at the present time is worth more than the same amount in the future due to potential earning capacity.
10 *Return on investment* is the benefit to the investor resulting from an investment of some resource.
11 *Internal rate of return* is the discount rate, commonly used in budgeting, that makes the net present value of all cash flows in a specific project equal to zero.
12 *Payback period* is the time required to regain costs of an investment or to reach the break-even point.

Appendix F: Building Taxonomy

INTRODUCTION

Taxonomy is the name given to describe a controlled grouping of terms and language used to find and provide consistency within a specific subject field. It is a living document that might never be considered finished because it is constantly evolving alongside of changes to the organization's business operations and functions. A good taxonomy should be flexible enough to adapt to any changes so it does not have to be re-created.

Through taxonomy, organization can provide their stakeholders (ie, employees, investors, etc.) with a set of terms and language that are:

- common and support the aggregation of common information across the organization
- comprehensive and thoroughly identify components of the subject field
- stable and help the comparative analysis of the subject field over time

DEVELOPMENT METHODOLOGY

Creating taxonomy is a demanding task that requires the coordination of resources, tools, and processes to optimally implement it. In the following sections, the process of creating taxonomy is performed in three stages as illustrated in Figure F.1.

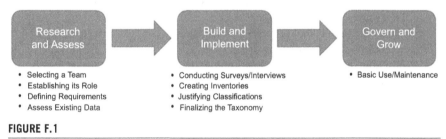

FIGURE F.1

Taxonomy development methodology.

STAGE 1: RESEARCH AND ASSESS

In this stage of the methodology, a team of key individuals is assembled to manage the entire development process. Once established, the team focuses on gathering information throughout the organization specific to the relevance of the taxonomy, the role it will have, and where there is existing information to be consumed.

Selecting a Team

The job of creating taxonomy cannot be achieved successfully by a single individual. Rather, it requires a systematic approach where key stakeholders with a specific or specialized knowledge of the subject field are involved. While the inclusion of team members can be based on the subject field the taxonomy is being developed; at a minimum, resources from the following teams should be included.

- *Information technology (IT)* support staff has a good understanding of the current technology environments. These resources can provide the team with insight into planned technology changes, help to discover opportunities for other technology, or identify limitation that should be addressed.
- *Legal* staff knows of current legal and litigation matters facing the organization and how they will impact the subject field.
- *Compliance* staff can advise the team of current or potential regulatory impacts that must be considered for the subject field.
- *Records management* staff has a good understanding of end user computing practices and can advise on how to maintain good business practice by avoiding compliance gaps within the subject field.

Establish Its Role Within the Organization

The incentive for an organization to create taxonomy can be either tactical, provide guidance during daily operations, or strategic, contribute to improvement of operational efficiencies. Generally, taxonomy can be seen as both a tool and opportunity to establish a foundation for all activities relating to a specific subject field.

- *Tool*: The taxonomy can be used as an incentive to address organizational objectives, such as:
  - improving efficiencies by making employees more effective at performing their duties
  - protecting intellectual property by identifying assets and documenting where/how they interact
  - providing a foundation for determining the subject field's relevant components
- *Opportunity*: The taxonomy can be used to assign responsibility and accountability for a subject field, such as:
  - developing a high expectation about roles and responsibilities
  - creating a self-reinforcing sense of morale and assurance

Define Business Requirements and Value Proposition

At this stage of the development process the team should meet with different business lines, if the organization is large enough to have more than one business line, to determine what, if any, challenges exist that require the creation of taxonomy. In preparation for these meetings, a survey should be used to initiate conversation in the subsequent meetings about subject fields that could benefit from taxonomy.

First and foremost, the team must clearly articulate the strategy for how the taxonomy will function throughout the organization and the issues (ie, legal, IT, compliance) it will address. In doing so, the survey can be designed to deal with these aspect through the use of terms and language that are simple, direct, and translatable throughout the organization. As the survey is being built, each question included should be structured in this way so that the surveyed individual(s) are not led into a specific response. As an example, the question "What is the most challenging task facing your business line?" allows the reader to objectively identify any subject field they consider needs attention.

Approximately 1–2 weeks following the distribution of the survey, all responses should be collected. These responses should be thoroughly reviewed to get an appreciation of the subject fields that have elevated urgency for the creation of taxonomy. From here, a prioritized list of subject fields can be drafted and used to prepare questions as part of the interviews with the surveyed individuals and various business lines.

Interviews are intended to serve two purposes: the first being a tool for gathering information to further develop the business requirements for the taxonomy; and the second being an opportunity to educate on what value the taxonomy will bring to the organization. During these interviews, it is important that the interviewee is permitted to do most of the talking so that as much information as possible can be captured.

Having completed all interview sessions, the team should now combine all results and prepare a list, sorted by interviewee, of the challenges and concerns identified during the sessions. With the aggregated interview results, the team will have a clear and holistic perspective into the subject fields where that should be prioritized for creating taxonomy. The prioritized listing should be reviewed with each interviewee to ensure they understand the findings and how it aligns with the organizational strategy.

Assess Existing Data

Input into the taxonomy should not have to be entirely recreated from scratch. For the most part, there is a good chance that throughout the organization, existing information can be used as source material to the taxonomy. Gathering relevant information for the taxonomy can happen from such data sources as the survey and interview results or preexisting documentation, such as organizational policy documentation or IT system architectures.

After reviewing the compiled information, the team will have a clear indication of how prepared the organization is for the taxonomy. The gap between readiness expectations and completeness of the preexisting materials will determine which business lines will have difficulty with implementing the taxonomy. Identifying the degree of readiness for each business line will allow the team to focus on getting additional clarity by conducting subsequent rounds of surveys and interviews.

STAGE 2: BUILD AND IMPLEMENT

In this stage of the methodology, the team conducts a series of interviews and surveys with subject matter experts to gather information necessary to develop the taxonomy. Using the aggregated results, the hierarchical classification scheme is built, evaluated and implemented throughout the organization.

Conduct Surveys and Interviews

The majority of content in the taxonomy will be drawn from surveying and interviewing people in business lines throughout the organization. Quite often, interviewing or surveying a group of individuals with a high-level understanding of how things should be done will be ineffective in gathering relevant information.

Alternatively, individual people with a detailed understanding of their job(s) or those who pay attention to detail can bring more value to the creation of the taxonomy. The reality is that the "go to" people in the organization are the best source of information for developing the taxonomy. This is because they are the best at describing what it is they do every day, what resources they need to do their job(s), and can directly identify any challenges or issues in performing their job(s).

At this point, there are plenty of source materials that can be drawn from to create the survey targeting the individuals who can provide the most value to creating the taxonomy. The process of surveying and interviewing are the organization's best opportunity to educate and help business lines better understand the scope, value, and relevance of taxonomy.

This round of surveys and interviews is designed so that the interviewee can further elaborate and provide greater details on the operations and functions they are involved in; that are relevant to the taxonomy's subject field. To facilitate the level of discussion held during the interview sessions, the team should consider distributing the survey beforehand to allow people additional time to review and absorb information such as the survey's context, definitions, purpose of the project, and goals of the survey.

As interviews are completed and the associated surveys are received, the team must thoroughly review the results. This time around, the goal of reviewing results is to ensure the responses align with the business line interviews and survey so that the team can identify any unresolved challenges that stand in the way of completing the taxonomy. To do so, the team must ensure they have a complete view of the business line from the interviewee's perspective which requires that, where needed, unfinished survey submission must be returned for completion with an explanation of the deficiencies needed resolution.

Processing through the aggregate results, the team will begin to realize the challenges that will affect how the taxonomy is created. For example, individual employees may not know how their job(s) relates to or impacts operations or processes in other business lines. This gap is where the team must note the exception and, depending on how severe the effect is to the taxonomy, determine the best course of action.

At a minimum, the team may need to reinterview individuals to gain additional details on the gap or conducting a new set of interviews and surveys with additional business lines. Alternatively, the team might determine that there is an absense of policies, procedures, or governance that needs to be implemented throughout the organization in order to address the gap.

Create Inventories

The collective information from interviews and survey with each business lines must now be consolidated into a single repository. Whether a single table or series of tables is needed to track the inventory, the team will need to ensure the information has been normalized and standardized in a format that it can be examined for consistencies and inconsistencies.

Once the information has been arranged into a record set(s), the team must review the complete inventory to ensure all aspects of the organization's security, privacy, and confidentiality have been dealt with. During the inventory review, the team might identify inconsistencies in the record set(s) that could also affect how the taxonomy is created. Similar to the resolution of gaps in the previous stage, the team must document the inconsistencies and potentially reinterview individuals to clarify the information before proceeding.

With the inventory confirmed to be consistent, the team will then provide each business line with the consolidated information to allow them an opportunity to provide their feedback and modifications. Quite often a business line will identify a record, such as a procedure of function, that is no longer relevant and request that it be removed from the inventory. The team should note these findings but not remove it until it has been confirmed that there are no other business lines that have procedures or functions depending on it.

Feedback from each business line must be reviewed by the team and a determination if modifications are consistent with the scope of the taxonomy. In some cases, the team may come across feedback where a business line has noted the need for modification that is specific to their operation or functions. For the taxonomy to be effective throughout the organization, the team must ensure that while feedback from each business line must be considered for inclusion to the taxonomy, it has to be consistent and realistic for the entire organization.

Justify a Classification Scheme

All the information gathered and consolidated from interviews, surveys, the inventory, and business line feedback should provide the team with a good idea of how the classification scheme and associated categories within the taxonomy will be structured. The classification scheme should be structured hierarchically using generic terms and language that clearly illustrate how it will be commonly referred to, so underlying categories can be aggregated from across the organization.

Similar to the service catalog hierarchy discussed in, Appendix D: Service Catalog, the taxonomy must also use a consistent and relevant series of categories to aggregate information. There should be a reasonable number of categories to simplify the classification scheme hierarchy; but not too few so that the purpose of the scheme becomes meaningless. Taxonomies should be personalized to meet the specific needs of each organization.

For example, organizations should customize the categories to better reflect the taxonomy's mandate, accurately align with existing structures or classification schemes, or to introduce subcategories that are relevant to its parent. In some instances, there could be an existing taxonomy throughout the organization that serves a purpose for a specific business operation or function. As mentioned previously, these taxonomies should be considered as reference or source data when developing an organizational taxonomy; as they may be existing categories that are applicable and can be reused.

After the classification scheme has been rationalized, the team must distribute it to stakeholders and business lines affected by its implementation. Where feedback is received questioning the scheme, such as terminology or hierarchy, the team may need to reinterview individuals to ensure they understood information was captured accurately. When the team has resolved the issues and modifications to the classification scheme have been completed, where and if needed, the first draft of the taxonomy can be developed.

Finalize the Taxonomy

Each draft of the taxonomy should be reviewed by stakeholders and business lines affected by its implementation. At this stage of the taxonomy development, the majority of modifications should be focused on addressing issues with terminology and clarity and could potentially span multiple rounds of review.

With the final revision completed, the team must perform one last check for defects and ensure what is being delivered aligns with the original scope and purpose. Additionally, the team will also need to ensure that the final revision is an accurate representation of the organization's current state in terms of security, privacy, confidentiality, legal and regulatory compliance, and technology management.

STAGE 3: GOVERN AND GROW

In this stage of the methodology, the team is focused on planning the long-term stability and sustainability of the taxonomy. With the final revision implemented, the team must develop a governance structure focused on the continued lifecycle including the:

- creation of policies and procedures to support its implementation and ongoing maintenance
- definition of the roles, responsibilities, and accountabilities throughout the organization
- establishment of training and awareness programs for support resources and employees

With the governance structure in place, the taxonomy should now be communicated and made available to employees throughout the organization so that the terminology, classification scheme, and categorization of the subject field can be commonly and consistently used.

SUMMARY

Creating a grouping of terms and language that is commonly and consistently used can drastically improve communication between individuals throughout an organization. It is important that as the organizations change, the terms and language also adapt to accommodate business operations and functions.

Appendix G: Risk Assessment

INTRODUCTION

Risk management is the process of selecting and implementing countermeasures to achieve an acceptable level of risk at an acceptable cost; beyond the cost–benefit analysis discussed previously in chapter "Understanding Forensic Readiness." By examining in depth the potential threats faced by an organization, a better understanding of business risk can be gained that subsequently leads to identifying strategies, techniques, approaches, or countermeasures that reduce or mitigate impact. At a high level, this can be achieved by asking three basic questions:

- What can go wrong?
- What will we do?
- If something happens, how will we pay for it?

Thinking about these questions in context of a particular organization, it might become clear that there are some areas where risk management could be applied, such as weaknesses in the software development life cycle or manual processes that are prone to human error. Since the potential damage or loss to an asset exists, the level of risk is based on the value given to it by its owner and the consequential impact. Additionally, the probability and likelihood of a vulnerability to be exploited must also be taken into consideration. Therefore, as illustrated in Figure G.1, risk cannot exist without the intersection of three variables: assets, threats, and vulnerabilities.

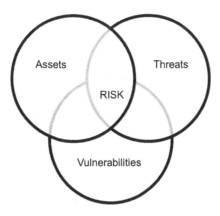

FIGURE G.1

Risk management variables.

WHAT IS A RISK ASSESSMENT?

A risk assessment is simply a thorough examination of what could cause harm to assets so that an accurate decision of how to manage the risk can be made. Risk assessments do not require an overengineered approach of new processes, methodologies, or loads of paperwork. There are several industry-recognized methodologies available to use during the analysis stage of the risk management program.

Depending on the type of business offered by an organization, one methodology may be preferred over another; while others may be mandated through regulations to use a particular methodology or a decision is made to develop one that meets their specific business needs. Generally, organizations have the option of conducting a risk assessment by following one of these two approaches.

QUALITATIVE ASSESSMENTS

Qualitative assessments are focused on results that are descriptive as opposed to measurable; where there is no direct monetary value assigned to the assets and its importance is based on a hypothetical value. Organizations should typically look to conduct a qualitative assessment when the:

- assessors have limited expertise
- time frame allocated for the assessment is short
- organization does not have data readily available to accommodate trending

Analysis commonly performed in this type of assessment can include several layers of determining how assets are susceptible to risks. This includes the correlation of both assets to threats and threats to vulnerabilities, as described further in Appendix H: Threat Modeling, as well as the determination of likelihood and the level of impact that an exploited vulnerability will create, as illustrated in Figure G.2.

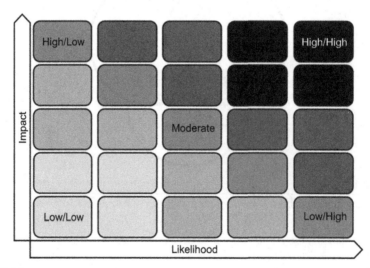

FIGURE G.2

Risk likelihood/severity heat map.

In a qualitative assessment, the output generated from the comparison of likelihood and the level of impact is the severity the risk has on assets. Generally, the higher the risk level the greater the priority on the organization to manage the risk and protect its assets from potential harm.

QUANTITATIVE ASSESSMENTS

The primary characteristic of a quantitative assessment is its numerical nature. Use of variables, such as frequency, probability, impact, or other aspects of a risk assessment are not easily measured against mathematical properties like monetary value. Quantitative assessments allow organizations to determine whether the cost of a risk outweighs the cost of managing a risk based on mathematics instead of descriptive terms.

Organizations that have invested in gathering and preserving information, combined with the enhanced knowledge and experience of staff, are better equipped to conduct this type of assessment. For this reason, getting to end of job requires a larger investment in resource knowledge and experience, time, and effort.

Knowing that quantitative assessments follow a mathematical basis, organizations that decide to conduct this type of analysis should consider performing the following series of calculations.

Single Loss Expectancy

The first calculation to be completed is the single loss expectancy (SLE). The SLE is the difference between the original and remaining monetary value of an asset that is expected after a single occurrence of a risk against an asset. The SLE is calculated as

$$\text{Single Loss Expectancy (SLE)} = \text{Asset Value (AV)} \times \text{Exposure Factor (EF)}$$

where AV is the monetary value assigned to an asset, and EF is an percentage representing the amount of loss to an asset.

For example, if the AV has been identified as $5000 and the EF is 40%, then the SLE would be calculate as

$$\text{Single Loss Expectancy (SLE)} = 5000 \times 0.40 = 2000$$

Annual Rate of Occurrence

Following the SLE, the next calculation to be completed is the annual rate of occurrence (ARO). The ARO is a representation of how often an identified threat will successfully exploit a vulnerability and generate some level of business impact within the period of a year. The ARO is calculated as

$$\text{Annual Rate of Occurrence (ARO)} = \#\,\text{impact/time period}$$

For example, if trending data suggest that a specific threat is likely to generate business impact one time over four periods, then the ARO would be calculated as

$$\text{Annual Rate of Occurrence (ARO)} = 1/4 = 0.25$$

Annualized Loss Expectancy

Having values for both SLE and ARO, the next calculation to be completed is the annualized loss expectancy (ALE). The ALE is the expected monetary loss of an asset that can be realized as a result of actual business impact over a 1-year period. The ALE is calculated as

$$\text{Annual Loss Expectancy (ALE)} = \text{SLE} \times \text{ARO}$$

For example, if the ARO is 0.25 and the SLE is 2000, then the ALE would be calculated as

$$\text{Annual Loss Expectancy (ALE)} = 2000 \times 0.25 = 500$$

With the ALE completed, organizations can use the resulting value directly in a cost–benefit analysis as described in, Appendix E: Cost–Benefit Analysis. For example, where a threat or risk has an ALE of $500, then the cost–benefit analysis would identify that investing $5000 per year on a countermeasure would not be recommended.

ADVANTAGES AND DISADVANTAGES

Depending on the goals for performing an assessment, both the qualitative and quantitative approach present its own benefits. Neither approach should be overlooked as a tool for performing risk assessment because they are unique in how they demonstrate risk to stakeholders.

With qualitative assessments, the approach is simpler because it does not require the in-depth analysis of numerical values through formulas and calculations. Analysis results are simpler for stakeholders to understand because it leverages business terms to communicate the level of risk involved. However, there is no escaping the fact that qualitative assessments are more subjective because they are based on the organization's experience and judgment which makes it more difficult to defend. The ability to monitor the implementation of countermeasures using labels and terms is difficult because it cannot be measured.

On the other hand, a quantitative assessment is considered objective because it is not influenced by subjective experience or judgment. It relies on predetermined formulas and calculations to arrive at the valuation of a risk decision based on numerical measurements. However, this approach requires organizations to have existing data, more experience, and be willing to invest more time because it is based on factual numbers and predetermined formulas.

TOOLS, METHODOLOGIES, AND TECHNIQUES

Organizations will select their risk assessment tools, methodology, and techniques based on what works best for their specific needs, capabilities, budget, and timelines.

Tools

Given the availability of industry resources, completing a risk assessment does not need to be an overly complicated process. Several tools are readily accessible to make the risk assessment tasks easier; including software, checklists, and templates.

Depending on volumes, gathering and processing data can be demanding and require significant efforts. Organizations should look to invest in automated tools that can alleviate the time needed to complete these tasks. Regardless of whether the organization plans on purchasing or building tools, this decision should be based on aspects such as appropriate timelines, skill sets, and the need to follow a proper system development life cycle (SDLC).

As organizations perform more risk assessments, they will begin to identify patterns where there are similarities in tasks being completed, such as cataloging threat agents and threats. In these situations, the use of checklists may be beneficial to ensure that the risk assessment considers all relevant information even if it may not apply in each instance.

Reviewing existing policies and procedures for relevant security gaps can be a complex and time-consuming task. When used properly, templates can be effective in improving operational efficiencies and accuracy of the risk assessment results.

Methodologies and Techniques

Generally, all risk assessments follow a similar methodology consisting of the same techniques to arriving at a final risk decision, including analyzing threats and vulnerabilities, asset valuation, and risk evaluation.

However, there is no single risk assessment methodology that meets the needs of every organization because they were not designed to be "one-size-fits-all." Ultimately, each organization is unique in its own respect and has their own reasons for why they would complete risk assessments. Therefore, a variety of industry-recognized risk assessment methodologies have been developed to address the varying needs and requirements.

Contained in the "Resources" section of this chapter, a series of different risk assessment methodologies have been provided as references. It is important to note that inclusion of a methodology below does not suggest that these are better or recommended over other models that were not included.

RISK LIFE CYCLE WORKFLOW

An assessment of risk at any given time will naturally evolve over time and the exposure to the organization will either increase or decrease accordingly. Supporting constant changes in business risk requires that the risk management process is performed regularly; not as a one-time exercise.

FIGURE G.3

Risk management life cycle workflow.

Effectively managing risk should be shared between multiple stakeholders because the responsibility and accountability of doing so cannot generally be placed on a single party. For example, while information security is responsible for providing guidance and oversight, accountability for implementing recommendations is with the business line that owns the risk.

Several well-established risk management frameworks are available that, while slight differences exist in terminology and stages, all use a very similar approach to the risk management life cycle. Described in the following sections, Figure G.3 illustrates the four-stage workflow involved in the risk management life cycle.

VISUALIZING RISK

Challenges with demonstrating business risk to stakeholders are largely attributed to delivering information in a format that is difficult to interpret. Illustrated in Figure G.4, a mind map is an excellent tool for conceptually representing risk in a nonlinear format to build out the framework for assessing and managing the risk.

Mind maps are a type of diagram that is based on a centralized concept or subject, such as risk management, with the components revolving around it like a spiderweb. The use of a mind map not only enhances communications through the use of categorized groupings, but also allows the risk management team to quickly record and capture ideas being discussed during meetings.

FIGURE G.4

Risk management mind map—communication.

COMMUNICATION

Communication is an integral component of risk management. It is essential that the key stakeholders responsible for managing risk throughout the organization, such as upper management, understand the reasons why decisions are being made and why the selected strategies, techniques, approaches, and countermeasures are necessary. For this reason, the communication activities performed in this workflow should not be viewed as a sequential stage, but instead represented as a continuous activity.

By having consistent communication, risk information can be more effectively reused throughout the organization; reducing the need to conduct more than one risk assessment on the same area for different purposes (ie, planning, auditing, resource allocations). When defining communication activities, organizations might include details that provide direction on the:

- types of information that needs to be communicated at various stages (ie, what information do stakeholders need or want)
- target audience for the various types of information (ie, management)
- means used to distribute communication to the target audiences

Stage #1: Identify

Risk cannot be managed without first recognizing, describing, and having a solid understanding of what potential risks can significantly impact an organization. To start, stakeholders (ie, employees, investors, etc.) should be provided with clear direction on what the organization's expectations are when it comes to identifying risk. Once informed, all stakeholders should be provided with the appropriate tools and techniques—such as training, workshops, checklists, etc.—that will be used to accurately identify risk.

To facilitate stakeholder involvement in the process of identifying risk, organizations should provide them with a taxonomy to ensure the use of consistent and common risk terminology and classifications throughout the risk management process. Further details about how to build a taxonomy can be found in, Appendix F: Building a Taxonomy.

Through a series of face-to-face or virtual sessions, stakeholders should contribute to the identification of risks as both collaborative and individual participation. After the collective results have been reviewed, the risk management mind map can be expanded further to include the specific components of the identification stage as illustrated in Figure G.5.

Stage #2: Analyze

Having identified all relevant assets, threats, and vulnerabilities that constitute risk, the next step is to individually analyze and prioritize all risks that have any potential of generating business impact. Analyzing each risk individually helps to prioritize them so that organizations can focus resources and efforts to managing the most appropriate risk first. When defining assessment activities, organizations might include details that provide direction on:

- who should be involved
- the level of detail required
- what type of information needs to be gathered
- how the risk assessment should be documented to deal, for example, with planning activities

As each risk is analyzed, organizations should take into consideration their risk tolerance as a factor in risk scoring. By doing so, organizations will get a better representation of risk by being able to identify the delta between the assessed risk level and what they consider to be an acceptable risk level. Generally, there are several tools and techniques available to analyze and prioritize risks. As illustrated previously in Figure G.2, at a minimum performing a risk assessment involves determining the likelihood of a risk occurring and the level of impact it will generate, ultimately achieving the severity valuation of the risk.

Output from the risk assessment will create an understanding of the nature of the risk and its potential to affect business operations and functions. After determining the impact of each risk, which is the combination of likelihood and severity, the risk management mind map can be expanded further to include the specific components of the identification stage as illustrated in Figure G.6.

Stage #3: Manage

Completion of the preceding assessment has resulted in each risk being assigned a ranking in terms of the level of impact it has on business operations and functions. With this knowledge, the organization must determine how to minimize the probability of negative risks while improving its security posture. This requires that, for each risk, a decision is made on how best to respond and manage the level of impact. Illustrated in Figure G.7, the four responses to risk include:

- *Mitigate* risk, where likelihood is high but severity is low, through the implementation of countermeasures to reduce the potential for impact
- *Avoid* risk, where likelihood and severity are high, by keeping clear of activities that will generate the potential for impact

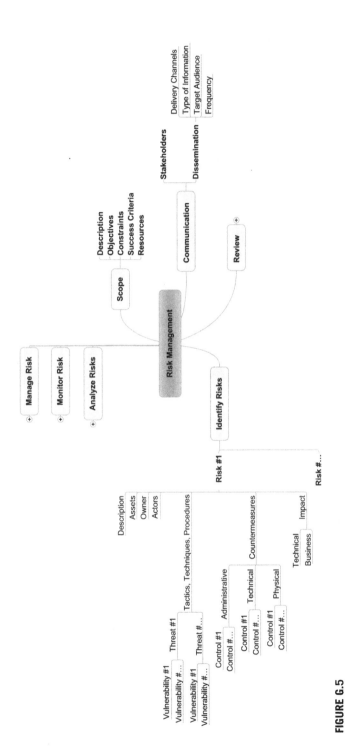

FIGURE G.5

Risk management mind map—identifying.

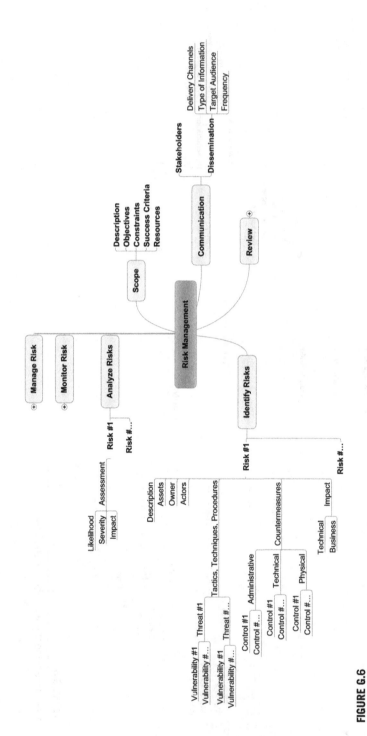

FIGURE 6.6

Risk management mind map—analyzing.

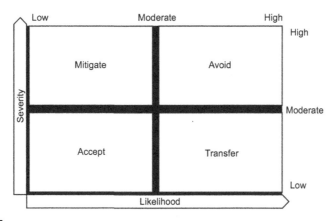

FIGURE G.7

Risk management responses.

- *Transfer* risk, where likelihood is low but severity is high, by shifting all—or a portion of—the risk to a third party through insurance, outsourcing, or entering into partnerships.
- *Accept* risk, where likelihood and severity are low, if the result of a cost–benefit analysis determines that the cost of mitigating the risk is greater than the cost to implement the necessary countermeasures. In this scenario, the best response is to accept the risk and continuously monitor it. Details on how to perform a cost–benefit analysis can be found in, Appendix E: Cost–Benefit Analysis.

Where the organization has determined that the best response to a risk is by implementing countermeasures, it is important to remember that these controls can be applied in the form of administrative, physical, or technical controls. After determining the best response, the risk management mind map can be expanded further to include the specific components of the identification stage as illustrated in Figure G.8.

Stage #4: Monitor

Generally, risk is all about uncertainty. Even though a formalized risk management program has been implemented, and up to this stage has been able to identify and get control over known risks, organizations need to ensure that the process is not performed as a one-time activity. Instead, the need to implement continuous monitoring within the risk management program has two fundamental aspects that are essential to ensuring its effectiveness.

The first aspect is about keeping a close and steady watch on previously identified risks. The advancement in technology evolves the way modern threats, vulnerabilities, and risks can impact business operation. To counterbalance this effect, organizations must be vigilant in how they monitor this anomaly to determine if a previously documented risk has changed. If a change has been detected, the

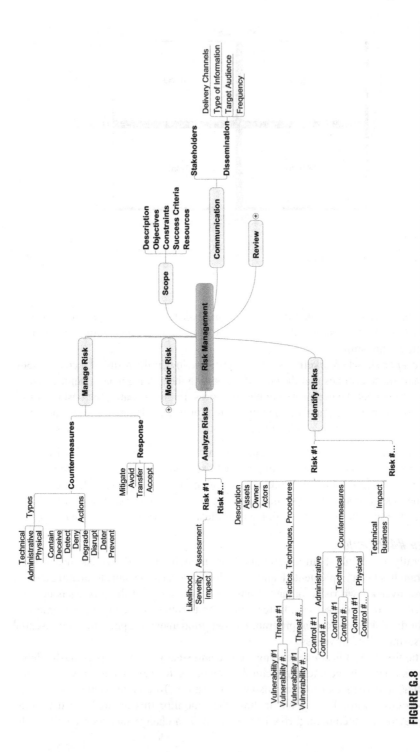

FIGURE G.8

Risk management mind map—managing.

organization has to reassess the original risk to determine if their risk response also needs to be changed.

The second aspect is about identifying any new risks that have emerged. The advancement in technology also introduces new threats, vulnerabilities, and risks that have the potential to generate new kinds of business impact. To counter balance this effect, organizations must implement and diligently follow a proactive management program to identify when new risks surface. Through a proactive approach, there will be greater opportunities to manage risks before they materialize and avoid impulsive risk response decisions.

The best method of risk monitoring comes from the combined implementation of administrative, physical, and technical solutions. After selecting the most appropriate risk monitoring solution(s), the risk management mind map can be expanded further to include the specific components of the monitoring stage as illustrated in Figure G.9.

REVIEW

Activities performed while reviewing the risk management are an important aspect of continuous process improvement. Reviewing the collective risk management approach and process is essential to providing stakeholders (ie, management, investors, etc.) with awareness and assurance that the organization's overall risk management approach is performing effectively, efficiently, and is still relevant. For this reason, the review activities performed in this workflow should not be viewed as a sequential stage, but instead represented as a continuous activity.

Information gathered during review activities helps organizations to identify opportunities to improve their risk management approach and process to ensure its overall performance remains consistent. To support the activities performed during the review stage, organizations should consider:

- clearly defining the accountabilities, roles, and responsibilities of all stakeholders involved in maintaining the performance of the risk management approach and process
- using existing governance and assurance functions (ie, internal audit) to assess the performance of the risk management approach and process
- documenting the expected outcomes of risk response decisions, such as reducing negative impact or capitalizing on opportunities
- defining key performance indicators (KPI) to measure the performance of the risk management approach and process
- building the necessary systems, processes, etc. to demonstrate the findings relevant to the performance of the risk management approach and process
- establishing a timeline for when and how (1) governance and assurance assessments will be conducted; (2) the outcome decisions will be communicated to stakeholders

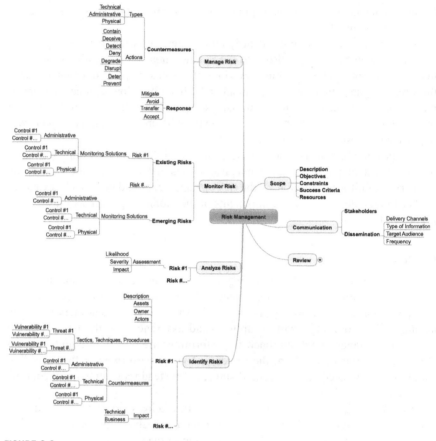

FIGURE G.9

Risk management mind map—monitoring.

Essential to every activity performed during the review stage is the measurement of the overall performance against the overall implementation strategy. Working together with the communication activities, and in parallel to the remaining risk management activities, review activities validate that the risk management approach and process meet the organization's need by adding value as a contributor to decision-making, business planning, and resource allocation. Where the review activities have identified gaps in the risk management approach and process, such as regulatory compliance or operational efficiencies, actions can be taken to identify opportunities to use more effective approaches, improve processes, or leverage new tools and ideas.

Generally, the documentation and communication of review activities support the organization's capability to improve its risk management performance through

FIGURE G.10

Risk management mind map—reviewing.

dissemination of best practices and lessons learned. After building the review activities, the risk management mind map can be expanded further to include the specific components of the review stage as illustrated in Figure G.10.

SUMMARY

While there is no "one-size-fits-all" approach to performing a risk assessment, the overall goal is to gain a better understanding of the business risk so organizations can identify appropriate strategies, techniques, approaches, or countermeasures to manage the impact. Through the use of any industry-recognized risk assessment methodology, organizations can avoid an overengineered approach of establishing new processes, approaches, or generating loads of paperwork.

RESOURCES

Alberts, C., Dorofee, A., Stevens, J., Woody, C., 2003. Introduction to the OCTAVE Approach. http://resources.sei.cmu.edu/asset_files/UsersGuide/2003_012_001_51556.pdf. Carnegie Mellon University.

Peltier, T.R., 2000. Facilitated Risk Analysis Process (FRAP). http://www.ittoday.info/AIMS/DSM/85-01-21.pdf. CRC Press.

Ionita, D., Hartel, P., 2013. Current Established Risk Assessment Methodologies and Tools. http://doc.utwente.nl/89558/1/%5Btech_report%5D_D_Ionita_-_Current_Established_Risk_Assessment_Methodologies_and_Tools.pdf. University of Twente.

Appendix H: Threat Modeling

INTRODUCTION

The threat landscape is constantly evolving and escalating as more and more business operations are relying on complex technology infrastructures. Building and sustaining effective mitigating and defense-in-depth strategies requires organizations to have a balanced understanding of both their adversaries and themselves so they can comprehend the nature of threats they face.

Threat risk modeling is an essential exercise that must be viewed as a component of every organization's overall risk management program. This exercise should be completed to build appropriate countermeasures that effectively reduce business risk impact through the identification of contributing threats. It is important that a structured threat risk assessment is completed to better understand the individual security threats that have potential to affect their business assets, operations, and functions.

WHY THREAT MODELING?

Specific to information security, a threat is any intentional (eg, cybercrime) or accidental (eg, natural disaster) course of action with the potential to adversely impact people, processes, or technology. Similar to business risk, threats can be classified according to their types, such as:

- Physical damage (eg, fire, water)
- Service impact (eg, electrical, telecommunication)
- Information compromise (eg, eavesdropping, media theft)
- Technical failures (eg, software defects, performance, and capacity)
- Operational compromise (eg, abuse of rights, denial of service)

It is important to recognize that even though the resulting impact(s) of individual security threats can be different, there are commonalities in how all threats are structured and work. Under the structured threat information expression (STIX) framework, illustrated in Figure H.1, organizations can utilize a common language for representing the nine constructs of how threats work. STIX is designed to improve the overall management and understanding of threat information so that organizations can develop mitigation strategies and countermeasures that are meaningful, adaptable, extensible, and automated.

- *Observables* are the resulting outputs that might be or have been seen across an organization (ie, service degradation)
- *Indicators* describe one or more observable patterns that, combined with other relevant and contextual information, represent artifacts and behaviors of interest (ie, file hashes)

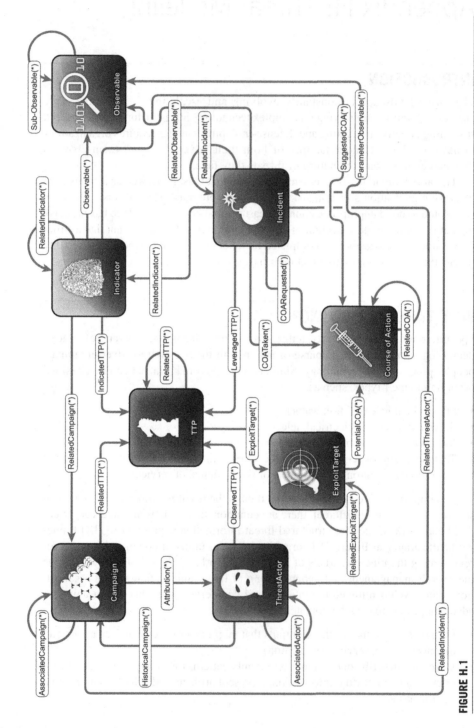

FIGURE H.1

Structured threat information expression framework. TTP, *tactics, techniques, and procedures.*

- *Incidents* are distinct instances of indicators that are affecting an organization accompanied by information discovered or decided upon during an investigation
- *Adversary tactics, techniques, and procedures* (*TTP*) describes the attack patterns, tools, exploits, infrastructure, victim targeting, and other methods used by the adversary or attacker
- *Exploit targets* describe vulnerabilities, weaknesses, or configurations that can be exploited
- *Courses of action* are specific countermeasures taken as corrective or preventative response actions to protect an exploit target or mitigate the potential impact of an incident
- *Campaigns* are event occurrences where threat actors perform a set of TTPs or incidents that are potentially experienced throughout an organization
- *Threat actors* identify and characterize the malicious adversary with intent and observed behaviors that represent a threat to an organization

It is not realistic or feasible to implement strategies that will mitigate all known threats to business assets, operations, or function. Alternatively, by completing a threat modeling exercise organizations can get a better understanding of threats targeting them and be better prepared to prioritize strategies for reducing their attack surface. STRIDE (Spoofing, Tampering, Repudiation, Information disclosure, Denial of service, Elevation of privilege) is a threat classification scheme that can be used to characterize individual threats based on TTP commonalities and implement countermeasures to reduce the overall attack surface.

Application of the STRIDE scheme as part of the overall risk management program allows organizations to meet the requirements for maintaining security properties of confidentiality, integrity, and availability, along with authorization, authentication, and nonrepudiation. The STRIDE acronym is formed using the first letter of the following six threat categories:

- *Spoofing* is the unauthorized use of authentication information, such as a user name and password, to gain access into objects[1] or assets[2].
- *Tampering* involves the malicious and unauthorized (1) alteration of data communication between subjects[3] such as business workflows or (2) modification to persistent objects or assets such as database content.
- *Repudiation* is the explicit denial of performing actions where proof cannot be otherwise obtained, such as executing unauthorized acts against an object or asset. Nonrepudiation is the mitigating control where a record of actions is maintained such as generating an audit log event for specific acts against an object or asset.
- *Information disclosure* involves exposure of information to subjects that are, under normal circumstances, not authorized for gain access, such as an intruder reading data communications between two systems.

- *Denial of service* attacks decrease the availability and reliability of objects or assets by making them temporarily unavailable or unusable, such as overwhelming a system with access requests.
- *Elevation of privilege* occurs when unprivileged subjects obtain privileged access and are subsequently authorized to gain access to objects or assets, such as exploiting defenses and impersonating a trusted system.

BUSINESS RISK ASSOCIATION

As business operations become much more interrelated with complex technologies, it is crucial that organizations do not continue to manage threats on a case-by-case basis. Alternatively, instead of managing threats through specific technology functionalities, organization should manage their attack surface with the goal of reducing a much larger number of threats without getting into the specifics.

To manage threats from a risk-based approach, organizations should put focus on assessing threats as part of their overall risk management program. The relationship between threats and business risk is illustrated in Figure H.2 whereby threats are represented as direct contributors and drivers for impact to business operations and functions.

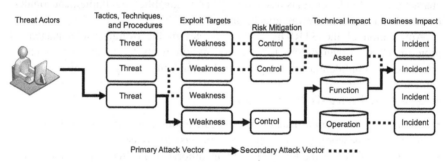

FIGURE H.2

Threat tree workflow.

THREAT MODELING METHODOLOGIES

Threat modeling is a process used to identify objectives and vulnerabilities, quantify the organization's exposure, and develop strategies to mitigate and countermeasure threats. Through the creation of a structured representation of all collected information, organizations are better informed and can make prioritized decision-making to improve their risk posture.

Organizations should ensure that threat modeling is performed as an iterative process and not as a one-time exercise. Threat modeling should be performed consistently throughout each phase of the system and software development to:

- ensure threats that are not identified during initial assessments are subsequently discovered; and
- adapt to changes in system or software designs and evolving business requirements

Several threat models have been published to enable the classification and categorization of individual threats in different ways. In some instances, organizations might find that adopting one threat model over another may not be appropriate for them because it does not meet their business requirements. In all cases, a functional run-through of threat models should be performed so that organizations can determine which one aligns best to their specific needs. While there might be threat models not specified below, the following are examples of methodologies that can be adopted to support a risk management program.

MICROSOFT THREAT MODELING

Developed by Microsoft in 2003, this threat model allows organization to systematically identify and prioritize threats that have the greatest potential impact to business assets, operations, and functions. Leveraging the STRIDE classification scheme, organizations can address individual threats by executing the following six stages:

- *Identify assets* documents all systems and objects that need to be protected
- *Create an architecture overview* uses data flow and workflow diagrams to illustrate the relationships and connectivity between systems and objects
- *Decompose the application* provides further details of the architecture to uncover weaknesses and vulnerabilities in design, implementation, or configuration
- *Identify the threats* discovers the exact weaknesses and vulnerabilities that could affect the systems and objects
- *Document the threats* records the attributes of each weakness and vulnerability using a common classification scheme
- *Rate the threats* scores threats to determine the priority for implementing mitigating countermeasures

Microsoft's threat modeling methodology is designed to address the unique challenges faced by organization when it comes to reducing the attack surface and improving security of their systems and software. Those involved in performing threat modeling using Microsoft's methodology will find that, while it focuses more on the technical aspects of business risk, it is easy to learn and adopt throughout any organization.

PROCESS FOR ATTACK SIMULATION AND THREAT ANALYSIS (PASTA)

Developed by Marco Morana and Tony UV., this is a threat model that is platform agnostic and can be applied to most systems or software development methodologies. This model is focused on aligning business objectives with technical requirements through the completion of the following seven steps:

- *Define the business and security objectives* documents functional capabilities by completing a business impact analysis from the security and regulatory compliance requirements perspective
- *Define the technical scope* describes the inclusion of technical assets and components that will be enumerated for threats
- *Decompose the application* identifies the individual component data flows from which threat and vulnerability assessments are performed
- *Threat analysis* extracts detailed threat intelligence and assesses the likelihood of attack scenarios occurring
- *Weakness and vulnerabilities analysis* involves mapping threat analysis results with enumerated weaknesses to develop use/abuse cases and vulnerabilities scoring systems
- *Attack/exploits enumeration and modeling* establishes an attacker's perspective of the attack surface including exploit targets or TTP's
- *Risk and impact analysis* provides qualitative and quantitative assessments of the business risk and impact along with mitigation strategy options

PASTA was designed by combining several threat modeling approaches to give organizations an attacker's perspective of threats so that they can identify mitigation strategies that follow an asset-centric approach. While there are technical aspects included in this methodology, the inclusion of business relevant aspects changes it from a purely technical exercise into a process that requires the involvement of key organizational stakeholders.

TRIKE

Developed by Eleanor Saitta, Brenda Larcom, and Michael Eddington, version 1.0 of this threat model was published in 2005 as a way of providing organizations with a unified framework for security auditing from a risk management perspective. The intention of using this methodology was to enable communication between multiple stakeholders to describe security characteristics of a system or software from the high-level architecture to the low-level implementation details.

TRIKE follows a risk-based approach where organizations sequentially complete four models to determine the impact threats have to assets, operations, and functions:

- *Requirements* focus on obtaining an understanding of the target system or software, including: the intended operations, all subject interactions, the actions that trigger what functionality, and rules that constrain actions.

- *Implementation* focuses on gathering information about the implementation. From previously documenting what operation(s) the system or software is intended to perform, the following assessments can be made:
  - Identifying the actions that do not align within the scope of the intended actions for the system or software
  - Examining the individual components and develop data flow diagrams for how they are interconnected
  - Creating a workflow that illustrates the relationship between subjects, actions, triggers, and operations.
- *Threat* focuses on identifying the threats against the implementation model. By developing an attack graph for a specific component or against the entire system or software, weaknesses can be identified and subsequently mitigation strategies created.
- *Risk* focuses on understanding the risk factors that are in and out of scope for each components of the system or software. Risks identified can be assumed resulting in changing the prioritization of weaknesses and vulnerabilities documented during the threat model. It is important to note that this risk model is still considered experimental within the TRIKE methodology and is subject to change.

Under version 1.0, organizations may experience performance issues after reaching a certain threshold of actors, and assets are included in a single system assessment. Since the initial release, there have been subsequent versions of the methodology, both versions 1.5 and 2.0, which are only partially documented and are still currently experimental. Organizations must exercise caution when considering the use of the latter versions of this methodology as they have not been fully tested against real systems or software.

THREAT RISK MATRIX

From the threat modeling exercise, a formalized report should be created to document the security aspects of the system or software architecture including additional attributes that link the identified threat to a business risk mitigation strategy. Publishing a threat report helps to prioritize, manage, and align potential threats across the organization with communication to key stakeholders such as:

- designers who can use secure software engineering principles relating to technologies and functionality;
- developers who author systems or software following recommended mitigation strategies; and
- testers and auditors who can verify and validate that the application security components were built as designed.

As a supplement to the overall risk assessment report provided in the *Templates* section of this book, a dedicated threat and risk assessment (TRA) report can be included to illustrate how the assessed threats contribute to the overall business risk.

Even though this additional report is included as part of the larger risk report, it should still contain sufficient information so that it can be used as a stand-alone report. At a minimum the TRA report, as provided in the *Templates* section of this book, should include:

- *Executive summary:* provides a high-level summary of the threat assessment and findings
- *Overall risk statement:* presents justification for the final risk score of each security principle specified in the assessment matrix
- *Methodology:* provides an explanation of how the threat modeling exercise was conducted
- *Assumptions:* identifies circumstances and outcomes taken for granted during the assessment
- *Threat tree workflows:* demonstrates how each threat can lead to business impact
- *Threat assessment matrix:* addresses, in sections, each security principle (ie, confidentiality, integrity, availability, etc.) with details about each individual threat including the:
  - unique identifier for recognizing a specific threat
  - name and description of the threat that was assessed
  - risk score that was assigned to the threat
  - description of countermeasures identified to mitigate the threat
  - description of residual risk remaining after countermeasures are implemented

THREAT MODELING: NEXT STEPS

Organizations must acknowledge that over time, threats evolve resulting in changes to the business risk and impact. While countermeasures can be implemented to reduce an attack surface, it is important to remember that threats exist regardless of the mitigation strategies previously implemented and cannot be completely eliminated as a potential business risk impact.

Threat modeling should not be treated as a program that is executed as a one-time exercise. It must be performed as an iterative process that is capable of adapting to the evolving threat landscape, changes to systems and software designs, and shifting business requirements.

SUMMARY

As part of an overall risk management strategy, threat modeling focuses specifically on security threats that have potential to affect their business assets, operations, and functions. By performing threat modeling, organizations will gain a better understanding of the threats they face so that more effective defense-in-depth strategies can be implemented.

TAXONOMY

1 *Objects* are passive elements that contain or receive information.
2 *Assets* are any resource of value such as people, information, or systems.
3 *Subject* is an active element that operates on information or the system state.

Appendix I: Data Warehouse Introduction

INTRODUCTION

At the core of a successful data warehouse implementation comes proper planning. As part of this planning, it is critical that organizations do not underestimate the importance and complexity of completing their requirements analysis.

Data warehousing is first and foremost a business discipline that leverages technical infrastructures to deliver the final solution. Achieving a successful data warehouse implementation requires a strategic approach that consists of the most suitable project team members, is focused on both business and technical requirements, and has a sound and thorough project plan.

WHAT IS A DATA WAREHOUSE?

An enterprise data warehouse (EDW) provides a centralized repository of integrated data from multiple disparate sources to allow for quicker and better informed decision-making capabilities. Collected data is commonly maintained within the EDW to provide organizations with the ability to trend data over a longer period of time for improved data mining, analytics, and reporting.

First defined by William Inmon, the four common characteristics of every EDW include the following:

- *Subject-oriented data*: all relevant data is gathered, stored, and organized as a set of information that can be used for a specific subject area
- *Integrated*: all data contained within the EDW in a consistent structure that allows it to always be integrated to all other data without exception
- *Nonvolatile*: all data is loaded and accessible in the EDW in a read-only presentation
- *Time variant*: all data is accurate as of some point in time and is represented over a long period of time, such as 5–10 years

DEVELOPMENT CONCEPTS

Traditionally, an EDW's functionality was scoped to provide functionality specific to analyzing their business data. Supporting business reporting, the data contained within the EDW is classified as either:

- *Operational data* that is commonly stored, retrieved, and updated by an online transaction processing (OLTP) system[1] for the purpose of running the business, such as an order-entry application.

247

- *Informational data* that is created from operational data sources and is typically:
  - summarized operational data
  - denormalized and replicated
  - optimized for decision-making
  - accessible in read-only formats

Illustrated in Table I.1, the difference between operational databases and data warehouses has been identified.

Table I.1 Online Transaction Processing and Online Analytical Processing Differences

Operational Databases (OLTP)	Data Warehouses (OLAP)
Lack of integration	Integrated data sources
Focused on database and process design	Focused on data modeling and database design
Data is accurate as if the last time it was accessed	Data is accurate the period of time
Data can be updated	Data cannot be modified
Current data available 60–90 days	Historical data available 50–60 years
Operations performed on database are changes, insert, delete, replace	Operations performed on database are load and access
Regular updates made record-by-record	Once data is loaded into the database, no updates are made
Data is very fresh	Data is very old
Database contains detailed information	Database contains summarized data

In order to analyze and report on business trends, organizations need to have a large amount of different data sources available for a long period of time. In the case of OLTP systems, they are designed to complete online transactions and query processing that requires historical data to be archived so that performance demands can be met. Alternatively, an EDW serves as solution for organizations to mine and analyze data trends over time, which makes it an online analytical processing (OLAP) system.[2]

Illustrated in Table I.2, the major features between OLTP and OLAP systems have been identified.

ARCHITECTURAL MODELS

From the comparison between OLTP and OLAP systems, the purpose for implementing an EDW is better understood in the role it plays within an organization. However, as EDWs become more common, organizations are constantly evolving their capabilities by finding new ways to use these infrastructures to collect, analyze, and process data for other business purposes.

Essentially every EDW is considered a living ecosystem that is developed using both business and technical architectural components. Without a sound

Table I.2 OLTP and OLAP Features

Feature	OLTP	OLAP
User/system orientation	Custom oriented for real-time transactions and querying	Market oriented[3] for historical trending and reporting
Data contents	Small amount of current and up-to-date data	Large amount of historical and accurate data
Database design	Entity-relationship model[4] and application oriented[5]	Star[6] or snowflake[7] model and subject oriented[8]
View	Current data	Historical data
Unit of work	Short and simple transactions	Complex operations
Characteristic	Operational processing	Informational processing
Orientation	Transaction	Analysis
User	Clerical, DBA	Analyst, manager
Function	Day-to-day operations	Long-term decision-making
Summarization	Highly details and flat relationships	Summarized and consolidated
Access patterns	Read/write	Read only
Focus	Data in	Information out
Number of records	Tens of thousands	Hundreds of millions
Number of users	Thousands	Hundreds
Database size	Less than 1 GB	Greater than 100 GB
Priority	High performance and availability	Highly flexible

OLTP, online transaction processing; OLAP, online analytical processing.

architecture, the solution cannot support the organization's strategic direction because the system will not function effectively as a complete and integrated solution.

The best way to approach developing the EDW architecture is to use the analogy of constructing a real building. Although the components of an EDW are different to those in a real building, the fundamentals for how they are both architected are identical whereas they both require a set of models, specifications, and structures that integrate several key components into a complete and final working solution.

Designing both the business and technical components of the EDW involves the following three distinct layers of functionality that seamlessly work together in support of the overall solution capabilities.

- *Extraction* identifies and collects disparate data from distributed repository
- *Transform* reconstructs collected data into structured data sets that can be used for mining and analysis
- *Load* writes structured data sets into target storage for mining, analytics, and reporting

The methods for how the extraction, transformation, and loading (ETL) functionality of collected data is implemented depends on the organization's requirements for developing the EDW. As an example, the following architectural reference models are commonly used when developing EDW solutions.

BASIC ARCHITECTURE

Illustrated in Figure I.1, this is the simplest type of architecture where users are permitted direct access to data stored in the EDW. This architecture requires that organizations preprocess their data outside of the solution before being placed into the EDW. The components of this architecture include:

- Repositories of data located in the multiple disparate sources
- Warehouse containing the centralized repository of collected data sources
- Entities that interact with centralized data sets

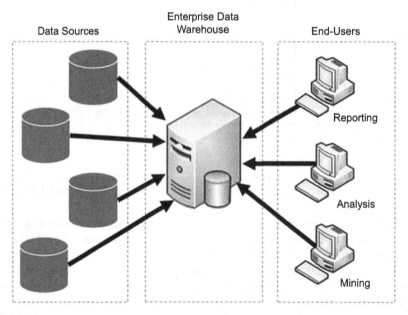

FIGURE I.1

Basic data warehouse architecture.

ARCHITECTURE WITH STAGING

Illustrated in Figure I.2, this type of architecture includes an intermediate staging area where ETL functions automate the preprocessing of data into a structured format before being stored in the EDW. The components of this architecture include:

- Repositories of data located in the multiple disparate sources
- Staging area where collected data sources is transformed into relevant structures
- Warehouse containing the centralized repository of structured data sets
- Entities that interact with centralized and structured data sets

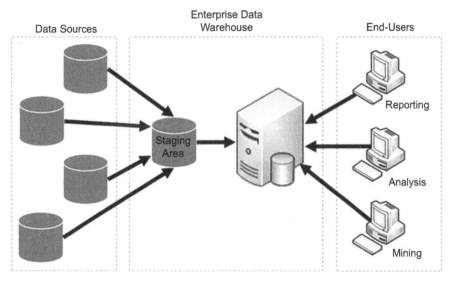

FIGURE I.2

Data warehouse architecture with staging.

ARCHITECTURE WITH DATA MARTS

Illustrated in Figure I.3, this type of architecture is similar to the basic deployment; however, it includes data marts that contain specific structured data sets designed for a particular use case, such as compliance, governance, etc. The components of this architecture include:

- Repositories of data located in the multiple disparate sources
- Warehouse containing the centralized repository of structured data sets
- Data mart of separate structured data sets designed for specific uses
- Entities that interact with specific data marts of information

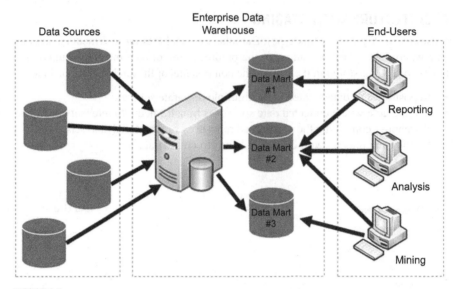

FIGURE I.3

Data warehouse architecture with data marts.

ARCHITECTURE WITH STAGING AND DATA MARTS

Illustrated in Figure I.4, this type of architecture is a combination of all previous architecture where it includes both a staging area and several data marts. The components of this architecture include:

- Repositories of data located in the multiple disparate sources
- Staging area where collected data sources are transformed into relevant structures

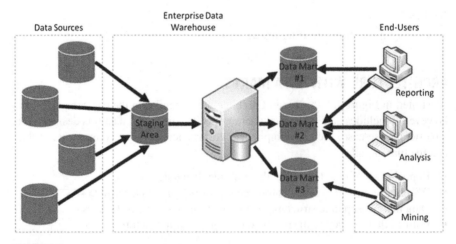

FIGURE I.4

Data warehouse architecture with staging and data marts.

- Warehouse containing the centralized repository of structured data sets
- Data mart of separate structured data sets designed for specific uses
- Entities that interact with specific data marts of information

DESIGN METHODOLOGIES

No matter which EDW architectures best fits an organization's requirements, to successfully design an effective EDW, organizations must understand and analyze their business need for why the system is being developed. Referring back to the analogy of constructing a real building, the EDW owner, architect, and engineer will all have a different perspective on how to achieve the final solution. The different views on how to build the EDW can include the following:

- *Top-down view* supports the selection of relevant data, as identified by current and ongoing business needs, which is necessary for the EDW. This viewpoint provides organizations with a systematic solution with minimal integration issues; however, it can be more expensive because it takes longer to develop and does not provide a great deal of flexibility.
- *Bottom-up view* supports the creation of data marts to provide reporting and analytical capabilities for a specific business process. This viewpoint provides organizations with more flexibility and quicker implementation of the data marts; however, it is problematic when having to integrate the individual data marts into the larger EDW.
- *Data source view* depicts the data being gathered, stored, and managed by the system.
- *Data warehouse view* includes both fact tables[9] and dimension tables[10] representing data stored within the EDW as well as data included to provide context.
- *Business query view* represents the EDW data from the end-use perspective.

By combining each of these viewpoints into a single design plan, a business analysis framework can be created that will represent the different perspectives of how the EDW solution will be constructed. This overall framework guides the organizations in determining how the EDW will actually be constructed to ensure they meet their intended business need(s). Generally, the four steps that must be completed when designing the EDW include the following:

- *Step #1*: Identify a business process to model the EDW after, such as compliance, governance, etc. If the business process spans the entire organization and involves several complex data collections, the suggested EDW architecture is either a basic deployment or with staging area; depending on the need to preprocess collected data. If the analysis is focused on a single business process and is limited to a department, the suggested EDW architectures are those that contain data marts, where implementing a staging area depends on the need to preprocess collected data.

- *Step #2*: Determine the level of granularity for how much detail about the business process will be represented in fact tables. For example, a decision must be made whether each individual record with metadata be recorded, will individual record summaries be recorded, and so on.
- *Step #3*: Select the dimensions, values such as time stamps, that will be stored inside of dimension tables and both how and where these values are associated with records stored inside fact tables.
- *Step #4*: Select the measures, values that are represented as numerical units, which will be stored inside each fact table record.

IMPLEMENTATION FACTORS

Among many other factors, the most common reason why organizations experience implementation failures is because of improper planning and inadequate project management. Before work begins on developing the EDW, thorough consideration needs to be given to some key areas that are essential to the successful implementation of the system.

BUSINESS DRIVEN, NOT TECHNOLOGY-CENTRIC

Business requirements are the primary driver for the use of all technology within an organization. While this should be common knowledge, there continue to be projects that are overshadowed by exploiting the capabilities of a technology instead of focusing on what the business need for using the technology really is. It is important that the designing and planning aspects of the EDW system are completed only after the business requirements have been well established.

With an understanding of the overall requirements, focus can be turned towards planning the development and eventual implementation of the EDW system. Regardless of which architecture model has been selected, it is recommended that the implementation of the EDW should be carefully planned and executed in incremental stages as the system grows and evolves within the organization.

VALUE AND EXPECTATION

In some instances, organizations implement their EDW without having a thorough understanding of the benefits that will be gained from implementing the solution. While the thought of having an EDW is appealing, first and foremost a requirement analysis needs to be completed, as discussed further in Appendix J: Requirements Analysis, to determine if implementing an EDW solution is a worthwhile initiative.

If this assessment identifies that there is a value proposition with implementing an EDW, the benefit(s) need to be measured against the cost to implement the system. This can be completed through a cost–benefit analysis, as discussed in Appendix E: Cost–Benefit Analysis.

RISK ASSESSMENT

Every project has risks that need to be acknowledged and accompanied by mitigation strategies to ensure that those risks do not significantly impact the successful EDW implementation. Completing a risk assessment, as discussed in Appendix G: Risk Assessment, organization can identify and get a better understanding of what factors have potential to impact the project.

BUY OR BUILD

A common sticking point for organizations is whether they invest resources into building their EDW system in-house or to buy a commercial-off-the-shelf (COTS)[11] solution. Realistically, there is a wide range of solutions available today that puts into question why organizations would invest resources to reinvent the wheel and build an in-house solution from the ground up. However, it is important to keep in mind that there is no silver bullet in terms of finding a COTS solution that will meet all the business requirements.

EDW's provide a wide range of functionality which, for the most part, COTS solutions allow for customizations to be made so that organizations can configure the look, feel, and functionality to meet their specific business needs. Performing these customizations is where leveraging internal resources comes into use to further enhance the COTS solutions or to build out elements such as data marts. Organizations need to evaluate their options and find the right balance between in-house development and COTS solutions.

"EGGS-IN-ONE-BASKET"[12] OR "BEST-OF-BREED"[13]

There are a wide range of COTS solutions catering to varying levels of EDW functionality. If a decision is made to purchase a COTS solution, the next option to consider is whether to invest in a complete EDW solution from a single vendor or to use the best COTS solution for the individual EDW functionalities (ie, OLAP, database, repository, etc.). Some considerations that should be noted when selecting a single EDW solution provider include the following:

- A higher level of integration throughout the EDW ecosystem
- Centralized management and support interface exchanges
- Lower total cost of ownership (TCO)[14]
- Common look and feel
- Limited vendor offerings of fully integrated EDW solutions

Alternatively, selecting multiple vendors for specific EDW functionality also comes with its own considerations such as:

- Increased EDW customization to fit business requirements
- Minimal compromises made on technology components
- Acquisition of solutions that are best suited to your organization
- Compatibility between different vendors can be troublesome
- Assurance of cross-vendor support for the overall system

PROJECT PLANNING

At the end of the day, a project is a project and the approach used follows much the same methodology as any technology-based initiative. However, EDW projects are slightly different where they have a much broader project scope, can have more complex architectural designs, and involve many different technologies.

Creating a project charter, as found in the *Templates* section of this book, is an excellent way of communicating the business value of implementing the system. This document should include, at a minimum, the following sections:

- *Introduction*: Describes the problem statement to be addressed, the purpose of the project, scope of the project's deliverables, and defines the intended audience
- *Business justification*: Illustrates the business need for the project and the strategic alignment to the organization's goals
- *Impact and constraints*: Highlights the risks, assumptions, and constraints that have potential to impact the success of the project, mitigating strategies for containing the impact, and dependencies prior to project execution
- *Timing/schedule*: Demonstrates the sequence of tasks that will be completed and highlights the key milestone throughout the timeline
- *Financial statements*: Details both one-time, ongoing funding sources, and financial assumptions
- *Project structure*: Details the executive sponsorship, roles and responsibilities, and both internal and external stakeholders

SUMMARY

An EDW solution is a living and evolving ecosystem that provides data mining, analytical, and reporting benefits throughout an organization when it is first and foremost driven by business requirements. Although its construction can be complex and involves a proportionate amount of moving parts, taking the time to develop a thorough plan to identify and mitigate the risk of failure is resources well spent.

TAXONOMY

1 *Online transaction processing (OLTP) system* is a type of system that manages and facilitates the operations of an application typically focused on data entry.
2 *Online analytical processing (OLAP) system* is a type of system that performs multidimensional analysis of data to provide complex modeling and trend reporting.
3 *Market oriented* is a methodology focused on discovering and meeting the needs and wishes of customers through products.
4 *Entity relationship model* describes the connections between other objects typically used in regard to the organization of data or information aspects.

5 *Application oriented* Is a methodology focused on interactions with complimentary modules that provide analytical or reporting capabilities.

6 *Star model* is a database schema where a central table contains the bulk of data and smaller sets of related table contain values for each linked dimension tables.

7 *Snowflake model* is a database schema where a central table contains the bulk of data and the smaller sets of related tables containing both values for linked dimension tables as well as volumes of data volumes with further linked dimension tables.

8 *Subject oriented* is a methodology focused on building systems that can be used to analyze a particular focus area.

9 *Fact tables* consist of measurements, metrics, or fact of a business process that are located at the center of a data warehouse schema.

10 *Dimension tables* consist of descriptive attributes that are used in support of fact table measurements.

11 *Commercial-off-the-shelf (COTS)* describes items that are available for purchase through the commercial marketplace, including, but not limited to, software or hardware products, installation services, training services.

12 *Eggs-in-one-basket* is a term used to describe the increased risk of losing an investment as a result of concentrating all resources into a single item.

13 *Best-of-breed* is a term used to describe the solution that generates the most value by providing the greatest functionality for a specific niche or subject area.

14 *Total cost of ownership* is a financial estimate to determine the direct and indirect expenses and benefits of an investment.

Appendix J: Requirements Analysis

INTRODUCTION

Generally, requirements must be actionable, measurable, testable, related to a business need or desire and defined at a level of detail that is sufficient for design criteria. They are commonly driven by some type of business need or desire where organizations are looking to improve a specific set of functions or processes.

Requirements analysis is a critical process to toward achieving success in a project. Also referred to as requirements gathering or requirements specifications, it involves a series of steps and activities that allow organizations to determine what conditions must be met during the system design.

THE IMPORTANCE OF REQUIREMENTS

Organizations must ensure that the process of requirements analysis is not confused or mistaken for as being the same with the system design process. Essentially, analysis is concerned with what needs to be done, such as studying the current state of a process or function and determining how it works. On the other hand, design is focused on how it needs to be done, such as applying a particular technology to improve the current state of a process or function.

Knowing the scope of what requirements analysis is, the process is essential in translating business needs or desires into an architectural view than can be used as the basis for systems design. Within the context of the systems development life cycle (SDLC), requirements analysis focuses on identifying gaps within a particular area within the organization and is performed:

- after the organization strategies are thoroughly understood
- before developing architectural design specifications

The process of defining requirements involves giving careful consideration to how they are built. When organizations do not allow sufficient time to ensure that requirements are accurate and complete, the resulting consequences will be a finalized set of requirements that are ambiguous, untestable, and not capable of satisfying the business needs or desires. Ultimately, the effect from these downfalls will lead to an unsuccessful project due to collateral damage such as:

- higher development costs
- schedule slippage
- scope creep
- system defects
- customer dissatisfaction

It is important that organizations define their requirements to be clear, meaningful, effective, and aligned with business needs and desires.

DEFINING REQUIREMENTS

Requirements analysis is centered on addressing the needs and desires of business strategies. From this, the requirements analysis process is performed to translate these needs and desires into a comprehensive architecture model that can be used throughout the organization.

As described in the following sections, requirements analysis encompasses several phases to interpret the business language and arrive at a deliverable solution. Understanding that the methodology used is subjective to the needs of each organizations, the approach illustrated below is intended to provide a simplified workflow to performing requirements analysis.

PHASE #1: DEFINING SCOPE

Similar with how any business project is initiated, boundaries must be set around what business strategy will be assessed. Without determining the scope for which requirements will be identified, the architecture model that will be delivered will not address the business needs and desires resulting in an unsuccessful project as explained previously in this chapter.

Contributing to the scope definition, the following elements must be captured in terms of the specifics that will play a factor in the architectural model.

- *Data*: What facts of significance are used to describe the organization and what do they mean?
- *Activities*: What processes, functions, etc. need to be included in this assessment?
- *Locations*: Where in the organization will the activities be addressed?
- *People and organizations*: What resources are involved in the activities that need to be included in this assessment?
- *Timing*: Which business events are drivers being activities included in this assessment?
- *Motivation*: What objectives, goals, policies, etc. affect the activities included in this assessment?

There are no predefined rules or guidelines that dictate how to define scope; it is subject to every organization's interpretation. Organizations have to rely on their experience and common sense when determining the width and depth of where to set the scope boundaries. At the completion of this phase, a detailed scope statement is produced and will be used as the basis for executing the remaining phases.

PHASE #2: PREPARE ASSESSMENT

Although the scope has already been defined, there has yet to be a plan put together to outline the activities, people, and schedule that will be needed to complete this assessment. In establishing these components, it is important to keep in mind that there is traditionally a trade-off where only two out of three can be maximized.

FIGURE J.1

Priority triad.

To avoid unexpected surprises later on in the process, it is important that the organizations decide what the priorities for this assessment are. Figure J.1 illustrates the three scenarios that will occur from deciding which components are priorities:

- If the goal is to have a shorter schedule and maintain higher quality through increased activities, then there will be an increased cost
- If the goal is to have a shorter schedule and reduce cost, there will be fewer activities resulting in lower quality
- If the goal is to reduce cost and maintain higher quality through increased activities, then there will be a longer schedule

PHASE #3: GATHER REQUIREMENTS

Identifying and capturing a baseline set of requirements must be done in a business language. In order to arrive at a model that encompasses a complete set of business needs and desires, this baseline set of requirements needs to be drawn from various sources throughout the organization; such as:

- operational support documentation
- stakeholder interviews
- formal proposals
- industry best practices
- strategic roadmaps
- (international, federal, local) legal and regulatory requirements

As the baseline set of requirements is being gathered from the multiple sources, it is important to recognize that while they are all related, each requirement is separate and distinct. Generally, requirements can be grouped into one of the following categories:

- *Functional requirements* define features of the deliverable(s) that will specifically meet a business need or desire
- *Operational requirements* describe the "behind the scene" functions needed to keep the deliverable(s) working over time

- *Technical requirements* identify conditions under which the deliverable(s) must function
- *Transitional requirements* outline aspects of the deliverable(s) that must be met to handover support responsibilities

As requirements are identified, each item should be documented in a centralized register that will be used throughout the analysis process, such as a database or spreadsheet. A requirement analysis report template has been provided as a reference in the *Templates* section of this book which includes a matrix which can be used to capture requirements.

PHASE #4: INTERPRET REQUIREMENTS

Using the aggregated set of baseline requirements, stakeholders now need to review what was documented to ensure that proper business language used in the requirements and that they were captured correctly. Depending on the availability and location of stakeholders, performing these reviews in-person might not be possible and alternative methods of meeting can be used, such as conducting interviews, distributing surveys, holding workshops, or conducting focus groups.

Having stakeholders validate and verify the baseline set of requirements at this stage in the process is a critical activity. Not only will stakeholder review ensure that requirements are as clear and concise as possible, but it also helps to eliminate any confusion of having to translate business requirements into technical specifications by:

- not combining separate requirements
- removing subjective wording, ambiguities, or opinions
- avoiding scope creep
- preventing scheduling delays

Following the stakeholder review, it is important that the baseline set of requirements is signed off by all stakeholders as part of the requirements analysis report; discussed further on in this Appendix. Documenting stakeholder agreement is important because these individuals may not be present throughout the remaining phases of the analysis or afterward during the system design process.

PHASE #5: FINALIZE REQUIREMENTS

By now the baseline set of requirements has been agreed to by all stakeholders and can be finalized as the foundation for upcoming planning and architectural design activities. For each requirement that has been accepted, the following additional contexts are needed to determine how it will be actioned and turned into a deliverable.

- *Aligning* the requirement to the scope of the project
- *Categorizing* the requirements based on how they relate to the business needs and desires

- *Prioritizing* the requirements according to the criticality to the business needs and desires by determining if they are:
  - "core" requirements which the deliverable will not be able to function without
  - "essential" requirements which a short-term work-around could be implemented; but in the long-term must be addresses
  - "desirable" requirements which are viewed as the "bells and whistles" that are not critical to the deliverable(s) functionality

As part of the requirement analysis report template provided as a reference in the *Templates* section of this book, the requirements matrix can be used to further expand on the context of each requirement as discussed above.

PHASE #6: PREPARE SPECIFICATION DOCUMENT

The specification document, also viewed as the final report, essentially outlines the organization's understanding of its business needs and desires as related to a specific business strategy. It provides a level of assurance that all stakeholders within the organization understand and agree to the requirements that were captured at that point in time.

It is important that this document is created in a clear and concise business language because it will be used as the basis for subsequent project activities such as design and architectural specifications, statements of work, and testing and validation plans. Because it will be used as a governing document, it is also important that it remains objective by not providing suggestions, solutions, or other information other than that related to the requirements analysis activities. When completed, the specification document will contain enough information that it:

- provides assurance that all business needs and desires have been well understood and translated into clear and concise requirements
- structures the requirements in a way that helps organizations to maintain appropriate control over scope and schedule
- contains sufficient details to serve as input into subsequent design specification activities
- acts as a governing document for the testing and validation activities that will be used to verify the requirements

A requirement analysis report template has been provided as a reference in the *Templates* section of this book.

SUMMARY

Requirements analysis is an essential part of the SDLC process to ensure that the needs and desires of an organization's business strategy are identified and documented as clear and concise as possible. Once completed, the specification document is used as a governing document to direct the subsequent activities of system design.

Appendix K: Investigative Workflow

INTRODUCTION

From the time when the initial event occurs, organizations must follow a consistent and repeatable process that encompasses several stages of information gathering (ie, preserving digital evidence, conducting interviewing), communication (ie, stakeholder reporting, escalations), and documentation (ie, standard operating procedures, incident/case management knowledgebase).

The goal of following a logical investigative process is to reduce the possibility for quick and uninformed decisions to be made at any time. However, understanding that the context of every investigation can be uniquely different, the logical workflow should still provide organizations with the ability to make the best and the most educated decision for what actions are performed next.

The investigative workflow illustrated in Figures K.1–K.4 encompasses each business risk scenario as discussed further in chapter "Define Business Risk Scenarios." While the specific business risk naming conventions have not been

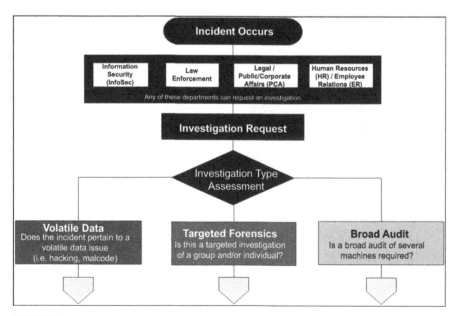

FIGURE K.1

Investigative workflow—process initiation.

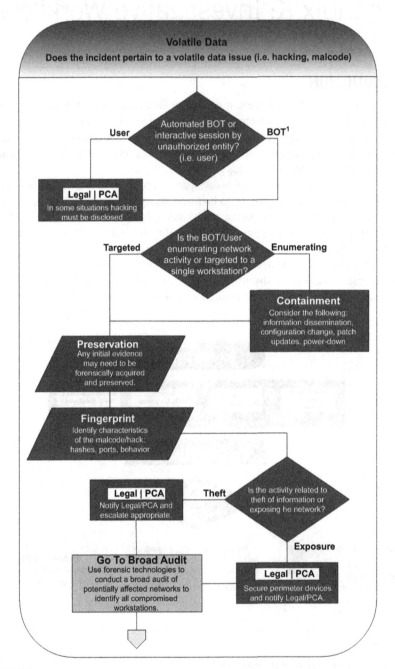

FIGURE K.2

Investigative workflow— volatile data process. *PCA*, public/corporate affairs.

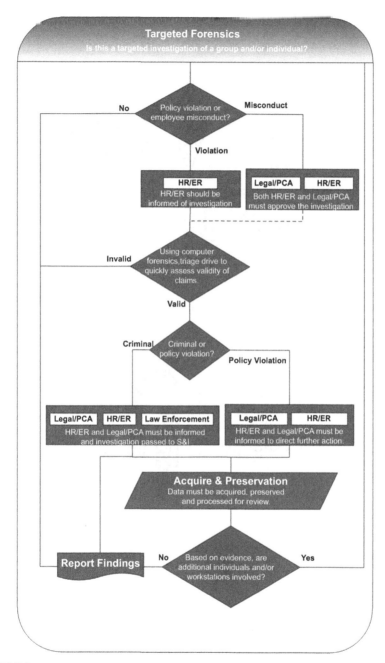

FIGURE K.3

Investigative workflow—targeted forensic process. *HR*, human resources; *ER*, employee relations; *PCA*, public/corporate affairs.

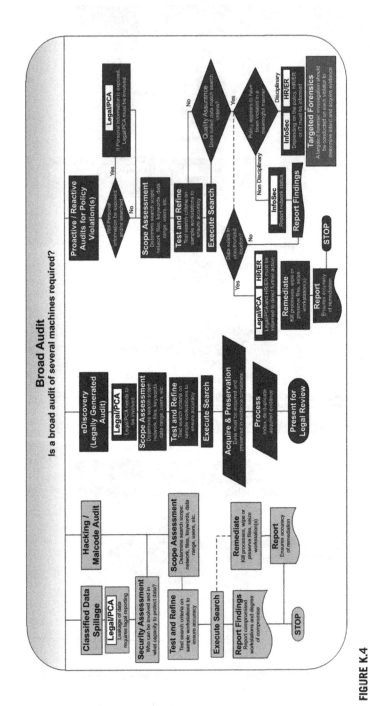

FIGURE K.4

Investigative workflow—broad audit process. *PCA*, public/corporate affairs.

used in the workflow that follows, the methodology and approach takes into consideration the workflow and activities required to address each risk scenario as they occur.

TAXONOMY

1   BOT (short for "robot") is a application that operates as an agent for a user, on behalf of another application, or to simulate human activity.

Templates

INTRODUCTION

This section includes all template materials that are representative and supportive of both digital forensic readiness and business process documentation. The templates provided in this section contain instructions to the author, standardized text, and fields that should be modified and replaced with values specified at the time of writing and include the following:

- Blue italicized text enclosed in square brackets (*[text]*) provide instructions to the author or describes the intent, assumptions, and context for content included in the template document. These fields must be deleted prior to finalizing the template document.
- Blue italicized text enclosed in angle brackets (*<text>*) indicates a field that should be replaced with information specific to a particular section or text within the template document.
- Text and tables in *black* are provided as standardized examples of wording and formats that may be used or modified as needed. These are provided only as reference and/or suggestions to assist in developing the template document; they are not mandatory formats.

When using a template document, the following steps are recommended to perform modifications:

1. Replace all text enclosed in angle brackets (ie, *<Project Name>*) with the correct field values. These angle brackets appear in both the body of the template document as well as in headers and footers.
2. Modify standardized text as appropriate for the template document's specific topic.
3. To update the table of contents, right-click on it and select "Update field" and choose the option "Update entire table."
4. Before submission of the first draft of this document, delete all instructions to the author throughout the entire template document.

Template A: Test Case Document

<Test Case Name>

Test Case Document

<Date>

Presented by:
<team/department name>

Document History

Version	Date	Comments
0.1	*<Date>*	Initial Draft

Approvals

Item Name	Authorizor	Comments
Business Objectives	*<Name & Title>*	*<approval terms or conditions, etc.>*
Test Environment	*<Name & Title>*	*<approval terms or conditions, etc.>*
Test Cases	*<Name & Title>*	*<approval terms or conditions, etc.>*

Table of Contents

Introduction

Overview and Scope

[Provide a summary on the objective of the testing, the tool or equipment name/version, and the business objectives for completing the testing]

This document outlines the results of assessing *<tool or equipment name/version>* for use in the digital forensics investigative workflow; focusing specifically on:

- *<high-level listing of focus areas for this testing>*

Summary of Findings

[Summarize the overall results from completing the test cases and note key observations and/or findings]

Conclusions / Recommendations

[Draw conclusions from the test results and provide recommendations, where/if needed, with justifications]

Product Overview

<Vendor Name>

[A brief background of the company and the solutions they offer; including links to online resources]

<Product Name>

[Details about the tool or equipment being tested; including, but not limited to: product name, current version, release date, key functionality]

Test Environment

Environment Baseline

[Administrative, physical and technical specifications describing the applications, systems, processes, resources, etc. used as the controlled configurations for performing testing]

Flow of Events

[Describe the flow of events that would be expected in normal conditions as well as any potential alternate flow of events, and exceptions/errors that may occur]

Assumptions

The following circumstances and/or outcomes have been assumed for the duration of this testing:

- *<detailed listing of assumptions>*

Test Cases

<Phase Name>

Step	Date	Step Description	Test Data	Expected Results	Status	Comments
01.						
02.						
03.						
04.						
05.						
End						

<Phase Name>

Step	Date	Step Description	Test Data	Expected Results	Status	Comments
06.						
07.						
08.						
09.						
10.						
End						

Template B: Investigator Logbook

Case/Incident	Date:	Description:	Investigator:

Time	Action(s) Taken

Prepared By   Signature

Template C: Chain of Custody Tracking Form

Case/Incident: _____ Exhibit/Property Number: _____

Date Acquired (mm/dd/yy): ____ / ____ / ____ Time Acquired (24hr): ____ : ____

Location of Seized: _____ Seized By: _____

Description of Item (ex. Model, Quantity, Serial #, Condition, Markings, etc):

Notes / Additional Comments:

Chain of Custody

Date / Time	Released By (Name & Signature)	Received By (Name & Signature)	Comments:

Authorization for Evidence Disposal

This item is no longer needed as evidence and is authorized for disposal through the following method:

☐ Return to Owner ☐ Destruction ☐ Donation ☐ Other_____

Release By: _____ Signature: _____ Date: _____

Witness to Evidence Disposal

I, _____, witnessed on the _____ day of _____ 20__ the disposal of
this item as performed by _____ in my presence.

Witness: _____ Signature: _____ Date: _____

Evidence Release to Lawful Owner

This item is no longer needed as evidence and has been released by me, _____,
to its lawful owner

Owner _____

Address: _____

Telephone Number: (_____) _____

Signature: _____ Date: _____

Template D: Investigative Final Report

<<Case Number and Name>>

Investigative Final Report

<<Date>>

Presented by:
<<team/department name>>

Document History

Version	Date	Comments
0.1	*<Date>*	Initial Draft

Table of Contents

Executive Summary

Background

[Description of the incident including: when it occurred, how it was detected, who identified it, where it tookplace, what happened, and who authorized the investigation]

Summary of Findings

[Summarize the significant findingsof the investigation]

Conclusions

[Establish conclusions from the investigative findings and provide expert opinions where/when needed]

Investigative Details

Chain of Evidence

[Details describing where evidence was identified, techniques used to seize it, methods used to transport it to a secure location, and its continuous custody records]

Gathering of Evidence

[Methodologies, tools, and equipment used to collect and preserve digital evidence]

Processing of Evidence

[Methodologies, tools, and equipment used to perform examination of digital evidence]

Analysis of Evidence

[Details describing the meaningful, relevant, and factual findings from the analysis of digital evidence]

Addendums

References

[Details of professional reference used during the investigation to validate and/or verify findings]

Glossary

[Definition of technical terms, phrases, or words used throughout the final report]

Template E: Service Catalog

Service Catalog - ABC Company							
Service Name	**Department**	**Service Owner**	**Service Manager**	**Description**	**Category**	**Group**	**Family**
[Name of the service being offered]	*[Name of department owning the service]*	*[Name of the Executive Management funding the service]*	*[Name of the individual functioning as the key contact for the service]*	*[Detailed description of the service]*	*[Illustrates the individual service function where the service aligns]*	*[Illustrates the individual business function where the service aligns]*	*[Illustrates the core business function where the service aligns]*

Unit Cost / Driver / Year			Service Cost per Year		
Driver	**Total Driver Units**	**Fixed Cost per Unit**	**Total Operational Costs**		**Total Service Cost**
[Illustrated the Fixed/Variable units used to measure activity of the service]	*[Number of Fixed/Variable units contained within the service]*	*[Calculated as: (Total fixed costs + Total variable costs) / Total units produced]*	*[Costs associated with fixed funding elements; including software licensing and capital expenditures]*		*[Calculated as: Total fixed costs + Total variable costs]*

Business Line #1			Business Line #2			
Department #1	**Department #2**	**Department #3**	**Department #1**	**Department #2**	**Department #3**	**Total %**
[Percentage this department utilizes the service activities]	*[Percentage this department utilizes the service activities]*	*[Percentage this department utilizes the service activities]*	*[Percentage this department utilizes the service activities]*	*[Percentage this department utilizes the service activities]*	*[Percentage this department utilizes the service activities]*	*[Total percentage the service is utilized by departments specified]*

Template F: Business Case Document

<Project Name>
Business Case

Recommendation

[Insert a new signature line for each additional stakeholders providing approval. The signature of each stakeholder confirms that all impacted business lines are informed and consulted. Approval of the business case provides agreement by stakeholders for shared responsibility of both one-time/ongoing cost and acceptance of project benefits. <u>Delete this comment once completed</u>.]

We recommend approval of this business case for *<Project Name>* initiative.

_____   _____
<Name – Technology Sponsor>   *<Name – Business Sponsor>*
<Title/Department>   *<Title/Department>*

I / We concur:

_____
<Name – Executive Sponsor>
<Title/Department>

Date Prepared   *<Date>*
Presented By   *<team/department name>*

Document History

Version	Date	Comments
0.1	<date>	Initial Draft

Table of Contents

1. Executive Summary

[This section highlights the key points required to demonstrate the business rational for decision-makers. It includes a summary of the current situation (i.e. risks/issues), identifies what needs to be done to remediate this situation, how the solution aligns to business strategies, and high-level illustration of costs and benefits. The executive summary should be no longer than one page in length. Delete this comment once completed.]

The cost and benefits illustrated below are in *<specify financial currency>*.

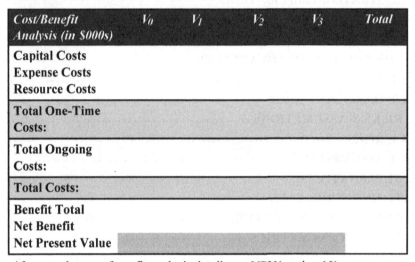

Cost/Benefit Analysis (in $000s)	V_0	V_1	V_2	V_3	*Total*
Capital Costs					
Expense Costs					
Resource Costs					
Total One-Time Costs:					
Total Ongoing Costs:					
Total Costs:					
Benefit Total					
Net Benefit					
Net Present Value					

*for complete cost/benefit analysis details see NPV(section 10)

2. Business Analysis

2.1. Background/History

[Describe the risk/issues that need to be addressed, reasoning for why the recommended solution needs to be implemented, and implications of not approving the solution. <u>Delete this comment once completed</u>.]

2.2. Strategic Implications

Organizational Focus

☐ Revenue/Cost   ☐ Risk Mgt.   ☐ Regulatory   ☐ Strategic
☐ Operational

[Select one or several of the strategic focus the recommended solution has on the organization. <u>Delete this comment once completed</u>.]

This initiative aligns with the business strategy by:

[Provide justifications, in bullet form, to illustrate the details of how the recommended solution aligns with the selected strategic focus. Specify details of how the solution will be implemented to support business functions throughout the entire organization and enhancements to operational efficiencies. Briefly highlight the impact on business plans, budgets, or forecasts. <u>Delete this comment once completed</u>.]

2.3. Purpose/Scope

[Document the objectives for evaluating alternatives specific to the details specified in Section 2.1. If this project is a subset of a larger project, ensure an overview of the larger project is provided. <u>Delete this comment once completed</u>.]

2.4. Business Need/Justification

[Elaborate in details on the business justifications specified in Section 2.2 including any internal and external considerations that will influence the need for the recommended solution. <u>Delete this comment once completed</u>.]

3. Advantages/Disadvantages

[Briefly illustrate the advantages/disadvantages of the recommended solution. <u>Delete this comment once completed.</u>]

3.1. Advantages:

[Provide advantages, in bullet form, to illustrate positive aspects of implementing the recommended solution. <u>Delete this comment once completed.</u>]

3.2. Disadvantages:

[Provide disadvantages, in bullet form, to illustrate negative aspects of implementing the recommended solution. <u>Delete this comment once completed.</u>]

4. Risks & Assumptions

4.1. Risks

[Describe the significant events or conditions that, if they occur, will have either positive or negative effects on the objectives specified in Section 2.3. <u>Delete this comment once completed.</u>]

4.2. Assumptions

[Describe the circumstance and outcomes that if taken for granted in the absence of concrete information will have either positive or negative effects on the objectives specified in Section 2.3. <u>Delete this comment once completed.</u>]

5. Alternatives

[Document the recommended <u>and alternative</u> course of action for this project. The last alternative to be specified in this section is DO NOTHING. Complete details about the recommended and alternative course of action can be documented in Appendix A. <u>Delete this comment once completed.</u>]

- Alternative 1: *<summarize the recommended course of action>*
- Alternative 2: *<summarize the alternative course of action>*
- Alternative 3: Do Nothing

6. Timing/Schedules

[Include an implementation date for the project. Use multiple rows if the project is being implemented in several phases. Include a high level schedule of the projected implementation plan; critical dates including additional funding checkpoints and any interdependencies with other initiatives. <u>Delete thiscomment once completed</u>.]

Implementation/Phase/Major Milestone	Target Date (Month, Year)
<specify the name of the phase>	*<specify the delivery year/month>*
<specify the name of the phase>	*<specify the delivery year/month>*

7. Governance Structure

[Document the controls and mechanisms put in place to ensure compliance with rules and regulations for how the project functions. While the roles included in the governance structure may not initially have names allocated, at a minimum representation from different levels throughout the organizations should be specified: Executive Sponsor, Business Sponsor, Technology Sponsor, and where needed those located in other business areas of the organization such as project management, back offices, operational support. Complete details about the governance structure can be documented in Appendix B. <u>Delete this comment once completed</u>.]

8. Key Success Metrics

[Baselines that will be used for measuring the success criteria against each test case including the criteria for measuring success or failure, scenario for how the test will be executed, tools or equipment subject to the test, and the business value for conducting the test case. Delete this comment once completed.]

#	Objective	Key Success Metric	Target	Baseline	Data Source
1					
2					
3					

[Details about the type of information to be provided in the above table is provided below:

Objective: description of benefit to be realized (i.e. improved operational efficiencies)

Key Success Metric: the item that will be measured(i.e. reduced work hours)

Target: the targetof change, either percentage or actual value, which must be measureable

Baseline: the starting point, either percentage or actual value, used to measure against

Data Source: the origin for where metrics used to measure success will be provided (i.e. reporting system)

Delete this comment once completed.]

9. Funding

[Indicate the funding source(s) that have been allocated and are available within approved budgets. If necessary, provide alternate funding options where funding is not allocated or available. Delete this comment once completed.]

10. Financial Analysis

[Specify for each funding year: the year, total $$ amount to be funded, the business area providing funding and the budget source for where funding is to be drawn. Delete this comment once completed.]

Details of cost/benefit analysis for the project are provided in the NPV schedule found in Appendix C.

[Complete details about the best and worst case scenarios identified through sensitivity analysis can be documented in Appendix C. Delete this comment once completed.]

10.1. Financial Assumptions

[Describe assumptions used during the financial analysis including the drivers being costs/benefits, business areas accepting ongoing costs or receiving benefits, justification for making the assumption, and the effect to the project if the assumption proves to be false. Complete details about assumption made during sensitivity analysis can also be documented in Appendix C. Delete this comment once completed.]

10.2. Cost Allocation

[Using the service catalogue as the authoritative source, indicate how ongoing funding of the implemented solution will be allocated across business areas sharing the costs. Delete this comment once completed.]

			1st Year Costs(V_0)		Ongoing Costs		
Business Line	% Total Allocation	$ Total Allocation	One-Time	Ongoing	V_1	V_2	V_3

Cost Driver Statement

[Describe the cost allocation driver, as documented in the service catalogue, used to calculate the business line cost allocations. Delete this comment once completed.]

11. Contact Persons

[List the individuals who should be contacted for questions regarding the content of this document. Complete details about the roles and responsibilities for individuals involved with this project can be documented in Appendix B. Delete this comment once completed.]

In case of any questions, contact the following individuals:

Name	Title	Email	Phone Number

12. Appendix A – Alternative Analysis

[Describe the alternative recommendations that were considered and have been discarded as the final solution. Explain the justifications for why these alternative recommendations were not identified as the final solution. <u>Delete this comment once completed.</u>]

13. Appendix B – Roles & Responsibilities

[Provide detailed contact information for those individuals who are involved in this project as part of either the Governance Structure or as a Contact Person. Specify the role played by the individual, reporting hierarchy, and escalation process. <u>Delete this comment once completed.</u>]

14. Appendix C – Sensitivity Analysis

[Insert a print screen of the NPV. Provide details about the best and worst case scenarios identified during the sensitivity analysis. <u>Delete this comment once completed.</u>]

Template G: Net Present Value

Cost/Benefit Analysis	V_0	V_1	V_2	V_3	Total
<insert project name>					
One-Time Costs					
Capital Costs:					
<insert line for each captial cost>	$ -	$ -	$ -	$ -	$ -
<insert line for each captial cost>	$ -	$ -	$ -	$ -	$ -
Total Capital	$ -	$ -	$ -	$ -	$ -
Expense Costs:					
<insert line for each expense>	$ -	$ -	$ -	$ -	$ -
<insert line for each expense>	$ -	$ -	$ -	$ -	$ -
Total Expenses	$ -	$ -	$ -	$ -	$ -
Resource Workdays (V_0 wkd V_1 wkd V_2 wkd V_3 wkd)					
<insert line for each busines line>	$ -	$ -	$ -	$ -	$ -
<insert line for each busines line>	$ -	$ -	$ -	$ -	$ -
Total Resource Workdays	$ -	$ -	$ -	$ -	$ -
Total One-Time Costs (Future Value)	$ -	$ -	$ -	$ -	$ -
Total One-Time Costs (Present Value)	$ -	$ -	$ -	$ -	$ -
Ongoing Costs					
<insert line for each ongoing cost>	$ -	$ -	$ -	$ -	$ -
<insert line for each ongoing cost>	$ -	$ -	$ -	$ -	$ -
Total Ongoing Costs (Future Value)	$ -	$ -	$ -	$ -	$ -
Total Ongoing Costs (Present Value)	$ -	$ -	$ -	$ -	$ -
Benefits					
<insert line for each benefit>	$ -	$ -	$ -	$ -	$ -
<insert line for each benefit>	$ -	$ -	$ -	$ -	$ -
Total Benefits (Future Value)	$ -	$ -	$ -	$ -	$ -
Total Benefits (Present Value)	$ -	$ -	$ -	$ -	$ -
Net Benefits / (Costs)	$ -	$ -	$ -	$ -	$ -
Cumulative Benefits / (Costs)	$ -	$ -	$ -	$ -	$ -
Net Present Value	$0.00				
Benefit / Cost Ratio	0.00				

Template H: Threat/Risk Assessment Report

\<Initiative Name\>

Threat Risk Assessment Report

\<Date\>

Presented by:
\<team/department name\>

Document History

Version	Date	Comments
0.1	*<Date>*	Initial Draft

Table of Contents

Executive Summary

[Provides a high-level summary of the threat assessment including why it was performed, key findings, and any conclusions or recommendations to be made. Delete this comment once completed.]

Assessment Details

Risk Statements

[A statement justifying the final and overall risk score of the threat modelling exercise. Delete this comment once completed.]

Confidentiality	Integrity	Availability	Authorization	Authentication	Non-Repudiation
<Score (i.e. Critical, High, Medium, Low>	<Score (i.e. Critical, High, Medium, Low>	<Score (i.e. Critical, High, Medium, Low>	<Score (i.e. Critical, High, Medium, Low>	<Score (i.e. Critical, High, Medium, Low>	<Score (i.e. Critical, High, Medium, Low>

Methodology

[Explanation of the stages, phases, steps, and processes used throughout the threat modelling exercise. Delete this comment once completed.]

Assumptions

[Identifies circumstances and/or outcomes that have been taken for granted without. Delete this comment once completed.]

Threat Tree Workflows

Threat *<#X: ThreatName>*

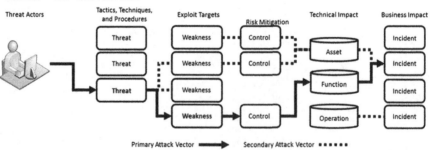

Threat Assessment Matrix

[Documents the details of each threat as relates to the security principle it affects.
Delete this comment once completed.]

Confidentiality Threats

Unauthorized viewing or disclosure of information that compromises privacy and/
or secrecy.

UID	Threat	Inherent Scoring (Critical / High / Med / Low)	Mitigating Controls (technical / administrative / physical)	Residual Risk (description)	Residual Scoring (Critical / High / Med / Low)

Integrity Threats

Unauthorized additions, changes or deletions that affect the completeness,
accuracy, authenticity, timeliness or currency of data or information.

UID	Threat	Inherent Scoring (Critical / High / Med / Low)	Mitigating Controls (technical / administrative / physical)	Residual Risk (description)	Residual Scoring (Critical / High / Med / Low)

Availability Threats

Interruptions in service that lead to loss of service for a longer period of time than
is acceptable, loss of a portion of expected functionality, degradation of response
time to an unacceptable level, missed delivery deadlines for required reports or
loss of use of resources (even though related software is functioning).

UID	Threat	Inherent Scoring (Critical / High / Med / Low)	Mitigating Controls (technical / administrative / physical)	Residual Risk (description)	Residual Scoring (Critical / High / Med / Low)

Continuity Threats
Major interruption of facilities, such that a loss of processing capability is
experienced that will last for an unacceptable period of time.

UID	Threat	Inherent Scoring (Critical / High / Med / Low)	Mitigating Controls (technical / administrative / physical)	Residual Risk (description)	Residual Scoring (Critical / High / Med / Low)

Authentication Threats

Proper identification of users and process requesting access into objects and assets.

UID	Threat	Inherent Scoring (Critical / High / Med / Low)	Mitigating Controls (technical / administrative / physical)	Residual Risk (description)	Residual Scoring (Critical / High / Med / Low)

Authorization Threats

Explicitly granting permissions to users or processes in order to read, write, or execute target information or processes.

UID	Threat	Inherent Scoring (Critical / High / Med / Low)	Mitigating Controls (technical / administrative / physical)	Residual Risk (description)	Residual Scoring (Critical / High / Med / Low)

Non-Repudiation Threats

Assurance that a user or process canntot deny the read, write, or execute access into target information or systems.

UID	Threat	Inherent Scoring (Critical / High / Med / Low)	Mitigating Controls (technical / administrative / physical)	Residual Risk (description)	Residual Scoring (Critical / High / Med / Low)

Template I: Data Source Inventory Matrix

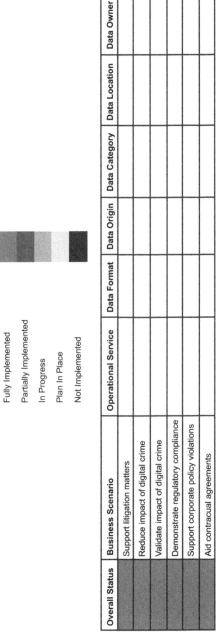

IMPLEMENTATION STATUS

Fully Implemented

Partially Implemented

In Progress

Plan In Place

Not Implemented

Overall Status	Business Scenario	Operational Service	Data Format	Data Origin	Data Category	Data Location	Data Owner
	Support litigation matters						
	Reduce impact of digital crime						
	Validate impact of digital crime						
	Demonstrate regulatory compliance						
	Support corporate policy violations						
	Aid contracual agreements						

Business Use Case	Technology Name	Technology Vendor	Technology Owner	Status	Status Details	Action Plan

Template J: Project Charter Document

<Project/Initiative Name>
Project Charter

Recommendation

[Insert a new signature line for each additional stakeholders providing approval. The signature of each stakeholder confirms that all impacted business lines are informed and consulted. Approval of this project charter provides agreement by stakeholders for shared responsibility of deliverables scope, schedule, and cost of this project. <u>Delete this comment once completed.</u>]

We recommend approval of this business case for *<Project Name>* initiative.

_____   _____
 <Name – Technology Sponsor>   *<Name – Business Sponsor>*
 <Title/Department>   *<Title/Department>*

I / We concur:

_____
 <Name – Executive Sponsor>
 <Title/Department>

Date Prepared	*<Date>*
Presented By	*<team/department name>*

Document History

Version	Date	Comments
0.1	<date>	Initial Draft

Table of Contents

1. Executive Summary

[This section highlights the key points required to demonstrate the business rational for decision-makers. It includes a summary of the current situation (i.e. risks/issues), identifies what needs to be done to remediate this situation, how the project aligns to business strategies, and a high-level illustration of costs and benefits. The executive summary should be no longer than one page in length. Delete this comment once completed.]

The cost and benefits illustrated below are in *<specify financial currency>*.

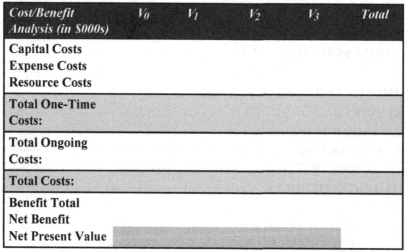

Cost/Benefit Analysis (in $000s)	V_0	V_1	V_2	V_3	Total
Capital Costs					
Expense Costs					
Resource Costs					
Total One-Time Costs:					
Total Ongoing Costs:					
Total Costs:					
Benefit Total					
Net Benefit					
Net Present Value					

*for complete cost/benefit analysis details see NPV(section 10)

2. Introduction

[This section documents the high-level summary about the project. If this project is a subset of a larger project, ensure an overview of the larger project is provided. Delete this comment once completed.]

2.1. Background/History

[This section describes the details of the problem statement that will be addressed, the reasoning for why the project must be executed, and the implications of not completing this project. Delete this comment once completed.]

2.2. Purpose

This project charter documents and tracks the information required by stakeholders and decision maker(s) to approve project funding. This document also includes the needs, scope, justification, and resource commitments so project sponsors have necessary information to determine if the project will proceed or not.

The intended audience of this project charter is the project sponsor and senior leadership.

2.3. Project Scope

[This section explains what deliverables will be produced through this project. Delete this comment once completed.]

The following are considered in-scope deliverables as part of this project:

#	Business Functionality
1	*<detail the business functionality to be delivered>*
2	*<detail the business functionality to be delivered>*

#	Technical Functionality
1	*<detail the technical functionality to be delivered>*
2	*<detail the technical functionality to be delivered>*

2.3.1. Out-of-Scope

[This section explains what deliverables will not be produced through this project. Delete this comment once completed.]

The following are considered in-scope deliverables as part of this project:

#	**Business Functionality**
1	*<detail the business functionality to be delivered>*
2	*<detail the business functionality to be delivered>*

#	**Technical Functionality**
1	*<detail the technical functionality to be delivered>*
2	*<detail the technical functionality to be delivered>*

3. Business Justification

[Elaborate in detail the justifications including any internal and external considerations that will influence the need for executing this project. Delete this comment once completed.]

3.1. Strategic Alignment

[For each goal this project will achieve, illustrate the details of its priority, how it alignments with the organizations strategic focus, and any additional comments decision makers need to know. Delete this comment once completed.]

Goal	Priority	Focus	Comments
<Goal description>	☐ High ☐ Medium ☐ Low ☐ Not Applicable	☐ Revenue/Cost ☐ Risk Mgt. ☐ Regulatory ☐ Strategic ☐ Operational	*<Goal details>*
<Goal description>	☐ High ☐ Medium ☐ Low ☐ Not Applicable	☐ Revenue/Cost ☐ Risk Mgt. ☐ Regulatory ☐ Strategic ☐ Operational	*<Goal details>*

4. Impact and Constraints

4.1. Risks

[Describe the significant events or conditions that, if they occur, will have an effect on the project. <u>Delete this comment once completed</u>.]

Risk	Severity	Mitigation
\<Risk description>	☐ High ☐ Medium ☐ Low	*\<Risk mitigating controls>*
\<Risk description>	☐ High ☐ Medium ☐ Low	*\<Risk mitigating controls>*

4.2. Assumptions

The following circumstances and outcomes, which if taken for granted in the absence of concrete information, will have an effect on this project:

- *\<Assumption description>*
- *\<Assumption description>*

4.3. Constraints

The following limitations and restrictions must be taken into consideration prior to the execution of this project :

- *\<Constraint description>*
- *\<Constraint description>*

4.4. Dependencies

The following preceding element must be in place prior to the execution of this project:

- *\<Dependency description>*
- *\<Dependency description>*

5. Timing/Schedules

[Include an implementation date for the project and use multiple rows if the project is being implemented in several phases. Include a high level schedule of the projected implementation plan; critical dates including additional funding checkpoints and any interdependencies with other initiatives. Delete this comment once completed.]

Implementation/Phase	Target Date (Month, Year)
<specify the name of the phase>	*<specify the delivery year/month>*
<specify the name of the phase>	*<specify the delivery year/month>*

5.1. Milestones

[Key deliverables that will be used for measuring the project's success or failure. Delete this comment once completed.]

Deliverable	Target Date (Month, Year)	Success Metric
<specify the devlierable	*<specify the delivery year/month>*	*<specify how success is measured>*

6. Financial Statement

[Indicate the funding source(s) that have been allocated and are available within approved budgets. If necessary, provide alternate funding options where funding is not allocated or available. Delete this comment once completed.]

6.1. Funding Source

[Specify for each funding year: the year, total $$ amount to be funded, the business area providing funding and the budget source for where funding is to be drawn. Delete this comment once completed.]

Details of cost/benefit analysis for the project are provided in the NPV schedule found in Appendix C.
[Complete details about the best and worst case scenarios identified through sensitivity analysis can be documented in Appendix C. Delete this comment once completed.]

6.2. Financial Assumptions

[Describe assumptions used during the financial analysis including the drivers being costs/benefits, business areas accepting ongoing costs or receiving benefits, justification for making the assumption, and the effect to the project if the assumption proves to be false. Complete details about assumption made during sensitivity analysis can also be documented in Appendix C. Delete this comment once completed.]

7. Project Structure

[Document the controls and mechanisms put in place to ensure compliance with rules and regulations for how the project functions. While the roles included in the governance structure may not initially have names allocated, at a minimum representation from different levels throughout the organizations should be specified: Executive Sponsor, Business Sponsor, Technology Sponsor, and where needed those located in other business areas of the organization such as project management, back offices, operational support. Complete details about the governance structure can be documented in Appendix B. Delete this comment once completed.]

7.1. Contact Persons

[List the individuals who should be contacted for questions regarding the content of this document. Complete details about the roles and responsibilities for individuals involved with this project can be documented in Appendix B. Delete this comment once completed.]

In case of any questions, contact the following individuals:

Name	Title	Email	Phone Number
<full name>	*<job title>*	*<business email address>*	*<business phone number>*

8. Appendix A – Alternative Analysis

[Describe the alternative recommendations that were considered and have been discarded as the final solution. Explain the justifications for why these alternative recommendations were not identified as the final solution. Delete this comment once completed.]

9. Appendix B – Roles & Responsibilities

[The matrix below contains an example of common project roles and accompanying responsibilities. Depending on the organization, the roles outlined below may or may not be required or responsibilities distributed to other roles. Regardless, within the matrix below must be assigned an individual who will function in each specific role. Delete this comment once completed.]

Project Role	Responsibilities	Assigned To
Project Sponsor	• Has ultimate authority over the project • Is responsible for the project's overall success • Approves changes to the scope and objectives • Provides all funding approvals • Approves budget-related deliverables • Controls business aspects • Assists in developing the charter and plans • Makes user resources available • Approves delivered products • Assists in tracking action items and budgets • Responsible for functional quality	*<specify the individual assigned to this role and related duties>*
Project Manager	• Controls the day-to-day aspects of the project • Develops and maintains the charter and plans • Executes formal reviews and management reviews • Tracks and closes issues, action items, and budgets • Helps resolve issues and change requests • Responsible for the quality of all deliverables	*<specify the individual assigned to this role and related duties>*

Team Leader	• Manages one or more functional aspects • Helps the project manager with formal reviews and management reviews • Helps research issues and change requests • Helps the project manager create the work breakdown structure for his or her functional area • Helps the project manager develop the scope and estimates for his or her functional area • Maintains the scope, estimates, and work plans for his or her area • Tracks action items related to his or her functional area • Ensures the proper reporting of status by his or her team members	*<specify the individual assigned to this role and related duties>*
Business Area Team Leader	• Responsible for the technical quality of deliverables assigned to his or her functional area	*<specify the individual assigned to this role and related duties>*
Procurement Officer	• Liaises and coordinates all procurement and contract management activities	*<specify the individual assigned to this role and related duties>*
Financial Officer	• Provides the financial information needed to manage the project • Helps the project manager to define the budget, estimates, and allocations • Helps the project manager with the tracking and reporting of costs and expenditures against budget	*<specify the individual assigned to this role and related duties>*
Business Analyst	• Documents and maintains models of business requirements • Documents and analyzes business processes using value-added or non-value-added, process modelling tools, cost-time charts, and root cause analysis	*<specify the individual assigned to this role and related duties>*

Project Management Officer	• Ensures effective communications about the project across the organization • Helps the project teams create a quality management approach and plan • Provides support to the project sponsor and project manager • Assists in developing divisional implementation plans • Establishes standards (where necessary) for tool usage and project management • Reviews project performance	*<specify the individual assigned to this role and related duties>*
Subject Matter Expert (SME)	• Exhibits the highest level of expertise in performing a specialized job, task, or skill within the organization • Understands a business process or area well enough to answer questions from people in other groups • Explains the current process to the project team and then answers their questions • Has in-depth knowledge of the subject • Represents the users' area in identifying current or future procedures	*<specify the individual assigned to this role and related duties>*
Senior Review Board	• Approves project investments • Reviews the business rationale, projects, and resources • Prioritizes projects based on specific criteria • Resolves all cross-project issues • Reviews all cross-divisional issues	*<specify the individual assigned to this role and related duties>*

Executive Steering Committee	• Discusses and resolves issues that cannot be resolved by the project team • Reviews all budget-related information regarding deliverables for the project • Is responsible for organization-wide communications • Provides guidance and mentoring to the project sponsors, project manager, and teams • Ensures that requirements of the business are adequately represented to the individual projects • Represents all affected business areas as determined by the project sponsor and project manager (the executive sponsor extends invitations to members) • Reviews and makes recommendations on scope changes • Monitors project progress	*\<specify the individual assigned to this role and related duties\>*

10. Appendix C – Sensitivity Analysis

[Insert a print screen of the NPV. Provide details about the best and worst case scenarios identified during the sensitivity analysis. <u>Delete this comment once completed.</u>]

Template K: Requirements Specification Document

<Project/Initiative Name>
Requirements Specifications

Recommendation

[Insert a new signature line for each additional stakeholders providing approval. The signature of each stakeholder confirms that all impacted business lines are informed and consulted. Approval of this requirements specification document provides agreement by stakeholders for shared responsibility of the business and technical requirements. <u>Delete this comment once completed.</u>]

We recommend approval of this business case for *<Project Name>* initiative.

<Name – Technology Sponsor>
<Title/Department>

<Name – Business Sponsor>
<Title/Department>

I / We concur:

<Name – Executive Sponsor>
<Title/Department>

Date Prepared   *<Date>*
Presented By   *<team/department
                    name>*

Document History

Version	Date	Comments
0.1	*<Date>*	Initial Draft

Table of Contents

1. Introduction

1.1. Purpose

This requirement specifications report documents and tracks the activities performed to determine the needs and/or desires for the architectural design of *<Specify the system name>*.

This document also includes an overview of the assessment methodology used and details the findings of the requirements analysis so stake holders have necessary information to build system architectural designs.

1.2. Scope

[This section explains what business strategies will drive the results of this assessment. Delete this comment once completed.]

The following are considered in-scope deliverables as part of this project:

- *<Insert in-scope strategy>*
- *<Insert in-scope strategy>*

1.2.1. Out-of-Scope

[This section explains what business strategies will not drive the results of this assessment. Delete this comment once completed.]

The following are considered in-scope deliverables as part of this project:

- *<Insert out-of-scope strategy>*
- *<Insert out-of-scope strategy>*

2. Business Need

2.1. Benefits

[This section describes the benefit(s) to be achieved and the justification(s) for completing the assessment. Delete this comment once completed.]

2.2. Audience

[Modify the table in this section based on the individuals who have a vested interest in the outcome of this assessment; such as Executive Management, Subject Matter Experts, IT Support, or Sales. Delete this comment once completed.]

The intended audience of this requirements specification document includes the following:

- *<Insert the business lines or organizational role>*
- *<Insert the business lines or organizational role>*

2.3. Stakeholders

[This section lists the specific individuals and/or business lines who will participate either directly or indirectly in the completion of this assessment. The stakeholders listed in the table below are provided as examples and should be modified to match those individuals and/or groups specific to the organization. Delete this comment once completed.]

Stakeholder Group	Role
Chief Executive	• Functions as the overall champion for completing this assessment • Provides general sponsorship
Other executives	• Functions as an additional champion for completing this assessment • Provides mutual sponsorship
IT groups	• Concerned with data availability, definition, control and accessibility.
Business Heads	• Governs consistency between their own reporting and any consolidated reporting.
Head office departments	• Have interest in ensuring common data definitions, accounting methodologies and software choices.

3. Impact and Constraints

3.1. Risks

[Describe the significant events or conditions that, if they occur, will have an effect on this assessment. Delete this comment once completed.]

Risk	Severity	Mitigation
<Risk description>	☐ High ☐ Medium ☐ Low	*<Risk mitigating controls>*

3.2. Assumptions

The following circumstances and outcomes, taken for granted in the absence of concrete information, have effected this assessment:

- *<Assumption description>*
- *<Assumption description>*

3.3. Constraints

The following limitations and restrictions have been taken into consideration prior to the execution of this assessment:

- *<Constraint description>*
- *< Constraint description>*

3.4. Dependencies

The following preceding elements were performed prior to the execution of this assessment:

- *<Dependency description>*
- *<Dependency description>*

4. Timing/Schedules

[Include an implementation date for the project and use multiple rows if the project is being implemented in several phases. Include a high level schedule of the projected implementation plan; critical dates including additional funding checkpoints and any interdependencies with other initiatives. Delete this comment once completed.]

Implementation/Phase	Target Date (Month, Year)
<specify the name of the phase>	*<specify the delivery year/month>*

4.1. Milestones

[Describe the key deliverables that will be used for measuring the project's success or failure. Delete this comment once completed.]

Deliverable	Target Date (Month, Year)	Success Metric
<specify the deliverable>	*<specify the delivery year/month>*	*<specify how success is measured>*

5 Assessment Methodology

The section outlines the methodology followed to gather and validate the requirements in support of the business strategies described in Section 1.2.

5.1. Reference Materials

In support of this assessment, the reference materials specified in the table below were used to gather the baseline set of requirements.

[In the table below, specify the documentation, roadmaps, best practices, etc. used to gather the baseline set of requirements. Delete this comment once completed.]

Reference Name	Author(s)	Publication Date	Location
<specify the reference name>	*<specify the reference author(s)>*	*<specify the date the reference was published>*	*<specify the location where the reference was retrieved>*

5.1. Assessment Techniques

In support of this assessment, the baseline set of requirements were validated with stakeholders identified in Section 2.3 using the approaches listed in the table below.

[In the table below, specify the interviews, surveys, workshops, etc. used to validate the baseline set of requirements with stakeholders. Delete this comment once completed.]

Validation Approach	Date Completed	Stakeholders
<specify the type approach used>	*<specify the date performed>*	*<identify the stakeholders that participated in the validation>*

6. Requirements Analysis

The section outlines the finalized set of requirements in support of the business strategies described in Section 1.2.

6.1. Functional Requirements

This section describes the features of the deliverable(s) that will specifically meet a business need or desire.

ID	Requirement	Priority
<#>	*<input the requirement description>*	*<specify the priority>*

6.2. Operational Requirements

This section describes the "behind the scene" functions needed to keep the deliverable(s) working overtime.

ID	Requirement	Priority
<#>	*<input the requirement description>*	*<specify the priority>*

6.3. Technical Requirements

This section describes the conditions under which the deliverable(s) must function.

ID	Requirement	Priority
<#>	<input the requirement description>	<specify the priority>

6.4. Transactional Requirements

This section describes the aspects of the deliverable(s) that must be met to handover support responsibilities

ID	Requirement	Priority
<#>	<input the requirement description>	<specify the priority>

6.5. Out-of-Scope Requirements

This section describes the requirements that have been identified as out-of-scope.

Requirement	justification
<input the requirement description>	<specify why this requirement is out-of-scope>

Bibliography

Agrawal, A., Gupta, M., Gupta, S., Gupta, S.C., 2011. Systematic digital forensic investigation model. International Journal of Computer Science and Security (IJCSS) 5 (1).

Ahmad, A., 2002. The Forensic Chain-of-Evidence Model: Improving the Process of Evidence Collection in Incident Handling Procedures. http://citeseerx.ist.psu.edu/viewdoc/summary?doi=10.1.1.87.8677.

American Bar Association, September/October 2007. E-Discovery and electronic evidence in the courtroom. Business Law Today. 17 (1). https://apps.americanbar.org/buslaw/blt/2007-09-10/chorvat.shtml.

Association of Chief Police Officers, 2007. Good Practice Guide for Computer-Based Electronic Evidence. http://www.7safe.com/electronic_evidence/ACPO_guidelines_computer_evidence.pdf.

Australian Government – Civil Aviation Safety Authority, 2007. Cost Benefit Analysis Methodology Procedures Manual. http://www.casa.gov.au/scripts/257r005.pdf.

Australian Signal Directorate, 2014. Strategies to Mitigate Targeted Cyber Intrusions. Australian Government - Department of Defense. http://www.asd.gov.au/infosec/mitigationstrategies.htm.

Bahadur, P., 2014. Difference between Guideline, Procedure, Standard and Policy. http://www.hrsuccessguide.com/2014/01/Guideline-Procedure-Standard-Policy.html.

Baryamureeba, V., Tushabe, F., 2004. The Enhanced Digital Investigation Process Model. Institute of Computer Science, Makerere University, Kampala Uganda. http://dfrws.org/2004/day1/Tushabe_EIDIP.pdf.

Beebe, N.L., Clark, J.G., 2004. A Hierarchical, Objectives-Based Framework for the Digital Investigations Process. Digital Forensics Research Workshop (DFRWS). http://www.dfrws.org/2004/day1/Beebe_Obj_Framework_for_DI.pdf.

Bem, D., Huebner, E., Fall 2007. Computer forensic analysis in a virtual environment. International Journal of Digital Evidence. 6 (2). https://www.utica.edu/academic/institutes/ecii/publications/articles/1C349F35-C73B-DB8A-926F9F46623A1842.pdf.

Bennett, B.T., 2007. Understanding, Assessing, and Responding to Terrorism: Protecting Critical Infrastructure and Personnel. John Wiley & Sons. ISBN: 9780471771524.

Bragg, R., 2002. CISSP Training Guide. Pearson IT Certification. ISBN: 978-0-7897-2801-2.

Bretherton, F.P., Singley, P.T., 1994. Metadata: A User's View. IEEE. ISBN: 0-8186-6610-2.

Brunty, J., 2011. Validation of Forensic Tools and Software: A Quick Guide for the Digital Forensic Examiner. http://www.forensicmag.com/articles/2011/03/validation-forensic-tools-and-software-quick-guide-digital-forensic-examiner.

Canadian Government – Treasury Board of Canada Secretariat, 2007. Canadian Cost-Benefit Analysis Guide: Regulatory Proposals. ISBN: 9780662050391http://www.tbs-sct.gc.ca/rtrap-parfa/analys/analys-eng.pdf.

Carrier, B.D., Spafford, E.H., 2003. Getting physical with the digital investigation process. International Journal of Digital Evidence 2 (2).

Carrier, B.D., Spafford, E.H., 2004. An Event-Based Digital Forensic Investigation Framework. Digital Forensics Research Workshop (DFRWS). http://www.digital-evidence.org/papers/dfrws_event.pdf.

Casey, E., 2000. Digital Evidence and Computer Crime – Forensic Science, Computers and the Internet. Academic Press, San Diego.

Casey, E., 2011. Digital Evidence and Computer Crime – Forensic Science, Computers and the Internet, third ed. Academic Press, San Diego.

Ceresini, T., 2001. Maintaining the Forensic Viability of Log Files. System Administration, Networking, and Security Institute (SANS) – Global Information Assurance Certification (GIAC). http://www.giac.org/paper/gsec/801/maintaining-forensic-viability-log-files/101724.

Choksy, C.E.B., 2006. 8 steps to develop a taxonomy. The Information Management Journal. http://www.arma.org/bookstore/files/Choksy.pdf.

Chow, K.-P., Shenoi, S. (Eds.), 2010. Advances in Digital Forensics VI. Sixth IFIP WG 11.9 International Conference on Digital Forensics. China, Hong Kong. http://www.springer.com/us/book/9783642155055.

Ciardhuáin, S.Ó., 2004. An extended model of cybercrime investigations. International Journal of Digital Evidence. 3 (1). https://www.utica.edu/academic/institutes/ecii/publications/articles/A0B70121-FD6C-3DBA-0EA5C3E93CC575FA.pdf.

Cichonski, P., Millar, T., Grance, T., Scarfone, K., 2012. Computer Security Incident Handling Guide. National Institute of Standards and Technology (NIST). http://nvlpubs.nist.gov/nistpubs/SpecialPublications/NIST.SP.800-61r2.pdf.

Communication Safety Establishment, 2007. Harmonized Threat and Risk Assessment Methodology. Royal Canadian Mounted Police. https://www.cse-cst.gc.ca/en/system/files/pdf_documents/tra-emr-1-e.pdf.

Contesti, D.-L., et al., 2007. Official (ISC)² Guide to the SSCP CBK. Auerbach Publications. ISBN: 9780849327742.

Cornell University Law School, 2014a. Admissible Evidence. https://www.law.cornell.edu/wex/admissible_evidence.

Cornell University Law School, 2014b. Brady Rule. https://www.law.cornell.edu/wex/brady_rule.

Cornell University Law School, 2014c. Federal Rules of Civil Procedure. https://www.law.cornell.edu/rules/frcp/.

Cornell University Law School, 2014d. Federal Rules of Evidence. https://www.law.cornell.edu/rules/fre.

Daubert Standard, 2015. Cornell University Law School. https://www.law.cornell.edu/wex/daubert_standard.

Daubert Test, Legal Dictionary – the Free Dictionary, 2008. http://legal-dictionary.thefreedictionary.com/Daubert+standard.

Fenu, G., Solinas, F., 2013. Computer Forensics Investigation an Approach to Evidence in Cyberspace. University of Cagliari, Department of Computer Science Cagliari, Italy. http://sdiwc.net/digital-library/download.php?id=00000541.pdf.

Finkle, J., Heavey, S., 2014. UPDATE 2-Target Says it Declined to Act on Early Alert of Cyber Breach. Reuters. http://www.reuters.com/article/2014/03/13/target-breach-idUSL2N0MA1MW20140313.

ForensicFocus, 2015. Computer Forensics Education. http://www.forensicfocus.com/education.

Forrester, 2012a. Application Control: An Essential Endpoint Security Component. http://www.forrester.com/Application+Control+An+Essential+Endpoint+Security+Component/fulltext/-/E-RES78502.

Forrester, 2012b. Prepare for Anywhere, Anytime, Any-Device Engagement With A Stateless Mobile Architecture. http://www.forrester.com/Prepare+For+Anywhere+Anytime+AnyDevice+Engagement+With+A+Stateless+Mobile+Architecture/fulltext/-/E-RES61569.

Freiling, F.C., Schwittay, B., 2007. A Common Process Model for Incident Response and Computer Forensics. Laboratory for Dependable Distributed Systems, University of Mannheim, Germany. https://www1.informatik.uni-erlangen.de/filepool/publications/imf2007-common-model.pdf.

Gartner Research, 2013. Enterprise Endpoint Protection When the Consumer Is King. http://www.gartner.com/document/2402415.

Ghorbani, A.A., Lu, W., Tavallaee, M., 2010. Network Intrusion Detection and Prevention Concepts and Techniques. Springer. ISBN: 9780387887708.

Gregory, P., 2014. CISSP Guide to Security Essentials. Nelson Education. ISBN: 9781305840478.

Grobler, C.P., Louwrens, C.P., 2007. Digital Forensic Readiness as a Component of Information Security Best Practice. Springer.

Harris, E.A., Perlroth, N., 2014. Target Missed Signs of a Data Breach. New York Times. http://www.nytimes.com/2014/03/14/business/target-missed-signs-of-a-data-breach.html?_r=0.

Hay, D.C., 2003. Requirements Analysis: From Business Views to Architecture. Prentice Hall Professional. ISBN: 9780130282286.

Hernan, S., Lambert, S., Ostwald, T., Shostack, A., 2006. Uncover Security Design Flaws Using the STRIDE Approach. MSDN Magazine. https://msdn.microsoft.com/en-us/magazine/cc163519.aspx.

Hernandez, S., 2012. Official Guide to the CISSP CBK, third ed. CRC Press. ISBN: 9781466569782.

HG Legal Resources, 2015. Information Technology Law. HGEXPERTS. http://www.hg.org/information-technology-law.html.

Ieong, R.S.C., 2006. FORZA – Digital Forensics Investigation Framework that Incorporate Legal Issues. Elsevier. http://www.dfrws.org/2006/proceedings/4-Ieong.pdf.

InfoSec Reading Room, 2002. An Overview of Threat and Risk Assessment. SANS Institute. http://www.sans.org/reading-room/whitepapers/auditing/overview-threat-risk-assessment-76.

International Organization for Standardization (ISO)/International Electrotechnical Commission (IEC), ISO/IEC 27005, 2011. 2011 Information Technology – Security Techniques-Information Security Risk Management.

Investopedia. http://www.investopedia.com/ 2015a.

Investopedia, 2015b. Market-Orientation. http://www.investopedia.com/terms/m/market-orientation.asp.

Jarke, M., et al., 2013. Fundamentals of Data Warehouse. Springer Science & Business Media. ISBN: 9783662051535.

Kabay, M.E., 2008. A Brief History of Computer Crime: An Introduction for Students. http://www.mekabay.com/overviews/history.pdf.

Karake-Shalhoub, Z., Al Qasimi, L., 2010. Cyber Law and Cyber Security in Developing and Emerging Economies. Edward Elgar Publishing. ISBN: 9781849803380.

Kedar, T.J., 2008. Advanced Database Management. Technical Publications. ISBN: 9788184310962.

Kent, K., Chevalier, S., Grance, T., Dang, H., 2006. Special Publication 800–86: Guide to Integrating Forensic Techniques into Incident Response. National Institute of Standards and Technology (NIST). http://csrc.nist.gov/publications/nistpubs/800-86/SP800-86.pdf.

Kissel, R., et al., 2008. Special Publication 800–64 R2: Security Considerations in the System Development Life Cycle. National Institute of Standards and Technology (NIST). http://csrc.nist.gov/publications/nistpubs/800-64-Rev2/SP800-64-Revision2.pdf.

Kohn, M., Eloff, J.H.P., Olivier, M.S., 2006. Framework for a Digital Forensic Investigation. Information and Computer Security Architectures Research Group (ICSA), Department of Computer Science, University of Pretoria. http://icsa.cs.up.ac.za/issa/2006/Proceedings/Full/101_Paper.pdf.

Krebs, B., 2014. The Target Breach, by the Numbers. KrebsOnSecurity. http://krebsonsecurity.com/2014/05/the-target-breach-by-the-numbers/.

Kruse II, W.G., Heiser, J.G., 2004. Computer Forensics – Incident Response Essentials. Pearson, Indianapolis.

Landoll, D., 2011. The Security Risk Assessment Handbook: A Complete Guide for Performing Security Risk Assessments, second ed. CRC Press. ISBN: 9781439821497.

Law Crossing, 2015. Information Technology Attorney Job Description. Employment Research Institute. http://www.lawcrossing.com/job-description/6048/information-technology-attorney-jobs.

Law Donut, 2015. Employment Law – Discipline and Grievance. http://www.lawdonut.co.uk/law/employment-law/discipline-and-grievance/disciplinary-issues-faqs#7.

Lee, H.C., Palmbach, T.M., Miller, M.T., 2001. Henry Lee's Crime Scene Handbook. Academic Press, San Diego.

Lloyd, I., 2014. Information Technology Law. Oxford University Press. ISBN: 9780198702320.

MacDonald, N., 2010. The Future of Information Security Is Context Aware and Adaptive. G00200385. Gartner Research.

Malega, P., 2014. Escalation management as the necessary form of incident management process. CIS Journal of Emerging Trends in Computing and Information Science. http://www.cisjournal.org/journalofcomputing/archive/vol5no8/vol5no8_8.pdf.

Mandia, K., Prosise, C., Pepe, M., 2003. Incident Response & Computer Forensics, second ed. McGraw-Hill.

Marcella Jr., A., Menendez, D., 2007. Cyber Forensics: A Field Manual for Collecting, Examining, and Preserving Evidence of Computer Crimes, second ed. CRC Press. ISBN: 9781439848234.

Marquis, H., 2010. A Study Guide to Service Catalogue from the Principles of Itil V3, vol. 3. The Stationery Office. ISBN: 9780117063648.

Mellon, C., 2002. CMMISM for Software Engineering (CMMI-SW, V1.1). http://resources.sei.cmu.edu/asset_files/TechnicalReport/2002_005_001_14069.pdf.

Microsoft, 2003. Threat Modelling. https://msdn.microsoft.com/en-us/library/ff648644.aspx.

Microsoft, 2005. The STRIDE Threat Model. https://msdn.microsoft.com/en-us/library/ee823878%28v=cs.20%29.aspx.

Microsoft, 2014. Secure Boot Overview. https://technet.microsoft.com/en-ca/library/hh824987.aspx.

Mohay, G., Anderson, A., Collie, B., De Vel, O., McKemmish, R., 2003. Computer and Intrusion Forensics. Artech House, Massachusetts.

National Institute of Standards and Technology (NIST), 2012. Computer Forensic Tool Testing Project. http://www.cftt.nist.gov/CFTT-Booklet-Revised-02012012.pdf.

Nelson, B., Phillips, A., Enfinger, F., Steuart, C., 2004. Guide to Computer Forensics and Investigations. Thomson Learning, Massachusetts. ISBN: 0-619-13120-9.

Newsome, B., 2013. A Practical Introduction to Security and Risk Management. SAGE Publications. ISBN: 9781452290270.

O'Loughlin, M., 2010. The Service Catalog: Best Practices. Van Haren. ISBN: 9789087535728.

Office of Legal Education Executive Office for United States Attorneys, Department of Justic, 2009. Searching and Seizing Computers and Obtaining Electronic Evidence in Criminal Investigations. http://www.justice.gov/criminal/cybercrime/docs/ssmanual2009.pdf.

OLAP.COM, 2015. OLAP Definition. http://olap.com/olap-definition/.

Open Web Application Security Project (OWASP), 2010. 2010 T10 Architecture Diagram. https://owasp.org/index.php?title=File:2010-T10-ArchitectureDiagram.png.

Open Web Application Security Project (OWASP), 2015a. Threat Modeling. https://www.owasp.org/index.php/Threat_Modeling.

Open Web Application Security Project (OWASP), 2015b. Threat Risk Modelling. https://www.owasp.org/index.php/Threat_Risk_Modeling.

Palmer, G., 2001. DTR-T001–01 Technical Report. A Road Map for Digital Forensic Research. Digital Forensics Workshop (DFRWS), Utica, New York.

Perumal, S., August 2009. Digital forensic model based on Malaysian investigation process. IJCSNS International Journal of Computer Science and Network Security 9 (8).

People's Law Dictionary, 2015. Bad Faith. http://dictionary.law.com/Default.aspx?selected=21.

Peterson, G., Shenoi, S., 2013. Advances in Digital Forensics IX: 9th IFIP WG 11.9 International Conference on Digital Forensics. Springer. ISBN: 9783642411489.

Pilli, E.S., Joshi, R.C., Niyogi, R., 2010. A generic framework for network forensics. International Journal of Computer Applications. 1 (11). http://www.ijcaonline.org/journal/number11/pxc387408.pdf.

Pollitt, M.M., 1995. Computer forensics: an approach to evidence in cyberspace. In: Proceeding of the National Information Systems Security Conference, vol. II. Baltimore.

Ponniah, P., 2004. Data Warehouse Fundamentals: A Comprehensive Guide for IT Professionals. John Wiley & Sons. ISBN: 9780471463894.

Porterfield, J., 2014. File Sharing: Rights and Risks. The Rosen Publishing Group. ISBN: 9781477776407.

Press Release, 2002. FBI "hack" Raises Global Security Concerns. CNET. http://www.cnet.com/news/fbi-hack-raises-global-security-concerns/.

Press Release, 2005. Alexey Ivanov and Vasiliy Gorshkov: Russian Hacker Roulette. CSO. http://www.csoonline.com/article/2118241/malware-cybercrime/alexey-ivanov-and-vasiliy-gorshkov–russian-hacker-roulette.html.

Press Release, 2008. Profile Gary McKinnon. BBC News. http://news.bbc.co.uk/2/hi/technology/4715612.stm.

Press Release, 2009. Pirate Bay File-Sharing Trial to Start in Sweden. Telegraph Media Group Limited. http://www.telegraph.co.uk/technology/8580318/Top-five-internet-piracy-battles.html.

Press Release, 2014. SEC Charges Company CEO and Former CFO with Hiding Internal Controls Deficiencies and Violating Sarbanes-Oxley Requirements. US Securities and Exchange Commissions. http://www.sec.gov/News/PressRelease/Detail/PressRelease/1370542561150.

Queensland Government, 2014. Identifying Business Risk. https://www.business.qld.gov.au/business/running/risk-management/identifying-business-risk.

Ray, D.A., Bradford, P.G., 2007. Models of Models: Digital Forensics and Domain Specific Languages. Department of Computer Science, University of Alabama, Tuscaloosa, AL. Box 870290 http://www.ioc.ornl.gov/csiirw/07/abstracts/Bradford-Abstract.pdf.

Ray, I., Shenoi, S., 2008. Advances in Digital Forensics IV. Springer. ISBN: 978-0-387-84927-0.

ReelLawyers, 2013. Lessons of AMD v. Intel. https://www.youtube.com/watch?v=jQ_9uLkw_Uo.

Reith, M., Carr, C., Gunsh, G., 2002. An examination of digital forensics models. International Journal of Digital Evidence 1 (3).

Rogers, M.K., Goldman, J., Mislan, R., Wedge, T., Debrota, S., 2006. Computer forensics field triage process model. Journal of Digital Forensics, Security and Law 1.

Rooney, P., 2002. Microsoft's CEO: 80–20 Rule Applies to Bugs, Not Just Features. CRN. http://www.crn.com/news/security/18821726/microsofts-ceo-80-20-rule-applies-to-bugs-not-just-features.htm.

Rowlingson, A., 2004. Ten step process for forensic readiness. Elsevier International Journal of Digital Evidence 2 (3).

Royal Canadian Mounted Police, 2011. Crime Prevention Through Environmental Design. Government of Canada. http://www.rcmp-grc.gc.ca/pubs/ccaps-spcca/safecomm-seccol-lect-eng.htm.

de Rus, G., 2010. Introduction to Cost-benefit Analysis. Edward Elgar Publishing Inc. ISBN: 9781848448520.

Saitta, P., Larcom, B., Eddington, M., 2005. TRIKE V.1 Methodology Document. http://www.octotrike.org/papers/Trike_v1_Methodology_Document-draft.pdf.

SANS, 2001. Developing a Computer Forensics Team. http://www.sans.org/reading-room/whitepapers/incident/developing-computer-forensics-team-628.

SANS, 2015. Information Security Policy Templates. https://www.sans.org/security-resources/policies/.

Schmitt, V., Jordaan, J., 2013. Establishing the validity of MD5 and SHA-1 hashing in digital forensic practice in light of recent research demonstrating cryptographic weaknesses in these algorithms. International Journal of Computer Applications. http://www.lex-informatica.org/2%20Ensuring%20the%20Legality%20of%20the%20Digital%20Forensics%20Process%20in%20South%20Africa.pdf.

Schniederjans, M.J., Hamaker, J.L., Schniederjans, A.M., 2004. Information Technology Investment: Decision-Making Methodology. World Scientific Co. Pte. Ltd. ISBN: 9812386955.

Scientific Working Group on Digital Evidence (SWGDE), 2012. Model Standard Operation Procedures Version 3.0. https://www.swgde.org/documents/Current+Documents/SWGDE+QAM+and+SOP+Manuals/2012-09-13+SWGDE+Model+SOP+for+Computer+Forensics+v3.

Security Awareness Program Special Interest Group PCI Security Standards Council, 2014. Information Supplement: Best Practices for Implementing a Security Awareness Program. PCI Security Standards Council. https://www.pcisecuritystandards.org/documents/PCI_DSS_V1.0_Best_Practices_for_Implementing_Security_Awareness_Program.pdf.

State of North Dakota, 2001. Requirements Analysis. New York State Office for Technology. https://www.nd.gov/itd/files/services/pm/requirements-analysis-guidebook.pdf.

Stephenson, P., 2003. A Comprehensive Approach to Digital Incident Investigation. Elsevier. http://www.emich.edu/cerns/downloads/pstephen/Comprehensive-Approach-to-Digital-Investigation.pdf.

Sule, D., 2014. Importance of forensic readiness. ISACA Journal. 1. http://www.isaca.org/Journal/archives/2014/Volume-1/Pages/JOnline-Importance-of-Forensic-Readiness.aspx#11.

Tan, J., 2001. Forensic Readiness. http://home.eng.iastate.edu/~guan/course/backup/CprE-592-YG-Fall-2002/paper/forensic_readiness.pdf.

Taruu.com, 2009. ITIL v3 Study Guide. Taruu LLC. http://taruu.com/Documents/ITIL%20v3%20Foundation%20Study%20Guide%20v4.2.2.5.pdf.

TechTarget, 2015a. Cloud Computing. http://searchcloudcomputing.techtarget.com/definition/cloud-computing.

TechTarget, 2015b. Cloud Provider. http://searchcloudprovider.techtarget.com/definition/cloud-provider.

TechTarget, 2008. IT Asset. http://whatis.techtarget.com/definition/IT-asset.

TechTarget, 2015a. Principle of Least Privilege (POLP). http://searchsecurity.techtarget.com/definition/principle-of-least-privilege-POLP.

TechTarget, 2015b. Total Cost of Ownership. http://searchdatacenter.techtarget.com/definition/TCO.

TechTarget, 2015c. Cloud Computing. http://searchcloudcomputing.techtarget.com/definition/cloud-computing.

TechTarget, 2015d. Cloud Provider. http://searchcloudprovider.techtarget.com/definition/cloud-provider.

The MITRE Corporation, 2015a. About STIX. http://stixproject.github.io/about/.

The MITRE Corporation, 2015b. STIX Project. http://stixproject.github.io/about/.

Tipton, H.F., 2011a. (ISC)^2 Official Guide to the ISSAP CBK. CRC Press. ISBN: 9781439800935.

Tipton, H.F., 2011b. (ISC)^2 Official Guide to the ISSMP CBK. CRC Press. ISBN: 9781420094435.

Treasury Board of Canada Secretariat, 2011. Guide to Risk Taxonomies. Government of Canada. http://www.tbs-sct.gc.ca/tbs-sct/rm-gr/guides/grt-gtr01-eng.asp.

Treasury Board of Canada, 2012a. Guide to Integrated Risk Management. Government of Canada. http://www.tbs-sct.gc.ca/tbs-sct/rm-gr/guides/girm-ggir02-eng.asp.

Treasury Board of Canada, 2012b. Guide to Integrated Risk Management. Government of Canada. http://www.tbs-sct.gc.ca/tbs-sct/rm-gr/guides/girm-ggir04-eng.asp.

U.S. Department of Justice, 2001. Electronic Crime Scene Investigation: A Guide to First Responders. https://www.ncjrs.gov/pdffiles1/nij/187736.pdf.

United States District Court, 2009. Eastern District Court of Missouri, Eastern Division. U.S. Government Publishing Office. United States of America v. Joseph Schmidt, III. http://www.gpo.gov/fdsys/pkg/USCOURTS-moed-4_09-cr-00265/pdf/USCOURTS-moed-4_09-cr-00265-0.pdf.

US-CERT, 2008. Computer Forensics. https://www.us-cert.gov/sites/default/files/publications/forensics.pdf.

Versprite, 2013. PASTA Abstract. http://versprite.com/docs/PASTA_Abstract.pdf.

Webopedia, 2015a. Mandatory Access Control. http://www.webopedia.com/TERM/M/Mandatory_Access_Control.html.

Webopedia, 2015b. Metadata. http://www.webopedia.com/TERM/M/metadata.html.

Webopedia, 2015c. Role-Based Access Control (RBAC). http://www.webopedia.com/TERM/S/structured_data.html.

Webopedia, 2015d. Structured Data. http://www.webopedia.com/TERM/S/structured_data.html.

Webopedia, 2015e. Unstructured Data. http://www.webopedia.com/TERM/U/unstructured_data.html.

Webopedia, 2015f. Entity-relationship Diagram. http://www.webopedia.com/TERM/E/entity_relationship_diagram.html.

Wheeler, E., 2011. Security Risk Management: Building an Information Security Risk Management Program from the Ground Up. Elsevier. ISBN: 9781597496162.

Wilson, M., Hash, J., 2003. Special Publication 800-50: Building an Information Technology Security Awareness and Training Program. National Institute of Standards and Technology (NIST). http://csrc.nist.gov/publications/nistpubs/800-50/NIST-SP800-50.pdf.

Yasinsac, A., Manzano, Y., 2001. Policies to enhance computer and network forensics. In: IEEE Workshop on Information Assurance and Security.

Yusoff, Y., Ismail, R., Hassan, Z., 2011. Common phases of computer forensics investigation models. International Journal of Computer Science & Information Technology (IJCSIT). 3 (3). http://airccse.org/journal/jcsit/0611csit02.pdf.

Zeltser, L., 2014. The Many Fields of Digital Forensics and Incident Response. SANS Digital Forensics and Incident Response. https://digital-forensics.sans.org/blog/2014/01/30/many-fields-of-dfir.

Index

Note: Page numbers followed by "f" indicate figures, "t" indicate tables and "b" indicate boxes.

Printed in the United States
By Bookmasters